# NORWAY 1940

François Kersaudy

UNIVERSITY OF NEBRASKA PRESS
LINCOLN

∞

First Bison Books printing: 1998
Most recent printing indicated by the last digit below:
10   9   8   7   6   5   4   3   2   1

Library of Congress Cataloging-in-Publication Data
Kersaudy, François, 1948–
[1940. English]
Norway 1940 / François Kersaudy.
p.   cm.
Includes bibliographical references and index.
ISBN 0-8032-7787-3 (pbk.: alk. paper)
1. World War, 1939–1945—Campaigns—Norway.   2. Norway—History—
German occupation, 1940–1945.   I. Title.
[D763.N6K4413   1998]
940.54′281—dc21
98-33494   CIP

Originally published in 1990 in Great Britain by William Collins Sons and Co.
Limited. Reprinted from the 1991 edition by St. Martin's Press, New York.

# CONTENTS

# LIST OF MAPS

# LIST OF ILLUSTRATIONS

Winston Churchill
*Document Tallandier*
Paul Reynaud
*Document Tallandier*
The Supreme War Council, Paris, February 1940
*Roger Viollet*
Adolf Hitler with Generals Keitel and Jodl
*Document Tallandier*
General von Falkenhorst, Commander-in-Chief
of Operation Weserübung
*E.C.P. Armées*
The German cruiser *Blücher*
*Norges Hjemmefrontmuseum, Akershus*
The sinking of the *Blücher*
*Norges Hjemmefrontmuseum, Akershus*
The cutting of the iron ore supplies
*Norges Hjemmefrontmuseum, Akershus*
German troops entering Oslo, 9 April 1940
*Norges Hjemmefrontmuseum, Akershus*
German diplomat Bräuer
*Norges Hjemmefrontmuseum, Akershus*
King Haakon VII of Norway
*Norges Hjemmefrontmuseum, Akershus*
The King and Prince Olav rushing for cover,
Nybergsund, 11 April
*Norges Hjemmefrontmuseum, Akershus*
Norwegian troops manning a roadblock, April 1940
*Norges Hjemmefrontmuseum, Akershus*
Namsos, before and after the German air raid
of 20 April
*Document Tallandier*

A German armoured column forcing a
roadblock north of Lillehammer
*E.C.P. Armées*
Admiral of the Fleet Sir Roger Keyes
*Imperial War Museum*
Lord Cork and Orrery, naval commander at
Narvik
*Keystone Paris*
General Bethouart
*Document Tallandier*
General Dietl
*Roger Viollet*
General Otto Ruge
*Norges Hjemmefrontmuseum, Akershus*
The cruiser *Warspite* entering Narvik fjord,
13 April
*Norges Hjemmefrontmuseum, Akershus*
British naval artillery pounding Bjerkvik,
13 May
*Document Tallandier*
German troops storming a hamlet near
Lillehammer
*E.C.P. Armées*

# INTRODUCTION

One look at the map was enough to understand Norway's unique strategic importance: facing the British Isles to the west, it opened the way to the north Atlantic; towards the south, it gave access to the Baltic Sea and the German coast; in the far north, it bordered on the Arctic Ocean and lined the northward approaches to the Soviet Union. Last but not least, it controlled the north-western route of Sweden's iron ore, which passed through Narvik and the Norwegian Leads – the narrow sea corridor lining the whole western coast of Norway – before reaching both Germany and Great Britain.

During the inter-war years, admittedly, no one had expressed much interest in such geostrategic considerations. The French, for instance, could find in their *Dictionnaire des arts et métiers* a rather peculiar map of Scandinavia: Sweden remained nameless, but Norway was called . . . Sweden! The Germans did little better, since the capital of Norway was nowhere to be seen on their maps: Christiania had been renamed Oslo in 1924, but this had not been registered in Germany. Were the British much better informed? Probably not: in 1940, the Foreign Secretary, Lord Halifax, glancing at a map of Scandinavia, was still mistaking the Norwegian border for a railway line. After all that, who could possibly have foreseen that France, Germany and Great Britain would soon be taking such extraordinary interest in the peaceful and somnolent little kingdom of Norway?

In 1935, for the first time in thirty years of independence, the 2.5 million Norwegians had elected a Socialist government, which included a number of decidedly colourful personalities. The Prime Minister, Johan Nygaardsvold, a former lumberjack, was in favour of a remarkably progressive social policy, but displayed precious little interest in foreign affairs and defence matters. His Foreign Minister, Halvdan Koht, a gifted scholar and eminent historian, was admittedly far more versed in questions of foreign policy;

9

unfortunately, he displayed a considerable degree of confidence in the power of neutrality and international law, which hardly seemed justified in the troubled world of the late 1930s. The new Minister of Justice, Trygve Lie, a former trade-unionist of imposing proportions, had directed fifteen years earlier a 'Bolshevik propaganda school' whose declared aim was to prepare for a takeover of Norway by distinctly illegal means . . . Yet the Defence Minister, Carl Fredric Monsen, was perhaps the most remarkable of the lot: a former pacifist and conscientious objector, he had joined the Socialist Party's Anti-Militarist Committee in the 1920s. Better still, he had been arrested for pacifist agitation among the soldiers! His brand-new responsibilities at the head of the Ministry of Defence were thus a fitting epilogue to an eventful career . . . and probably a unique case in contemporary history.

For all that, any pessimistic forecast would have been entirely unjustified: during the next five years, this rather eccentric government was to spare no effort in its pursuit of economic, political and social progress. By 1939, it had largely succeeded in all three fields; and yet a fourth field remains unmentioned, though it was hardly a negligible one by the summer of 1939: the defence of the kingdom.

The Norwegian army had a peace-time strength of six divisions, with 30,000 men in theory (and 7,000 in reality). In wartime, these divisions were to be split into brigades, which was already a source of weakness, since the reorganization would necessarily take a long time. Furthermore, the officers who were to command the brigades were unacquainted with them, they had never met their men, and in fact the men had never met each other . . . Field manoeuvres? Out of the question: they had been abolished years earlier as part of the economy drive.

Equipment was perhaps the sorest point: the army had only vintage .75 cannons, and its 6.5 mm Krag-Jørgensen rifles were decidedly obsolete; apart from that, there were no sub-machine guns, no grenades, no anti-aircraft guns and no tanks. Besides, troop deployment was bound to be difficult: there was no railway linking southern Norway to the northern provinces of Troms and Finnmark; no road either, except at the planning stage. There remained the sea route, of course; but then the navy was hardly in better shape than the army.

The Royal Norwegian Navy included seventy small units. The two largest ones, *Norge* and *Eidsvold*, were by 1939 the oldest ironclads in the world; the commanding admiral had affectionately dubbed them 'my old bathtubs'. Moreover, the Norwegian navy had never left its ports since 1918 – the economy drive again. The ports themselves were protected by a highly obsolete coastal artillery. The fortress of Oscarsborg, in the middle of Oslo fjord, was thus equipped with a nineteenth-century Krupp cannon, which had fallen into the water upon being mounted; once fished out, it was fittingly christened 'Moses'. The fortress of Agdenes, at the mouth of Trondheim fjord, was garrisoned only by a company of soldiers who had received 48 days of training a decade earlier. Besides, several of its batteries had only skeleton crews, others had none at all. In Bergen fortress, the artillery pieces were also undermanned – and somewhat rusty, as they had not fired a shot for the last two decades; had they done so, the results would probably have been disappointing: most of the shells were too old to explode on impact . . . In Narvik, the shells were somewhat more modern, but that did not really matter, since there were no cannons to fire them: several batteries had been sent there in 1912, but they were never mounted for lack of funds.

As for the air force, it did not exist as a separate entity; there was an army air force and a naval air force, which was clearly detrimental to co-ordination – though actually there was practically nothing to co-ordinate: apart from a few museum pieces, there were practically no aeroplanes.

The military had naturally done their best to remedy the situation within the framework of stringent financial constraints. Thus, according to the 1933 budget statement, the cavalry was to be equipped with tanks, but the sums earmarked were so insignificant that it took several years of savings to buy a single tank, 'so that the Norwegian soldiers could at least see one sample in their lifetime'.[1] The air force also bought Caproni aeroplanes from Italy, not because they were the best, but simply because they could be paid for in dried cod, which allowed the Norwegian authorities to help their fishing industry in the process. But the planes almost immediately proved inadequate, thus compelling the government to buy better ones from the United States – in hard cash, unfortunately.[2]

After 1937, the commanders of the armed forces, increasingly alarmed by the worsening international situation, undertook to inform the Norwegians of the woeful state of their defences; it was hoped that the citizens would in turn bring pressure to bear on the Storting – the Norwegian parliament – in favour of increased military expenditures. Their efforts were even backed by the Minister of Defence, who had definitely jettisoned his anti-militaristic background. Yet it was all in vain: the Prime Minister and the Foreign Minister were still clinging to their neutralist stance and their pacifist visions, and by the end of the 1930s Norway's defence remained extraordinarily vulnerable. In January 1939, the naval Chief of Staff confessed to the press that the Norwegian navy was 'worse off than in 1914, both in men and in equipment'[3]... Clearly a hopeless situation.

Among the Norwegian authorities, however, one man at least seemed to think otherwise; he was the King of Norway. A former naval officer, Prince Charles of Denmark, son-in-law of King Edward VII of England, had been elected by the newly independent Norwegians in 1905, and crowned king the following year under the name of Haakon VII. Since then, the tall, gaunt monarch had obviously taken his task to heart, and gradually earned the unswerving loyalty of his subjects. Moreover, his education at the royal court of Copenhagen as well as his family ties with the British Crown had made him a shrewd observer of European affairs; thus, in 1932, he confided to British Admiral Sir John Kelly: 'If Hitler comes to power in Germany and manages to hold on to it, then we shall have a war in Europe before another decade is over.'[4]

During the years that followed, King Haakon was to exert discreet pressure on Norway's successive governments in favour of drastic improvements in the country's defences. Unfortunately, Norway's constitution strictly limited the king's role, and his advice was almost entirely disregarded. Thus, when the Second World War broke out in Europe, the seventy-year-old monarch was left to reign over a country that was both strategically vital and militarily defenceless – a highly unhealthy combination. King Haakon thought so too, and never tired of repeating it; 'I dare say', one of his aides later confided, 'that in his own mind the King had practically experienced the whole disaster long before it actually struck'.[5]

# CHAPTER ONE

# Churchill's Solitary Crusade

By the summer of 1939, Neville Chamberlain had just turned 70. Slim and dapper, easily recognized by his trademark umbrella, he was still quite popular among his contemporaries. Had he not been an excellent Lord Mayor of Birmingham? a successful Chancellor of the Exchequer? a peerless Prime Minister? A great majority of his countrymen clearly thought so; and yet there was no denying the obvious: Chamberlain, no doubt a perfect gentleman, an efficient manager and a shrewd politician, was also disastrously incompetent in foreign affairs and, worse still, he was blissfully unaware of it. Hence his decision to negotiate personally with both Mussolini and Hitler in 1937, and the deplorable outcome of his efforts at Munich the following year. Since then, the hideous spectre of Nazism had never ceased to haunt the capitals of Europe; and yet Chamberlain, too confident in his diplomatic talents, too preoccupied with political popularity and financial orthodoxy, and too ignorant of military matters, had dismissed all proposals for an accelerated rearmament until his country stood at the very brink of the abyss. By the late summer of 1939, war was knocking at England's door, and yet Neville Chamberlain still could not see himself in the role of a war Prime Minister.

An entirely different man was Winston Spencer Churchill; the old bulldog, with his massive frame, pugnacious temper and formidable eloquence, had acquired in the course of thirty-five years a more varied experience of government than any Prime Minister in British history. A controversial Home Secretary and less than successful Chancellor of the Exchequer, Churchill had given the full measure of his abilities during the First World War; as First Lord of the Admiralty, infantry officer in the muddy trenches of northern France or Minister of Munitions, he had fought with amazing energy until the very end of the war – and even some time after that.

As a member of successive Coalition and Conservative administrations in the twenties, Churchill felt somewhat ill at ease in peace-time politics. As Chancellor of the Exchequer, he was directly responsible for the notorious Ten Years' Rule that considerably inhibited British defence planning. Besides, his hopelessly outdated views on India led him to disagree with his party over the India Bill, as a result of which he resigned from the Conservative Shadow Cabinet in 1931.

For the better part of the next decade, Churchill was to remain a solitary figure in Parliament, whose eloquence was feared but whose ideas were seldom taken seriously. Yet, unlike Stanley Baldwin or Neville Chamberlain, Churchill quickly grasped the mortal danger of Hitler's expansionist ambitions. For more than thirty years, he had known the exact state of Britain's defences, and was deeply convinced that in the event of war he alone had the energy, the drive and the imagination to galvanize them. In fact, a great majority of Englishmen thought so too, and curiously enough, so did all successive Prime Ministers from Ramsay MacDonald to Chamberlain himself. But of course, until the summer of 1939, practically no one really believed in the imminence of war.

In early September, however, when German troops entered Poland, a declaration of war became politically unavoidable, and in the ensuing Cabinet reshuffle Winston Churchill was appointed First Lord of the Admiralty. For Neville Chamberlain, this had obviously been a difficult decision to make; after all, Churchill had been for the last two years the most relentless, the best informed and the most eloquent detractor of Chamberlain's slow rearmament policy and weak appeasement diplomacy. Yet, once war had broken out, both the pressure of public opinion and simple common sense made it utterly impossible to keep Churchill out of the Cabinet.

Did Chamberlain really send Churchill to the Admiralty so that he would be too preoccupied with the affairs of his ministry to be tempted to meddle in those of the Prime Minister as well?[1] If so, Chamberlain was grievously mistaken, but at any rate Churchill was clearly delighted to return to the post he had left most unwillingly a quarter of a century earlier.*

---

* Winston Churchill had been compelled to resign from the Admiralty in May 1915, as a result of the failures of the Dardanelles campaign.

Upon arriving at the Admiralty, Churchill soon discovered that his staff was absorbed in the study of a momentous question: that of Germany's iron ore supplies. Experts from the Ministry of Economic Warfare and the Admiralty had indeed noted that, out of the 11 million tons of iron ore used by Germany, 9 million tons were imported from northern Sweden.[2] Such imports were therefore vital to Germany's armament industry. A closer look even showed that this iron ore was normally shipped through the Swedish port of Luleå, at the head of the Gulf of Bothnia, but that in winter, the gulf being frozen, the ore was sent by railway to the Norwegian port of Narvik. From there, it was shipped south to Germany through the Leads.[3] 'The Admiralty staff', Churchill later wrote, 'were seriously perturbed at this important advantage being presented to Germany.'[4] On 18 September, indeed, the Deputy Chief of the Naval Staff, Admiral Drax, had told Churchill how desirable it would be to interrupt the iron ore traffic from Narvik 'by diplomatic means'; if that failed, he added, 'more energetic means' would have to be contemplated . . .[5]

For Winston Churchill, inaction was clearly an unknown word. He immediately set to work producing a plan of action, and the very next day he wrote to the First Sea Lord: 'I brought to the notice of the Cabinet this morning the importance of stopping the Norwegian transportation of Swedish iron ore from Narvik, which will begin as soon as the ice forms in the Gulf of Bothnia. [. . .] The Cabinet, including the Foreign Secretary, appeared strongly favourable to this action. It is therefore necessary to take all steps to prepare it.'[6]

But Churchill's projects almost immediately ran into serious obstacles. Negotiations had been under way with the Norwegians since early September for the chartering of a large part of their merchant marine, including a fleet of modern tankers of vital importance for the Allied war effort. An operation in Norwegian territorial waters, in clear violation of international law, would surely induce the Norwegians to break the negotiations in reprisal. Any offensive operation was therefore out of the question before the conclusion of these negotiations. Besides, in spite of Churchill's optimistic statement, the Foreign Secretary, Lord Halifax, was by no means in favour of his plan; in fact, the former Viceroy of India, a high churchman and scrupulous civil servant, was resolutely opposed to any infringement of Norwegian neutrality, and he exercised

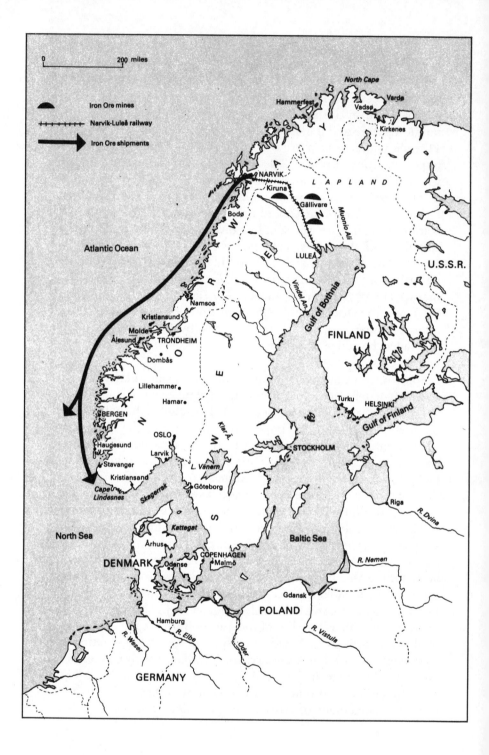

considerable influence over his Cabinet colleagues. Finally, the fragmentary information available by late September seemed to indicate a marked decrease in the iron ore traffic from Narvik to Germany, which of course robbed Churchill's argument of a good deal of its force.

All these uncertainties were reflected in Churchill's memorandum to the War Cabinet. On 29 September, having recognized that the operation could not be carried out right away, the First Lord of the Admiralty nevertheless asked his colleagues to 'remit the question to the various departments concerned in order that detailed plans may be made for prompt action'.[7] But it was all in vain: 'I was unable to obtain assent to action,' Churchill lamented; 'the Foreign Office arguments about neutrality were weighty, and I could not prevail'.[8]

By the end of November, however, the situation had evolved significantly. The negotiations for the chartering of Norwegian tonnage had not yet been concluded, but there was now much more information on the German iron ore traffic from Narvik, as the Admiralty had sent a few agents to make discreet enquiries in Norway.[9] Moreover, the Ministry of Economic Warfare had just informed the First Lord that 'a complete stoppage of Swedish exports of iron ore to Germany would, barring unpredictable developments, end the war in a few months'.[10] Thus fortified, Churchill outlined his new plan to the War Cabinet on 30 November: 'Just before the end of the last war, we had been able to deprive the Germans of their iron ore imports by mining Norwegian territorial waters, thus forcing the ore ships into the open sea. The time was coming when we should have to consider taking similar measures. A few small minefields, each of perhaps three or four square miles, would be enough for the purpose.'[11]

The historical part of Churchill's argument was shaky at best; British authorities had indeed contemplated the mining of Norwegian territorial waters in 1918, but in the end nothing had come of the idea.[12] Not that it really mattered, for the War Cabinet was no more inclined to action than it had been two months earlier. Lord Halifax was still vehemently opposed to Churchill's pet project, Chamberlain backed him, and in the end the Cabinet took no decision at all, except to ask the Chiefs of Staff for a report on the military aspects of the question.[13]

17

To be sure, Chamberlain, Halifax and their colleagues had grounded their objections on arguments of strategic caution, political expediency and respect for international law; but the truth was that three months after the outbreak of war Chamberlain remained a peace-time Prime Minister, and his only real strategy was to await the effects of the Allied blockade on the German war effort, while in the meantime carefully abstaining from any rash initiative.[14] Churchill's plan would therefore have been definitely doomed, but for the advent of the Finno-Soviet war.

The attack on Finland by the Soviet Union caused world-wide indignation; on 14 December, the Council of the League of Nations announced that the Soviet Union was no longer a member of the organization, and four days later its Secretary-General asked each and every member nation to give Finland all possible material and humanitarian assistance.[15] The appeal was warmly welcomed in France, whose authorities, while recognizing Britain's dominant role in the naval blockade of Germany,[16] had conducted a study of their own on the possibility of cutting Germany's strategic supply lines. Of particular interest were the waterways (especially the Danube), Germany's petroleum sources . . . and of course the iron ore traffic.

In fact, the French general staff had displayed considerably more interest in the first two targets, which led its planning services to conceive a series of particularly ambitious operation plans involving the Balkans, the Black Sea area and the Near East.[17] But as British authorities repeatedly and categorically refused to take such projects seriously,[18] the French were compelled to fall back on the iron ore traffic coming down the Norwegian Leads.[19] In this respect, the appeal by the League of Nations was nothing short of a blessing. France, encouraged by the initial successes of the Finnish army, answered the call with alacrity. 'Now of course,' Admiral Auphan later wrote, 'it's a little cynical to say so, but no one really hoped to stop the Soviet army and save Finland. The idea was to use the pretext of such an operation to lay our hands on the Swedish iron ore, and thus deny it to Germany.'[20]

It might seem surprising to witness such an overflow of strategic imagination on the part of the French government and General Staff; after all, the massacres of the First World War had effectively burnt the concept of offensive operations out of almost every

French mind. Yet the explanation was simple – and, as usual, almost purely political: three months after the outbreak of war, the French Premier, Daladier, was being fiercely attacked in Parliament, the press and the cafés for the conspicuous inertia of his war policy – a stinging rebuke for this former history teacher and radical socialist militant who had served several times as Defence Minister and considered himself a specialist in military affairs. Besides, his regrettable performance at Munich the year before made it all the more imperative to cultivate the image of an ardent and ruthless fighter. A direct attack on Germany was obviously ruled out – another legacy of the First World War – but a quick foray in some distant theatre like Finland, where the British allies could bear the brunt of the undertaking, was of course an entirely different matter; indeed, it would be a splendid way of winning laurels without having to pay a prohibitive price for them. On the strength of such considerations, the French began exerting considerable pressure on their British counterparts to participate in the operation to 'save Finland'; in fact, they put before them a whole series of plans for naval landings at Petsamo, Luleå, Narvik and Murmansk – in other words in Finland, Sweden, Norway and the Soviet Union.

*C'est magnifique, mais ce n'est pas la guerre!* In London, where no one relished the prospect of an open conflict with the Soviet Union, the French plans were greeted as usual with a healthy dose of scepticism. But Winston Churchill, who never lost sight of his ultimate goal – the complete defeat of Germany – swiftly realized that the latest turn of events could prove eminently favourable to the re-emergence of his pet project. 'If Narvik was to become a sort of allied base to supply the Finns,' he wrote, 'it would certainly be easy to prevent the German ships from loading ore at the port and sailing safely down the Leads to Germany.'[21]

Thus, in less than four months, British strategy had made a giant stride – on paper at least: in early September, the Admiralty and the Ministry of Economic Warfare were thinking of encouraging the Norwegians to interrupt the iron ore traffic themselves; by mid-December, the Cabinet was being presented with a plan to turn Narvik into 'a sort of allied base', after the mining of Norwegian territorial waters. For three months, the indomitable First Lord had been practically the only proponent within the Cabinet of any offensive action against Germany. But by December 1939, the situation had clearly turned in his favour. Even Lord Halifax was now publicly expressing his revulsion at the Soviet attack on Finland,[22] and Naval Intelligence had at last given Churchill the precise information he required: between 27 November and 30 November, three German ore ships had arrived at Narvik, two had departed and four others had been sighted further south along the Norwegian coast.[23] On 16 December, Churchill therefore submitted yet another memorandum to the War Cabinet: 'The effectual stoppage of the Norwegian ore supplies to Germany ranks as a major offensive operation of war. No other measure is open to us for many months to come which gives so good a chance of abridging the waste and destruction of the conflict, or of perhaps preventing the vast slaughters which will attend the grapple of the main armies. [...] The ore from Narvik must be stopped by laying successively a series of small minefields in Norwegian territorial waters at the two or three suitable points on the coast, which will force the ships carrying ore to Germany to quit territorial waters and come on to the high seas, where, if German, they will be taken as prize, or, if neutral, subjected to our contraband control.'[24]

Chamberlain having earlier expressed his fear of a negative reaction by the neutrals – particularly the United States – to a British mining operation, Churchill hastened to tell his colleagues that he had asked the American ambassador in London to ascertain President Roosevelt's position in such an eventuality, and he had received an answer 'which indicated that the President's reactions were more favourable than he had hoped'.[25] Finally, having also noticed that Lord Halifax was less hostile to a naval incursion in Norwegian territorial waters than to the mining of these waters, Churchill quickly altered his plan to oblige the Foreign Secretary: the German ore ships intercepted in Norwegian territorial waters would be captured instead of sunk.[26] But to carry the day, Churchill needed the backing of yet another influential personality: Sir Edmund Ironside, the Chief of the Imperial General Staff.

A dapper seven-footer in his early sixties, with a square jaw and drooping eyelids, General Sir Edmund ('Tiny') Ironside had seen action on innumerable battlefields from South Africa to Arkhangelsk – clearly not a man to be intimidated by the prospect of yet another overseas expedition. But General Ironside considered Churchill's naval action plan far too limited in scope. Instead, he contemplated a much more ambitious scheme, whose implementation would also require considerable delay: an overland expedition to occupy the iron ore mines.[27]

This was naturally most distasteful to Churchill, who was above all seeking immediate action, even on a limited scale; but to propitiate the Chief of the Imperial General Staff, he declared to the War Cabinet on 18 December: 'If land operations became necessary, it would be perfectly feasible to land British and French troops in Norway. [. . .] We might, at a later stage, even be able to establish air bases in the south of the peninsula, and so intervene in the Baltic.'[28] Last but not least, Churchill had also enlisted the backing of the French authorities, who were just then submitting to the Supreme Allied War Council a proposal for an Anglo-French memorandum assuring Norway and Sweden of Allied 'backing', in order to secure their acceptance of any subsequent Allied operation – should there be one.

Thus, by the time the War Cabinet met on 22 December, all the cards seemed to be stacked in Churchill's favour. But there remained a fatal flaw: two days earlier, at a meeting of the Military Co-ordination Committee, General Ironside had again mentioned his plan for the occupation of the iron ore mines, and strongly hinted that Churchill's naval project would compromise his own 'long term' plan.[29] This disagreement naturally resurfaced at the War Cabinet meeting, heavily exploited by both the Foreign Secretary and the Prime Minister;[30] the latter, like Lord Halifax, was indeed categorically opposed to any kind of intervention that could not be 'legally' justified.[31] Above all, he feared that any offensive operation would bring Germany to retaliate, and lead to a 'shooting war' – a bloody affair likely to reveal both England's weakness and the Prime Minister's utter incompetence in military affairs.

At the meeting of the War Cabinet, Chamberlain therefore pointed out that there were now two distinct projects: the original plan to stop the ore traffic along the Norwegian coast, either with mines or with direct naval action, and a 'major', 'long term' project to secure the iron ore mines by dispatching a complete expeditionary force to Scandinavia. To be sure, the Prime Minister continued, everyone agreed that the assent of Norway and Sweden was essential to the success of the 'major' project, but there was no doubt that the 'minor' operation would displease the Norwegians and embarrass the Swedes; it was therefore inadvisable to risk compromising the 'major' operation by carrying out the 'minor' one.[32]

For the next three months, this fatal dilemma effectively paralysed all Allied initiatives.[33] The 'major' project, requiring lengthy preparations, seemed eminently suitable to those members of the War Cabinet who dreaded any hasty initiative.[34] Besides, one could hardly conceive of a better way to silence the ebullient First Lord of the Admiralty . . .

Thus, at the War Cabinet sessions of 22 and 27 December, the ministers merely asked the Chiefs of Staff to devise plans for future operations in Scandinavia – which could do no harm – and agreed on the text of the memorandum which the French insisted on delivering to the Swedes and Norwegians – that could do no harm either. As a first step, the Swedes and Norwegians would be informed that they could count on Allied help if they undertook to assist Finland. Then, 'a little later', they would be told 'in general terms' that the Allies were preparing to dispatch warships to interrupt the German ore traffic in Norwegian territorial waters; but of course the Allies would do nothing at all until they had received an answer from the Scandinavian governments, and Chamberlain was confident that this answer would be anything but positive. Complete inaction would thus be eminently justified.

There the matter still rested on 28 December 1939. But it took much more than that to discourage Winston Churchill, who was spurred on by the Admiralty; that same day, indeed, he had received the following note from Admiral Drax: 'I had no idea until yesterday that the question of iron ore from Norway was not yet decided, especially in view of the fact that the Germans torpedoed ships without warning in Norwegian territorial waters on 8, 11 and 13 December. [. . .] Enclosed are suggestions for dealing with the difficulties.'[35]

Churchill needed very little prompting; the very next day, he sent his new plan directly to the Prime Minister:

I suggest the following time-table of action should be adopted:
1. Now (if not already done) the diplomatic communication to Norway and Sweden promising help from Britain and France in certain contingencies.
2. Saturday, 30 December, completion of technical report of Chiefs-of-Staff Committee on larger plan.

3. Monday, 1 January, notification to Norway of our intention to retaliate for the German sinkings in Norwegian territorial waters . . .
4. Thursday, 2 January, flotillas start for Norwegian coast.
5. Thursday, 4 January, we begin arresting German ships [. . .] inside Norwegian territorial waters.
6. 30 January, at the latest, __ measures __ against __ Oxelosund. We meanwhile and thereafter await German reactions, and study and implement Chiefs-of-Staff's report on larger project.'[36]

Chamberlain was clearly impressed by such determination; at the 2 January session of the War Cabinet, he spoke in favour of the 'minor project', but hastened to add that 'he was, however, seriously concerned by the emphasis which the Chiefs-of-Staff laid upon possible action by Germany in southern Norway'. Thereupon, with commendable patience and a slight tinge of exasperation, Winston Churchill replied that 'all preparations had been made to stop the Narvik traffic immediately. The naval forces were standing by. [. . .] It was impossible in any operation of war to see a way clear through all the objections that could be raised to any particular course of action. It was right that all the difficulties should be fully examined, but we should not be deterred from action simply because there were certain objections. The war was costing us six millions a day, and it would be disastrous to reach a negative decision on this proposal, which seemed to offer the best chance of ending the war quickly.'[37]

Endless and inconclusive debates followed the First Lord's intervention. That night, General Ironside noted in his diary: 'A long day. Actually 8½ hours in Conferences and Meetings. You cannot make war like that.'[38] But in fact the session had not been entirely without result: the ministers had at least decided in favour of an immediate delivery of the memorandum to the Norwegian government. This was done on 6 January, when Lord Halifax received Norwegian Minister Eric Colban; Sir Alexander Cadogan noted in his diary that Lord Halifax 'had a painful interview with Colban',[39] and indeed the memorandum, after having mentioned the torpedoing of British and neutral ships in Norwegian territorial waters, went on to state that 'by these hostile acts, German naval forces have made Norwegian waters a theatre of war and have in practice deprived them of their neutral character. His Majesty's Government are therefore taking appropriate dispositions to prevent the use of Norwegian territorial waters by German ships and trade. To achieve this purpose, it would be necessary for His Majesty's naval forces at times to enter and operate in these waters.'[40]

The Norwegian reply took the form of a private letter from the King of Norway to his nephew George VI, asking him to use his influence with his ministers to bring them to reconsider their plan.[41] Actually, the intervention of such an eminent personality as King Haakon of Norway was more than enough for Neville Chamberlain to give up even the semblance of any warlike initiative. But for Norway, this was to be only a very short lull; five weeks later, the danger returned in full force, under the guise of the *Altmark* incident.

*Altmark* was the auxiliary ship of the German pocket battleship *Graf Spee*, and had on board 299 British sailors captured from merchant ships sunk by the battleship. After *Graf Spee* herself was sunk near Montevideo in December 1939, *Altmark* hid in the South Atlantic for two months; then, believing he had shaken off his pursuers, *Altmark*'s commanding officer, Captain Dau, undertook to sail to Germany by the northward route, skirting the coasts of Greenland, Iceland, and finally Norway. He had almost succeeded when, on 14 February, *Altmark* was spotted by a British observation plane in Norwegian territorial waters.[42] Two days later, a destroyer flotilla under the command of Captain Philip Vian intercepted *Altmark*, which took refuge in a narrow fjord near Stavanger, the Jøssingfjord. Two British destroyers were ordered to board the German ship and search her; but they were met by two Norwegian gunboats, who informed them that *Altmark* was not armed, and had already been visited by the Norwegians themselves the day before. At that, the British destroyers withdrew.

There matters might have rested, but for the personal intervention of the First Lord of the Admiralty. That same day, at 5.25 p.m., he sent the following order to Captain Vian: 'Unless Norwegian torpedo-boat undertakes to convoy *Altmark* to Bergen with a joint Anglo-Norwegian guard on board, and a joint escort, you should board *Altmark*, liberate the prisoners, and take possession of the ship pending further instructions.'[43] That same evening, the destroyer *Cossack* entered the Jøssingfjord; after a short and fruitless parley with the captain of the Norwegian gunboat, Captain Vian steered his ship towards *Altmark*, and ordered his men to board her.

A fierce hand-to-hand fight ensued, in which four Germans were killed and five wounded. *Altmark* was finally captured, and the 299 British prisoners freed. By midnight, *Cossack* had departed, leaving *Altmark* stranded on a sand bank.

Needless to say, Mr Halvdan Koht sent off a strongly worded diplomatic note to protest at such blatant disregard of Norwegian neutrality.[44] The whole Norwegian political class clearly viewed the situation with alarm,[45] and King Haakon VII himself confided to the new French minister in Oslo, Count de Dampierre, that Norway was increasingly being used as 'a kind of football field by the two antagonists'.[46] The problem, of course, was that the game was fast getting out of hand.

In London, meanwhile, the *Altmark* affair had naturally enhanced the prestige of the Admiralty,[47] and strongly influenced the general strategic debate. In fact, even after the defeat of Churchill's naval action scheme in mid-January, the War Office had pursued its study of operation plans in Scandinavia, and in the process General Ironside's 'major project' had gathered considerable momentum – on a theoretical plane at least. The initial plan, dubbed 'Avonmouth', provided for a landing in the Narvik area by two divisions that were to occupy the Swedish iron ore mines and then – perhaps – proceed to Finland.[48] Yet it quickly appeared to the planners that the Germans could easily threaten the rear of the expeditionary corps by landing at Bergen, Trondheim and Stavanger. In order to forestall them, the British Chiefs of Staff therefore devised an additional plan for central Norway, involving five battalions and code-named 'Stratford'.[49] A week later, however, after receipt of the Scandinavian protest notes, it suddenly dawned upon the planners that the Swedes might well refuse to co-operate with the British expeditionary corps, for fear of armed German reprisals in southern Sweden. In order to 'reassure' them, a third expedition was therefore planned; known as 'Plymouth', it included at least two divisions that were to land at Trondheim and 'co-operate in the defence of southern Sweden'.[50] For the Chiefs of Staff, the idea was to launch all three operations simultaneously.

Actually, it was all quite simple: the plan for a naval operation in Norwegian territorial waters had been abandoned because it would have antagonized the Norwegians, thus compromising the 'major project' designed to capture the iron mines of northern Sweden –

under the pretext of helping Finland, of course . . . But northern Sweden could not be reached without first landing in northern Norway, and, in order to protect that operation from German attack, another landing in southern Norway was definitely called for; yet, if Swedish co-operation was to be forthcoming, it would clearly be necessary to land also in central Norway, and even enter southern Sweden.[51]

The tragi-comic aspects of this situation were somewhat aggravated by two crucial facts: on the one hand, the troops earmarked for all three operations existed only on paper; between October 1939 and March 1940, ten regular divisions had been sent to France, and less than two divisions remained in the British Isles. As for the territorial troops, they were almost entirely devoid of training and equipment, which seemed to preclude their deployment overseas. Besides, the plans described above had not been definitely agreed upon by the Chiefs of Staff Committee, a body whose individual members were still inclined to champion their own services – which in turn led to 'a certain lack of comprehension', as their secretary Lord Ismay was later to state with considerable understatement.[52] Should the Chiefs of Staff eventually agree, however, they were to write a report to the Military Co-ordination Committee,* which advised the War Cabinet on military matters. There the whole discussion began anew and, all going well, the members of the War Cabinet were finally presented with a recommendation . . . which they were entirely free to disregard if they deemed it expedient. At that stage, it must also be borne in mind that, with the exception of Winston Churchill, the War Cabinet ministers had not the slightest notion of strategy, and they knew it;[53] as for Churchill's notions, they were highly imperfect – and he did not know it.

In France, Prime Minister Daladier was being sharply attacked in both the press and parliament for the feebleness and inconsistency of his government's efforts to help the embattled Finns.[54] Yet there was certainly no lack of zeal on the part of the French strategic planners, who were contemplating innumerable plans of operations against the Soviet Union, at Petsamo, Murmansk, in the Balkans

---

* This committee was made up of the Ministers of War, Air, Supply, and the First Lord of the Admiralty, with the Minister for the Co-ordination of Defence in the chair and the three Chiefs of Staff acting as advisers.

and even in the Caucasus . . .[55] Alas, not one of these ambitious plans could be implemented without British participation, and the British, naturally enough, still refused to take such plans seriously.[56] Mr Chamberlain said as much with impeccable civility at the Franco-British Supreme War Council session of 5 February. However, no doubt because it would have sounded indecent to advocate complete inaction in wartime, Chamberlain discreetly recommended the three-part 'major project', which had miraculously survived the bureaucratic snares and pitfalls described above.

Daladier, desperately groping for some kind of military initiative to ensure the survival of his hard-pressed government, was not too difficult to persuade.[57] It was therefore agreed to set up and dispatch an Anglo-French expeditionary force, ostensibly to help Finland, but first and foremost to secure the Swedish iron ore mines. To be sure, both the Swedes and the Norwegians seemed unwilling to co-operate, but it was decided to exert 'vigorous moral pressure' on the two countries.[58] Besides, as soon as the expeditionary force was ready, the Finns would be asked to issue an official appeal for help, whereupon the Scandinavians would be morally compelled to let the Allies cross their borders.[59] The expedition was to set sail under British command by the third week of March. At long last, there was a measure of co-ordination between French and British plans.

In London, the military now proceeded to advance beyond the stage of hypothetical planning. By mid-February, under the command of General Massy, detailed plans had been feverishly worked out for the triple expedition: the 'Stratford' force, with five battalions, was to occupy Trondheim, Stavanger and Bergen; the 'Avonmouth' detachment, an infantry brigade created *ex nihilo* 'with any elements that could be dredged up in England',[60] would land at Narvik together with a brigade of French mountain troops and a Polish half-brigade. From there, it would proceed to occupy the Swedish iron ore mines, with the towns of Kiruna, Gällivare, Boden and Luleå.[61] Finally, the 'Plymouth' force, with a troop strength fluctuating wildly from week to week, would land at Trondheim to 'assist the Swedes' in southern Sweden. These plans were regularly discussed with General Audet, the newly appointed commander-in-chief of all French forces earmarked for the Scandinavian operation.[62]

Meanwhile, the training and equipment of all French and British forces proceeded at full speed, and Major-General Sir John Kennedy, who had been associated with the early stages of planning in January, was summoned to the War Office on 23 February. 'I found', he later wrote, 'that our hypothetical plan had become a reality, and that I was mooted as Chief of Staff to a combined Franco-British expedition to Narvik under Mackesy's command.'[63] His surprise was understandable: two weeks earlier, General Massy, who knew the Prime Minister well, considered it perfectly possible that neither 'Stratford' nor 'Avonmouth' would ever be implemented.[64] Yet during the second half of February three new factors conspired to bring Scandinavia back to the fore – the first being of course the *Altmark* affair.

Having reaped the laurels of that exploit, Churchill at once proceeded to unearth his Norwegian minelaying scheme, which for the last two months had been largely eclipsed by General Ironside's 'major project'. But the latter was now better disposed towards Churchill's scheme, the First Lord having represented that the minelaying action would not fail to bring a German retaliation, which in turn would fully justify Ironside's 'major project'. At this stage, Churchill had also enlisted the support of the Foreign Office, for whom a limited mining operation in Norwegian waters now seemed preferable to an army expedition that had gradually assumed such frightening proportions. Besides, Lord Halifax considered that the *Altmark* affair, by showing that Norway was unable to protect her territorial waters from German incursions, amply justified a naval operation. On 20 February, he cabled to the British Ambassador in Washington, Lord Lothian: 'Now that *Altmark* incident has shown [. . .] complete subservience of Norway to German pressure [. . .] question arises of taking permanent measures to stop German use of these waters, e.g. by laying a minefield in them.'[65] Thus the Admiralty, the War Office and the Foreign Office, heavily influenced by the *Altmark* affair, now agreed on the necessity of immediate action in Norwegian waters.

That was not enough; at the War Cabinet meeting of 23 February, Neville Chamberlain declared that 'although his instincts were in favour of taking action, he could not take the proposed step lightheartedly. We had entered the war on moral grounds, and we must be careful not to undermine our position, else we might lose the support of the world. In any case, it would be necessary to make quite certain that the Dominions were with us, and it would be advisable to consult the leaders of the opposition.'[66]

Six days later, the leader of the Liberal Party, Archibald Sinclair, having backed the proposed action, and the Dominions Prime Ministers expressing no strong opinions for or against, Chamberlain remained adamant: 'In principle, he was in favour of the project. [. . .] He was, however, not at all convinced that the measure proposed would be opportune at the present moment. [. . .] He had reluctantly come to the conclusion that he could not advise the War Cabinet to take action in Norwegian territorial waters for the present. The project could be put on one side, and its execution could be reconsidered as the situation developed.'[67] Needless to say, this 'decision' carried the day.

Unfortunately for Chamberlain, even inaction was not an entirely satisfactory option, for a second factor – the Finno-Soviet conflict – lingered on as a permanent inducement to Allied action. Indeed, the Soviets, having thoroughly reorganized their forces since the disastrous offensive of late December, had started rolling forward again on the Karelian isthmus, and by mid-February they already controlled several advanced outposts of the Mannerheim Line.[68] The Finns, knowing that it was only a matter of time before their defences were overwhelmed, made discreet enquiries through a third party as to Moscow's conditions for a cessation of hostilities.[69] But on 23 February, the British Minister in Helsinki was authorized to disclose to the Finnish authorities the Franco-British plan of 5 February, including the provision that the Finns should issue an official appeal for help. The Finnish ministers asked about the strength of the Allied contingents and their planned date of arrival, to which the British diplomat answered that they would arrive in mid-April, and would be about 20,000 strong.[70]

The Finns were thus confronted by a crucial choice: either accept the Soviet terms for ending the war, or appeal to the Allies for help. Yet as early as 28 February, they were informed that Sweden would not allow an Allied expedition bound for Finland to cross its territory.[71] Besides, the Finnish government and the Commander-in-Chief, Marshal Mannerheim, were aware that the Allies wanted above all to occupy the Swedish iron ore mines, and that their help for Finland would definitely take second place to that imperative.[72]

In the end, the Finnish decision was dictated by purely strategic considerations. By the end of February, Marshal Mannerheim, having recognized that his army was in imminent danger of collapsing, appealed to his government for an immediate opening of cease-fire negotiations. On 1 March, the Helsinki government decided to begin such negotiations. But this did not mean that they had lost all interest in the proposed Allied expedition; on the contrary, they assumed that the very threat of a Franco-British expedition would lead the Soviets to present more moderate peace conditions, in the hope of securing an agreement to end hostilities before the Allies entered the fray.*[73]

On 1 March, the Finnish Ambassador in London, Gripenberg, accordingly informed Lord Halifax that his government's decision to negotiate or to appeal for Allied help would be directly influenced by the strength and the sailing date of the proposed Allied expedition. He had therefore been instructed to ask 'whether the Allies could send 100 bombers and their crews at once and 50,000 men to reach Finland in March, with reinforcements later, whether this force could fight anywhere in Finland, whether the British government thought that they could persuade Norway and Sweden to allow passage to the Allied forces, and whether the refusal of passage would change Allied policy'.[75] Needless to say, Lord Halifax could give no encouraging reply to such questions, and neither could the War Cabinet members meeting that afternoon: it was technically impossible to send 50,000 men within the time specified, and there was little to be done about a Swedish and Norwegian refusal to allow passage through their territories. However, none of this could be told so crudely to the Finns, who had to be encouraged to keep fighting, to the British public, who expected a vigorous prosecution of the war, or – least of all – to the French, who were clamouring for the quickest possible intervention in the northern theatre.

They had good reason for that; in France, after the first Finnish setbacks, the government was subjected to increasing public pressure in favour of action – of whatever kind.[76] In the words of the

* Apparently not a bad calculation, since Soviet General Meretskov was to write thirty years later: 'Any delay in the victorious conclusion of the war could have allowed the French and the Swedes to send reinforcements, and instead of having to wage war against a single state, we would have been faced with a coalition.'[74]

French Commander-in-Chief, General Gamelin, 'Actually, public opinion did not know what it wanted done, but it wanted something else, and above all, it wanted action.'[77] Another observer was even more blunt: 'The idea was to do something, even something stupid.'[78] Naturally, the inference was not lost on Daladier that this was a *conditio sine qua non* for his government's survival; hence the pressure exerted through all possible channels on the British government for a speedy implementation of the decisions taken on 5 February. Indeed, when the Finnish ambassador in Paris came to the French Foreign Ministry on 1 March with the same questions as his London counterpart, he received positive answers to all his requests: the French troops were ready to start, and in the event of a Norwegian refusal, a 'forcible entry' would be made.[79] Daladier had not even found it necessary to consult with the British beforehand, and yet they, not the French, were to be responsible for the conduct of the operation . . .

In London, Lord Halifax and his colleagues greeted the news with surprise and consternation: 'The War Cabinet thought the French answers most disquieting. Their promises seemed to be bluff and to have been made in the knowledge that they could blame us for the failure to redeem them. We could neither spare the bombers nor transport 50,000 men to Finland in March.'[80] However, the Cabinet deemed it preferable not to turn down the Finnish requests categorically, for otherwise the Finns would probably sue for peace, and that in turn would mean the end of any Scandinavian undertaking. The Finnish ambassador was accordingly to be informed in general terms that the Allies 'would do everything in their power' to support Finland; simultaneously, the Scandinavian governments were to be handed a statement of His Majesty's government's 'intention to ask for passage', coupled with an offer of assistance in case such a decision on their part 'involved them in war with Germany'.[81] Finally, preparations for the expedition were to proceed apace, just in case they were required. No drastic decisions in all this, of course, just a conscientious effort to placate the Finns, the French, the First Lord of the Admiralty, the Chief of the Imperial General Staff – and of course public opinion at large – with a suitable display of martial rumblings.

On 4 March, both Sweden and Norway replied to the British note with a categoric refusal: granting passage to an Allied expedition was entirely out of the question.[82] As on the other hand no official request for intervention seemed to be coming from Helsinki, the British War Cabinet now had at least two excellent reasons for doing nothing. In Paris, however, Daladier was still planning to go ahead with the operation; but if he considered it quite possible to disregard Scandinavian opposition, he could not do without a Finnish appeal for help, which alone would legitimize the expedition in the eyes of the world. On 7 March, he accordingly declared to the Finnish ambassador: 'For the last few days, we have been expecting an appeal from Finland in order to rush to her assistance with all possible means, and it seems difficult to understand the delay in issuing such an appeal.'[83] Simultaneously, Daladier was showering the British authorities with telegrams, notes, appeals, aide-mémoires and memoranda exhorting them to set everything in motion before the Finns reached agreement with the Russians on the cessation of hostilities – a move that would swiftly sound the death knell of the proposed expedition, and quite probably that of M. Daladier's government as well.

On 11 March, French Ambassador Corbin accordingly called at the Foreign Office to apply the usual pressure, and the Under Secretary of State, Sir Alexander Cadogan, noted in his diary: 'Corbin appeared, to make a grand remonstrance about our backwardness in Scandinavia. I retorted – saying that it might be picturesque and romantic . . . to promise the Finns 200,000 men, but it wasn't playing the game. [. . .] How tiresome the French are.'[84] General Ironside clearly agreed, and noted in his own diary: 'Corbin [. . .] said that Daladier would resign if we did not do more over Finland. [. . .] That people were beginning to doubt whether we were in earnest. [. . .] The French, who are not responsible for the military execution of the plan, put forward the most extravagant ideas. They are absolutely unscrupulous in everything.'[85]

Perhaps . . . but that very day, the War Cabinet finally gave in to French pressures, and decided to go ahead with landing operations at Narvik, even without Norwegian consent.[86] 'We are now working away at this plan,' Ironside noted, 'which means that we must be prepared for some sort of an opposed landing. I can see our great big Scots Guards shouldering the sleepy Norwegians out of the way at 5 a.m. in the morning. It seems inconceivable that the Norwegians should put up any resistance if they are in any way surprised.'[87]

Winston Churchill: 'I am much concerned at the complete failure not only of our efforts against the enemy, but of our method of conducting war.'

Paul Reynaud: 'One must think big or stop making war, one must act fast or lose the war.'

The Supreme War Council Meeting in Paris, February 1940 (left to right: Lord Halifax, Daladier, Cadogan, Chamberlain, Churchill): 'Academic resolutions amounting to a fine exercise in non-commitment, in the best parliamentary tradition.'

Adolf Hitler with Generals Keitel and Jodl: 'I consider Operation Weserübung to be particularly daring – in fact one of the rashest undertakings in the history of modern warfare. Precisely that will help ensure its success.'

General von Falkenhorst, Commander-in-Chief of Operation Weserübung: 'I went to town and bought a Baedeker, a tourist guide, in order to find out what Norway was like . . . I had no idea.'

Preparations were now well advanced; in France, the troops and transports were ready to proceed with the operation, code-named 'BK'. In Britain, General Mackesy, the commander designate, had set up his headquarters in Yorkshire, and his Chief of Staff noted drily that 'on 11th March, the whole affair suddenly looked more realistic'.[88] But General Mackesy himself was not so sure; three days earlier, he had expressed his doubts in a note to the War Office: 'It is my considered view that the plan as it now stands may result in a dangerous if not disastrous situation, if and when the force arrives at its destination.'[89] The main reasons cited by the General: the last units of the force would arrive at Narvik 45 days after the first ones, so that it would take more than two months before the troops constituted a fighting force; besides, no co-ordination had been planned with the 'Plymouth' forces due to operate further south, and the Narvik expedition was due to receive *one* anti-aircraft battery, a whole month after the initial landing! Last but not least, Mackesy was amazed that his plans continued to allow for Swedish co-operation, when the Swedes had repeatedly stated that they would oppose any Allied passage.[90]

If the attitude of the Swedes was indeed important, that of the Norwegians was clearly crucial. At a meeting of the Chiefs of Staff on the morning of 11 March, as the British forces were about to embark, Admiral Evans, considered an expert on Norway, struck a reassuring note: the Norwegians loathed the Germans, and would surely do nothing to oppose the British. Still, the real issue was being deliberately avoided: if the Norwegians did resist, what was to be done? And yes, what about the Swedes? 'I think the whole thing is hare brained,' Air Marshal Sir Cyril Newall flatly asserted.[91] Lord Ismay agreed. So did General Kennedy.

On the next day, 12 March, the issue of a possible Scandinavian military opposition was finally brought up at the War Cabinet session, and no one seemed to agree on what was to be done. 'We had a dreadful Cabinet,' General Ironside noted. 'Everybody had a different idea upon how much force we would have to use at Narvik. In the end, the Prime Minister was persuaded to see the Admiral [Sir Edward Evans] and the General [Mackesy] ... When I explained to him that the men were commencing embarkation, they all seemed surprised. A more unmilitary show I have never seen. The Prime Minister began peering at a chart of Narvik and when he had finished he asked me what scale it was on. He asked what effect an 8-inch shell would have on a transport and finished up by saying that he was prepared to risk a 4-inch shell, but not an 8-inch shell. He then asked what the weight of the shells were. Chatfield, an Admiral of the Fleet, first said that we should not risk firing at the Norwegians, and then said he thought we ought not to be bluffed by a mere Lieutenant in charge of a shore battery. The Cabinet presented the picture of a bewildered flock of sheep faced by a problem they have consistently refused to consider. Their favourite formula is that the case is hypothetical and then they shy off a decision. I came away disgusted with them all.'[93]

That same evening, Halifax, Lord Chatfield, Lord Hankey, Sir Cyril Newall, Admiral Pound, Lord Ismay and General Ironside met with the Prime Minister at 10 Downing Street to review the operational instructions for the force commanders. General Mackesy was present, and so was his Chief of Staff, who noted that 'the meeting began with Evans giving an enthusiastic exposé of the whole plan, with all its details. The Prime Minister looked tired and lugubrious enough when he began. But as Evans warmed to his subject, Mr Chamberlain looked more and more horrified.'[94]

The instructions to the military commanders governing the use of force were in fact highly ambiguous – at times even ludicrously so: 'It is not the intention of this government that the force should fight its way through either Sweden or Norway. Nonetheless, should you find your way barred by Swedish forces, you should demand passage from the Swedish commander with the utmost energy.'[95] According to Sir John Kennedy, General Mackesy then said that 'he proposed to go up to the frontier in person to demand passage. The Prime Minister asked what he would do if the way was barred. Mackesy explained that if he could not get through without fighting, he would call it off.' Whereupon Lord Halifax interjected: 'Well, if we can't get in except at the cost of a lot of Norwegian lives, I am not for it – ore or no ore.'[96]

The operational orders were finally approved: the expedition was to establish itself at Narvik, secure the railway into Sweden, and then concentrate in Sweden in anticipation of its ultimate goal, which was of course to assist Finland. There was to be no fighting against the Swedes or the Norwegians, but on the other hand 'the commanders were not to be deterred by a show of resistance'.[97]

Some might ask how the force commanders would manage to distinguish a show of resistance from a genuine resistance if they were not allowed to fight, but that was left unspecified.

Thereupon the meeting ended, and General Kennedy noted: 'The Prime Minister shook hands with us as we filed out of the room, saying "Good-bye, and good luck to you – if you go". Once again, we resorted to betting. [. . .] Bridges said he thought the chances were against it. Newall was laying three to one against. Mackesy a hundred.'[98] All knew the irresolute temperament of the Prime Minister, and besides, there were persistent rumours coming from Helsinki about the imminent signature of a peace agreement . . .

There was clearly something behind these rumours. On 7 March, Finnish negotiators had been sent to Moscow. By then, Marshal Mannerheim's army could no longer delay the Soviet onslaught, the fall of Viborg was imminent, and Helsinki was directly threatened. On 12 March, the Finnish delegates in Moscow were granted full powers to reach agreement. Meanwhile, the French and British troops were embarking, and the politicians seemed to have finally made up their minds; the War Cabinet had even decided that there would be no diplomatic niceties prior to landing: 'No communication should be made to the government of Norway as to our intention to land a force at Narvik until transports have actually arrived.' The latest position on the use of force was also far more martial, though hardly more coherent: 'The naval and military commanders should not be instructed that they were not to fire in any circumstances . . .'[99]

In Moscow, late that night, agreement was finally reached, and the next day, 13 March, at 11 a.m., the Soviet and Finnish delegations signed the peace agreement. For General Sir John Kennedy, in Yorkshire, this was to be 'a very odd day': 'I was putting the finishing touches to our orders down to the minutest detail, while the news coming in from Finland about our impending peace with Russia made the expedition more and more unlikely. Ismay agreed to tackle the Prime Minister and persuade him that he must make up his mind: the ships were loaded, the troops were moving, and a decision was overdue.'[100]

The War Cabinet met at 11.30 to hear the news of the Finno-Soviet peace. Churchill naturally wanted to go ahead with the operation regardless of the new situation, as 'our real objective was of course

35

to secure possession of the Gällivare ore fields', but Chamberlain no less predictably rejected the idea, and proposed instead to send a mission to Norway and Sweden 'to improve our relations with them'. John Simon, Oliver Stanley, Samuel Hoare and Kingsley Wood immediately approved this suggestion; Lord Hankey alone seemed to have a few doubts. The War Cabinet finally decided to disperse all units that had been prepared for the Scandinavian expedition.[101]

That evening, Winston Churchill, completely discouraged, wrote to Lord Halifax: 'All has now fallen to the ground, because so cumbrous are our processes that we were too late. Now the ice will melt, and the Germans are the masters of the North. [. . .] Whether they have some positive plan of their own which will open upon us, I cannot tell. It would seem to me astonishing if they have not.'[102]

This was a highly prescient judgment, for the Germans did indeed have a plan of their own – and a formidable one at that.

# CHAPTER TWO

# Hitler's 'Rashest Undertaking'

By the autumn of 1939, Adolf Hitler had just turned fifty. Few destinies can be as amazing as that of the homeless, unemployed painter from Vienna who, in less than two decades, had made himself the absolute master of Germany. He had certainly been powerfully helped by the rancours of defeat, the fear of communism, a devastating economic crisis, the near-sightedness of the big German industrialists and the ineptitude of his political rivals. Yet none of the above would suffice to explain this solitary, uncultured and unbalanced Austrian's meteoric rise to power, unless one were to take into account his fanatical singleness of purpose, high degree of opportunism, and complete lack of scruples, added to an astonishing personal magnetism, undeniable talents both as an actor and as a stage manager, and of course an unrivalled ability to browbeat and paralyse through an expertly balanced combination of secrecy, surprise, verbal abuse and concentrated violence.

Having become at once Chancellor and President of the German Reich, leader of the country's only remaining party and master of both army and police, he had eliminated his rivals one by one, and could now rule supreme, guided only by his inspiration, 'with the assurance of a sleepwalker'. In the pursuit of his ultimate goal – the conquest of a vast *Lebensraum* in Eastern Europe – he had proved astonishingly adept at exploiting the rivalries, irresolution, pacifist inclinations and political paralysis of the Western powers to win a long string of bloodless victories: the rearming of Germany, the remilitarization of the Rhineland, *Anschluss* with Austria, and even the annexation of Czechoslovakia, thanks to the shameful episode of Munich in the autumn of 1938. Encouraged by this brilliant succession of strategic and diplomatic victories – crowned shortly thereafter by the conclusion of a Soviet–German pact – Hitler proceeded to invade Poland. Once again, he was counting on the passivity of London and Paris, and perhaps even on a new Munich, to swallow his prey without a fight. But, on 3 September 1939, Chamberlain and Daladier, well aware that their governments would be swept away by any new capitulation, summoned the courage to declare war on him. Henceforth, an armed conflict was inevitable.

The Führer was entirely prepared for it. In a three-week campaign, his Wehrmacht crushed the Polish army, while the French and the British remained passively on the sidelines. Yet Hitler now knew that he would be unable to avoid a general war in Europe, which he had hitherto hoped to unleash in 1943 at the earliest.[1] In October, as his shock troops returned from Poland, Hitler therefore proceeded to alter his plans, and prepare all German forces for the decisive blow in the West. The idea was definitely to strike before the end of the year, but several dates fixed for the attack were to come and go without any action being initiated; each time, the weather proved unfavourable.

Five years earlier, Hitler had told Hermann Rauschning that 'should war break out, one of his first moves would be the invasion of Sweden', for 'he could not abandon the Scandinavian countries to Russian or British influence.'[2] During the years that followed, the Scandinavian countries largely disappeared from Hitler's preoccupations, but at the beginning of October 1939, two Nazi dignitaries sought to persuade the Führer of the absolute necessity of invading Norway. The first was Admiral Raeder, Commander-in-Chief of the Kriegsmarine, who had just been instructed to draw up plans for a 'siege of Great Britain', and evidently thought that Norwegian naval bases would be invaluable in this respect. Hitler's second interlocutor was Reichsleiter Rosenberg, Party ideologist and chief of the NSDAP's 'Foreign Policy Office', which sought to compete with – and eventually replace – von Ribbentrop's Foreign Ministry through a highly complex and often amateurish network of intrigue at home and subversion abroad.[3] But Hitler, whose attention was now monopolized by his plans for an offensive in the west, had no intention of weakening them by a diversion in the north; Raeder's and Rosenberg's proposals were therefore categorically rejected. Nothing more would have been heard of the matter, but for the appearance at the Reichskanzlei in mid-December of a Norwegian named Quisling.

A strange and fascinating man was Vidkun Abraham Lauritz

Jonssøn Quisling. Born in 1887 in the Norwegian province of Telemark, he was the son of a clergyman, from whom he had inherited a passion for religion, metaphysics and mathematical sciences. At the early age of twelve, this tall lad with slightly bulging blue eyes had invented a mathematical demonstration still taught in Norwegian schools to this day; by the time he was 24, he had graduated from the military academy with the best marks ever granted in that institution – which earned him a formal presentation to the King. At 35, he had become nothing less than a benefactor of humanity: as the secretary of Fridtjof Nansen, he had organized the distribution of foreign help to whole regions of the Ukraine devastated by civil war, famine and epidemics; through his personal intervention, he had saved hundreds of thousands of lives, very often at the peril of his own.

Unfortunately, this brilliant personality was not without its weaker sides; indeed, ever since his childhood, Vidkun Quisling had been a loner, curiously obsessed with the idea that everyone was about to betray him – or had already done so. Besides, he often immersed himself in highly abstract metaphysical meditations, which further isolated him from his fellow men and from the plain realities of daily existence. To make things worse, this already fragile and tormented individual had remained far too long in the Soviet Union, at a time when it was surely preferable to be found elsewhere: that of the first great purges of Joseph Stalin. Quisling returned to Norway at the beginning of 1930, deeply shaken by this traumatic experience, but also firmly resolved to lead a great crusade against communism . . .

In Norway, the beginnings were clearly auspicious: a year after his return, thanks to his brilliant past and a few choice acquaintances, Quisling was named Minister of Defence in the new Norwegian government! In 1933, after the fall of that government, he set up his own political party, the Nasjonal Samling (National Union), which immediately undertook to compete in the legislative elections. At every stage, Quisling loudly proclaimed his intention of fighting communism. Unfortunately, he tended to see communists everywhere, he was decidedly mediocre as an orator, even worse as an organizer, and he drifted increasingly towards the extreme right of the political spectrum. All this scared away the average elector, and the Nasjonal Samling suffered two crushing electoral defeats.

Yet Vidkun Quisling, undeterred, pursued his solitary crusade against the ubiquitous spectre of communist expansionism.

It would not do, however, to dismiss the man as a hopeless visionary engaged in the quixotic pursuit of his pet chimera. Back in 1930, Quisling had written a little book entitled *Russia and Ourselves*.[5] Anyone reading this book could have found, nine years in advance, the exact path later followed by Stalin's policy of expansion; Poland was described as the first victim, and indeed, Soviet troops were to enter eastern Poland in September 1939. According to Quisling, the Baltic states were to be the next on the list, and sure enough, by early October, Soviet units had taken up positions in all strategic areas of Estonia, Latvia and Lithuania. For Quisling, Norway was to come next, but before that, he could see yet another victim of Soviet expansionism: Finland. Once again, he was entirely right: on 30 November 1939, Finland was attacked. After all that, no one could deny that Quisling was a good prophet; but unfortunately, he had also decided to become an actor in the great drama of the European conflict . . . and Quisling was a very bad actor.

Now that Finland was under attack, Vidkun Quisling predicted with increasing assurance that Norway would come next. For him, the Soviets would attack his country in order to counter a British landing. Could it be that Quisling had been informed of British strategic discussions concerning Norway? At any rate, he decided to step in, and he contemplated no half-measures: he would take power in Norway, with German assistance, 'in order to forestall occupation by the British, a civil war . . . and the Bolshevization of the whole country'.[6] Granted, not everyone will understand how a British occupation could lead to the Bolshevization of Norway, but it must be remembered that Quisling's anxiety and obsessive anti-communism could easily make him impervious to common logic.

As the success of Quisling's ambitious plan depended entirely on German assistance, it was of course necessary to approach the Führer – something the strangely hesitant, impractical and irresolute Quisling would have found almost impossible to do; but he had among his henchmen several determined, crafty and not overly scrupulous people for whom such matters were easily arranged. And indeed, it took them little time to contact two Nazi dignitaries with a tremendous interest in Norway: Admiral Raeder and Reichsleiter Rosenberg. Having quickly realized the relevance of

Quisling's plans to their own ambitions, they lost no time at all in securing for him an interview with the Führer; and so it was that Vidkun Quisling entered the Reichskanzlei on 14 December 1939, for a fateful meeting with the master of the German Reich.

One of Rosenberg's close collaborators, Gruppenleiter Hans Wilhelm Scheidt, was present at the interview, which he described in the following terms: 'In his halting German [. . .] Quisling began by saying that he was in no way an enemy of England, and that he deeply deplored that the war had broken out. Neither was he a National Socialist, but he considered himself a friend of Germany, which he hoped would participate in the struggle against Bolshevism. He considered that the propaganda campaign orchestrated by Great Britain in Norway was intended to prepare the ground for British strategic aims in Scandinavia. Quisling's knowledge of existing conditions in Norway and in all Scandinavia aggravated his fears. [. . .] He was the leader of a national-radical party that was demanding first and foremost an upgrading of military preparation and armament, which would allow Norway to oppose any attempt to violate her neutrality. To that effect, and considering the state of things as well as the fact that there was no time to be lost, he could see no other solution than an assumption of power by himself and his party. He was therefore thinking of a coup. Hitler listened very calmly and attentively to Quisling's statement. The latter's ideas about plans for a coup gave rise to a certain animation, and a kind of amused attention on the Führer's part. He did not declare himself categorically opposed to such a plan, but he made it plain that it raised considerable objections. Above all, he appeared unconvinced that such a small minority could impose itself when faced with the police, the army and the trade unions. On that matter, he concluded: "Believe me, Herr Major, we National Socialists are so to speak experts in revolutions." But he promised to give financial support for the development of Nasjonal Samling. As for Quisling's assertions concerning the political situation, he admitted to having been impressed by such arguments. Above all, the danger of a British occupation of Norway, in violation of that country's neutrality, appeared to him immediately as the crucial aspect of the problem. [The Führer] said that he had always been an Anglophile, and still was today, in spite of the war which he was being compelled to wage. [. . .] But should the danger of a British violation of

Norwegian neutrality [. . .] ever become acute, then he would land in Norway with six, eight, twelve divisions, and even more if necessary, to beat the British to the post. He was much in favour of Norwegian neutrality, and was not inclined to bind troops out there, when he could make much better use of them elsewhere. But if ever he detected the slightest British intention of entering Norway, he would be sure to intervene in good time.'[7]

Concerning the Führer's last words, Quisling was later to say that 'upon mentioning the eventuality of a violation of [Norwegian] neutrality, Hitler worked himself into a frenzy, culminating in a sort of ecstasy'.[8] No one should underestimate the part played by frenzy – and ecstasy – in the Führer's decision-making process; that same evening, at the Oberkommando der Wehrmacht (Armed Forces High Command), General Jodl entered in his diary: 'Führer orders investigation, with smallest possible staff, of how occupation of Norway can be carried out.'[9]

This, in Hitler's mind, was probably intended to be a theoretical study only. Four days later, indeed, he met Quisling a second time, and the conversation – or rather the monologue – was summarized thus: 'No infringement of Norwegian neutrality by Germany, on the contrary, Germany has an interest in the strict enforcement of neutrality. A sharp look-out to be held in Norway for any indication of an intended conspiracy with England, and close surveillance to be maintained of all activities in suspected gathering points and points of embarkation in England, as well as inception in Germany of preventive measures to cope with any British attack. Quisling was to build up his party legally, but intensively, and would receive financial means to that effect. There was no more serious discussion of the coup plan; or, rather, it was quite simply dropped. It was also mentioned that Nasjonal Samling would be entrusted with domestic policy, in case it became necessary to pre-empt a British occupation.'[10] The message was clear: Hitler was thinking of a contingency plan, to be carried out only in case of a British threat. He had as yet no substantial information concerning such a threat, and he clearly was not anxious to be dragged into a conflict in northern Europe.[11] The reason for that was obvious: on 27 December, Hitler had set a new date for the great offensive in the west: 14 January 1940.

Like all previous dates for the offensive, this one was soon to be cancelled on account of the weather. But, on 26 January, Hitler once again replied to Admiral Raeder, who was asking for permission to initiate operations against Norway, that 'at the present moment, both Sweden and Norway are firmly resolved to observe a strict neutrality'; to which he added that he 'considered that absolute priority ought to be given to the protection of the Ruhr area, which was essential to the prosecution of the war, as well as to the enlargement of the land base from which to carry out an offensive against Great Britain. It was necessary to defeat France, in order to deprive Great Britain of her base on the Continent.'[12]

Meanwhile, the investigation ordered by Hitler on 14 December was being pursued at the OKW (Oberkommando der Wehrmacht), under the code name of 'Studie Nord'. It included reports submitted by the staffs of all three branches of the armed forces, and not unnaturally, given Admiral Raeder's keen interest in the matter, the navy's report was by far the most exhaustive; it called for landings along the entire coast, from Oslo to Tromsø.[13] On 20 January, a first draft of Studie Nord was presented to the Führer, who issued the very next day an order for the formation of a Special Staff (Sonderstab) within the OKW, entrusted with preparing operational plans for what was henceforth to be known as Operation Weserübung.

On 5 February 1940, the three chiefs of the new 'Special Staff', Admiral Krancke, Colonel Knaus and Oberleutnant von Tippelskirch, gathered for the first time in the utmost secrecy at OKW headquarters, where the Commander-in-Chief, General Keitel, gave them a brief outline of their mission: 'Your task is to prepare an operation for the occupation of Norway, an operation which could prove necessary in certain circumstances. We are in possession of information from several sources indicating that the British themselves intend to occupy the ports of the western coast of Norway, in co-operation with the French. We are also informed that the British have already approached the Norwegian government in this matter. [. . .] Given our situation of naval inferiority, it would clearly be in our interest that Norway remain strictly neutral [. . .] On the other hand [. . .] the occupation of the western coast of Norway by Allied forces [. . .] would be a major setback for us. We must therefore prepare an operation ourselves, on a theoretical basis at first, so that it could be implemented rapidly in case of necessity. In view of our considerable naval inferiority, such an undertaking must remain absolutely secret. It is therefore necessary that all other political and military authorities [. . .] be kept in complete ignorance of the investigation of this matter.'[14]

The Special Staff accordingly set to work in the utmost secrecy. Its first task was to collect a huge amount of documentation on Norway, from both civilian and military sources. The navy's report, already the backbone of Studie Nord, was once again the main basis for all planning work. Indeed, the plan now drawn up by Admiral Krancke's Special Staff called for a simultaneous occupation of all main ports on the Norwegian coast by a lightning naval action. The first wave of assault troops, carried in warships, would land at Oslo, Kristiansand, Arendal, Stavanger, Bergen, Trondheim and Narvik. At the same time, parachute troops were to descend on the airports of Oslo and Stavanger. Reinforcements would then come in successive waves by sea and air during the following days.[15]

By mid-February, the operational plan was already well advanced, yet no one could tell whether it would ever be carried out. 'Inasmuch as both Hitler and Jodl allowed us to work in peace,' Admiral Krancke later noted, 'I was under the impression that they were not firmly resolved to execute the operation.'[16] Indeed, the Führer continued to view the whole plan as purely preventive: Norway would surely remain neutral, and dissuade the British from any rash undertaking in the north. Hitler seemed to believe this basically because it was convenient: nothing should be allowed to divert the Wehrmacht from its decisive stroke in the west. And yet in mid-February, a single incident was enough to overturn Hitler's conviction: the boarding of *Altmark*.

Upon hearing of the liberation of all British prisoners aboard *Altmark*, Hitler flew into a violent rage. 'The event threw a whole new light on the matter,' wrote Admiral Raeder, 'for it showed that the Oslo government was no longer capable of enforcing its neutrality.'[17] In his own diary, Rosenberg was even more specific: 'Really a stupid initiative on Churchill's part. It confirms Quisling's views and his warnings. I saw the Führer today and [. . .] there is nothing left of his determination to uphold the neutrality of the northern countries, and make preparations only for the eventuality of things taking a turn for the worse. No need to say what will happen next.'[18]

Perhaps there is ... Admiral Krancke, for one, immediately noted a change in the atmosphere at the OKW: 'When we received more detailed information on the un-neutral attitude of the Norwegian torpedo-boats, the operation, hitherto considered as purely prophylactic, was taken far more earnestly.'[19] That was an understatement; on 19 February, Hitler ordered a drastic speeding up of all work connected with Operation Weserübung. General Jodl suggested that a general and his staff be entrusted with the co-ordination and acceleration of all preparations, and Hitler immediately agreed.[20] From then on, everything proceeded at top speed. General Keitel put forward the name of General von Falkenhorst, and the very next day, 20 February, the latter was summoned to the Reichskanzlei.

Nikolaus von Falkenhorst had only recently been appointed general, and his aristocratic origins were unlikely to endear him to the Führer. But in 1918, von Falkenhorst had landed in Finland as Chief of Staff to General von der Golz,* and he therefore possessed valuable experience of combined operations in the north. Indeed, upon receiving von Falkenhorst in his study, Hitler immediately asked him about the co-ordination between army and navy during landing operations in Finland; after which he led the General to a table covered with maps and told him point blank that he intended to 'launch a similar operation in order to occupy Norway'. 'The Führer,' von Falkenhorst later declared, 'told me that the Reich had received information that the British intended to land in Norway, and had reached an agreement with the Norwegian authorities in this matter.† Besides, the events of the Jøssingfjord, with the boarding of *Altmark*, had dispelled all ambiguity as to British intentions.' 'I could feel', General von Falkenhorst added, 'the sheer nervousness caused by the Jøssingfjord affair.'[21]

For Hitler, it was now essential to beat the British to the post. The interview ended with a long monologue, in which the Führer explained the reasons behind the undertaking: 'Scandinavia constituted the northern flank of the European theatre of operations. Should the British gain a foothold in Norway, they would thereby be able to control Sweden and the Baltic. In the Baltic sector, Germany only had very few troops. The coast lay undefended, without artillery or fortifications [. . .] By crossing the Baltic, the British [. . .] could

---

* The operation was mounted to help General Mannerheim's 'White Guards' defeat the 'Reds'.

† The latter information was of course entirely incorrect.

make their way to Berlin, to the very heart of Germany. [. . .] A Norway occupied by the British, or under strict British control, would become a mortal danger to the German submarine weapon. [. . .] Swedish iron ore was indispensable to Germany. The Swedish port of Luleå, like the greater part of the Baltic, being ice-bound in winter, Germany depended on exports through Narvik. Should the enemy occupy the Norwegian coast, [. . .] the iron ore supply would be interrupted. That was why he had decided to take all principal ports of Norway in a surprise attack. [. . .] The idea was to cover his northern flank; hence the decisive importance of Norway.'22

According to General Keitel, Hitler had only summoned von Falkenhorst to sound him out. But perhaps because he got carried away by his diatribe, and more likely because he 'sensed' that he had found the right man, Hitler entrusted von Falkenhorst on the spot with the command of Operation Weserübung. The General was given a few additional indications: he was to have five divisions at his disposal; only the largest ports and the main cities need be occupied; some contingency plans had been worked out during the winter. The whole undertaking, Hitler underlined, was to be kept rigorously secret – this was an absolute precondition for its success. Upon ending the interview, Hitler ordered von Falkenhorst to report back to him at 5 p.m. that afternoon, in order to explain how he intended to make use of his five divisions to carry out the undertaking.

'Once outside,' von Falkenhorst noted, 'I went to town and bought a Baedeker, a tourist guide, in order to find out what Norway was like [. . .] I had no idea; I wanted to know where the ports were, how many inhabitants Norway had, and what kind of country this was. [. . .] I absolutely did not know what to expect.'23 The General then returned to his room at the Kaiserhof hotel, read the main chapters of his Baedeker, and studied the maps with particular care.

At 5 p.m., von Falkenhorst was back at the Reichskanzlei, and he proceeded to give Hitler a broad outline of his plan. It closely matched the conclusions of Admiral Krancke's Special Staff, probably because they were based on a study of the self-same Baedeker. At any rate, the Führer was fully satisfied, and he ordered von Falkenhorst to pursue his work along these lines; he repeated that there was no time to lose, and, according to the General, 'he seemed preoccupied by the idea that our undertaking might be compromised by an English operation'. By the evening of 21 February,

General von Falkenhorst had thus been entrusted with the execution of Operation Weserübung. Jodl noted in his diary that 'von Falkenhorst accepted with enthusiasm'; after the war, von Falkenhorst was to deny this categorically. Admittedly, Jodl was in no position to judge, and when von Falkenhorst offered this denial, he was himself facing judgment . . . After all, it hardly matters one way or the other.

On 26 February, the staff of a new unit known by the name of 'Group 21' began its work in several contiguous offices of a discreet building belonging to the OKW in Berlin's Bendlerstrasse. Only one unmarked door led into these offices; in the first one, several officers were painstakingly carrying out secretarial work – no question of employing real secretaries, of course; the next two offices were occupied by General von Falkenhorst and his new staff, Colonel Buschenhagen, Major Pohlmann, and two former members of the Special Staff, Colonel Knaus and Admiral Krancke. All these men worked in complete isolation from 7 a.m. to 11 p.m. every day of the week.[24] On the basis of Studie Nord and the work of the Special Staff, they set up an attack plan of conspicuous daring and impressive proportions. The first echelon of the landing forces, as well as all available ships, were to be divided among six attack areas: Group I, 'Narvik', with 2,000 men of the Third Mountain Division, embarked in ten destroyers and escorted by the battle cruisers *Scharnhorst* and *Gneisenau*; Group II, 'Trondheim', with four destroyers carrying 1,700 men, escorted by the heavy cruiser *Admiral Hipper*; Group III, 'Bergen', with 1,300 men aboard the cruisers *Köln* and *Königsberg*, and two destroyers; Groups IV and V, 'Kristiansand' and 'Egersund', with the cruiser *Karlsruhe*, the escort vessel *Tsing Tau*, three torpedo-boats and four minesweepers; finally, Group VI, 'Oslo', with the cruisers *Blücher*, *Lützow* and *Emden* and three destroyers, carrying shock troops of the 163rd Division, the General Staff of the expedition, as well as 'all the people that are immediately necessary for the occupation of a large city'[25] – no doubt a euphemism for Gestapo agents. At a late stage in their planning, General von Falkenhorst's staff were also to propose a simultaneous invasion of Denmark, the airports of Jutland having been found necessary to ensure the air cover of the operation.[26]

On 29 February, the revised plan was shown to Hitler, who expressed satisfaction and asked to be informed every other day of the exact state of preparations.[27] On 1 March, the General Staff of 'Group 21' received a document entitled 'Führer Directive No. 1 for Case Weserübung', which contained the following passages: 'Latest developments of the Scandinavian situation render it imperative that all preparations be made for an occupation of Denmark and Norway by units of the Wehrmacht. This will enable us to forestall British actions in Scandinavia and the Baltic, to safeguard our supplies of iron ore from Sweden, and to improve the starting positions of our naval and air forces against Great Britain [. . .] The crossing of the Danish border is to be carried out at exactly the same time as the landing in Norway. Preparations for the undertaking are to be completed as quickly as possible. It is of the utmost importance that both the Nordic countries and the Allies be caught unawares by our operation. All preparations must take this element into account.'[28]

Finally, on 3 March, Hitler decided to unleash Weserübung before Gelb – the decisive attack in the west.[29] During the next few days, the extreme agitation in the Allied camp just before the Finno-Soviet cease-fire was duly recorded by German Intelligence, and it almost prompted Hitler to order the early start of Weserübung. But the signing of the Moscow peace agreement was soon followed by a dismantling of the Allied naval build-up in the North Sea, and Hitler ordered that preparations for invasion be completed 'calmly, and with especial attention to camouflage'.[30]

While personally following the last preparations of Group 21 in minute detail, Hitler also displayed a keen – and highly exclusive – interest in the political aspect of the operation: 'In the course of Weserübung, all political measures to be taken in regard to the governments of Denmark and Norway, as well as German interventions in the administration and economy of both countries, are to conform with the requirements of a peaceful occupation, having as its aim the protection of the Nordic countries' neutrality. Great pains should be taken to dissuade the Danish and Norwegian governments from offering armed resistance, and to persuade them to accept a German occupation. [. . .] The mission of the commander of Group 21 is an exclusively military one. [. . .] Measures and interventions in political, administrative and economic fields are to be carried out by a civilian envoy, according to specific instructions issued by the Führer.'[31]

The German cruiser *Blücher*

Hit by a single salvo from the nineteenth-century cannon 'Moses', the *Blücher* goes down in the middle of Oslo fjord with the Gestapo, a military band . . . and the general staff of the attack force.'

'The permanent route of Swedish iron ore to Germany has been severed, and will remain severed.' (Paul Reynaud)

German troops entering Oslo, April 9, 1940: 'An irresistible onslaught, a slight hitch . . . and a disastrous political void.'

The intention was thus to secure the collaboration of the Norwegian government; in case of refusal, the latter would simply be dissolved, and King Haakon would be made to appoint a new one.[32] Of course, the King might seek to escape, but Hitler had anticipated that too; on 2 April, the staff of Group 21 received a new directive: 'Führer has ordered that the flight of Kings of Denmark and Norway from their countries at the time of occupation be prevented at all costs. Necessary steps to that effect are to be taken by plenipotentiaries of the Foreign Ministry, in co-operation with military commanders on the spot. It is essential that the sovereigns' residences be closely watched, and that they be prevented from leaving their palaces should they attempt to do so.'[33]

On 20 March, General von Falkenhorst informed Hitler that all preparations for Weserübung had been completed. On 1 April, all army, navy and air force officers responsible for the operation, including the commanders of the various landing corps, reported to the Führer. The latter, according to von Falkenhorst, 'conferred with each one of the generals, and each one of the admirals. He cross-examined every single general, who was to explain very precisely the nature of the task he was to carry out. He even discussed with the ship commanders whether they would land their men on the right or on the left of a given objective. He left nothing to chance; it was his idea, it was his plan, it was his war.'[34]

Finally, the Führer, according to the Naval War Diary, 'expressed his complete satisfaction with the way preparation had been made. He considered Operation Weserübung to be particularly daring – in fact one of the rashest undertakings in the history of modern warfare. Precisely that would help ensure its success. [. . .] He [the Führer] described the state of anxiety he would feel until the success of the operation as one of the strongest nervous tensions of his life. He had full confidence in the success of the undertaking. The whole history of warfare taught that carefully prepared operations usually succeeded with relatively insignificant losses. He pointed out that the strictest secrecy was vital to the success of the surprise attack.'[35]

On 2 April, Hitler held a top-level military conference attended by General von Falkenhorst, Marshal Goering, Admiral Raeder and General Keitel. Everything was ready, and both weather and ice conditions were favourable to the operation. Hitler thereupon ordered the attack to begin on 9 April at 5.15 a.m. on all objectives simultaneously, in both Denmark and Norway. At 5.20, the German minister in Oslo was to hand King Haakon VII a formal diplomatic note; at the very same time, his counterpart in Copenhagen was to deliver a similar one to King Christian X.

# CHAPTER THREE

# On the Brink

In London, the signing of the Finno-Soviet peace was considered a major defeat for the Allied cause.[1] During the debate in the Commons on 19 March, several MPs took to blaming Norway and Sweden for the defeat of Finland; thus Sir Archibald Southby considered that both countries 'deserved the contempt of the world' for having betrayed their 'brave little neighbour'.[2] Several of his colleagues were just as content to use the Scandinavian countries as scapegoats,[3] but many others, like Sir Archibald Sinclair, Major Rayner and Commander Stephen King-Hall, refused to be duped, and pinned the blame squarely on Mr Chamberlain's conduct of the war.[4] Their words were soon echoed by those of a Conservative MP, Harold Macmillan, who had just returned from Finland: 'I do not know enough of the strategy of war to know whether on the whole we gained or lost . . . But it does, I think, throw a piercing light on the present machinery and the method of government. The delay, the vacillation, change of front, standing on one foot one day and on the other the next before a decision is given – these are patently clear to anyone.'[5]

A violent scene ensued between Mr Macmillan and the Prime Minister, after which the debate ended in general confusion; but, though Mr Chamberlain remained in complete control of his parliamentary majority, his Tory supporters were clearly shaken by the accusations of ineptitude directed at the government's war policy. For many, the seeds of doubt were sown there and then; they would soon come to fruition.

Since mid-March, the attention of both ministers and Chiefs of Staff had gradually shifted away from Scandinavia. Discussions in the War Cabinet mostly revolved around the bombing of Scapa Flow, revelations about the disastrous weakness of Britain's anti-aircraft defences,[6] rumours about an impending attack on the Netherlands,[7] and the 'peace mission' undertaken by American

51

Secretary of State Sumner Welles in London and Paris; yet at least one member of the War Cabinet was still strongly pressing for offensive operations against Germany: Winston Churchill, of course. On 19 March, he proposed to 'send an aircraft carrier up the Norwegian coast, from which aircraft could lay mines in the approaches to Luleå and bombard the ships in that port'. He also presented a plan dubbed 'Royal Marine', which called for the mining of the Rhine;[8] and of course there was his pet project: the minelaying action in Norwegian territorial waters . . .

There was little opposition to 'Royal Marine' in the War Cabinet – after all, the French would bear the brunt of that operation – but the Scandinavian plans were greeted with the greatest scepticism. Lord Halifax pointed out that 'the Allies must not act in such a way as to force Norway and Sweden on the German side'.[9] All other ministers seemed to agree that 'it would be wrong to do something merely for the sake of doing something', but as on the other hand it was impossible to do nothing at all, Lord Halifax finally proposed a safe and reasonable course of action: a communication to both Scandinavian governments informing them that the Allies considered themselves free 'to seize any opportunity to interfere with supplies of iron ore to Germany'. 'In this way,' the noble Lord added, 'we might build up foundations that would make future action possible,' and besides, 'it might also help us to make clear to the French that we were not merely letting the situation drift.'[10]

This was indeed one of the War Cabinet's major preoccupations. Ever since the end of hostilities in Finland, Daladier's war policy had been fiercely attacked in parliament and in the press as half-hearted and vacillating.[11] The French ambassador in London had therefore been instructed to tell the British authorities that his government's survival depended on a quick decision to intervene in Scandinavia. Under-Secretary of State Cadogan was thus understandably reluctant to tell the French ambassador about the very meagre results of the War Cabinet session of 19 March: 'I felt', he wrote on the same day, 'that to tell him that [. . .] proposals for interrupting Norwegian shipments had been turned down might produce a rather depressing effect at what might be a critical moment.'[12] A commendable precaution, but a useless one: that same day, in Paris, a vote of confidence at the Chamber of Deputies had just sealed the government's fate; backed by only 239 deputies out of 540, with 300 abstentions, Daladier was forced to resign. Two days later, on 21 March, Paul Reynaud formed the new government.

At 62, Reynaud, a former lawyer, could look back on a brilliant political career; elected deputy of Paris in 1928, he had been successively Finance Minister, Minister of Colonies and Minister of Justice, before returning to the Ministry of Finance under Daladier. A man of small stature, with conspicuously foxlike features and an intelligence to match, Reynaud was widely recognized as an expert in financial matters and a master of parliamentary strategy. For all that, the new Premier set out with two very serious handicaps: as a peace-time leader, he was particularly ill-prepared to take strategic decisions of any consequence; and, as his new government depended for its survival on the support of the Radical-Socialist Party, he had been compelled to leave the Ministry of War to his predecessor Daladier. Unfortunately, for both personal and political reasons, the two men were at daggers drawn, and there was not the slightest hint of a reconciliation between them – all of which clearly boded ill for the future.

In London, the few proponents of an 'active blockade' of Germany were placing high hopes on Paul Reynaud; all reports reaching London had described him as a man of action, and on 22 March, Churchill was already submitting his 'Royal Marine' scheme to him.[14] Indeed, Reynaud was unambiguously in favour of a new and resolutely offensive strategy. But even a moderately sagacious observer could see that the real purpose of the new Premier's bold strategy was merely to ensure the political survival of his government: 'Paul Reynaud', one of his advisers noted, 'is casting about for some way of showing the country that something has changed with his arrival at the helm.'[15] But a frontal attack on Germany being entirely out of the question, there remained only the possibility of an offensive action on some external theatre of operation, for which the British would ideally bear the main responsibility.

Granted, this could hardly be called a new strategy; in fact, by the time Reynaud had finished poring over the maps, the plan he came up with was an almost perfect synthesis of some of the most outrageous schemes conceived under his predecessor between December 1939 and February 1940. 'The sudden outcome of the Finnish struggle', Reynaud wrote to the British War Cabinet on 25 March, 'has faced the Allies with a new and perhaps decisive situation. In order to seize again the initiative which they have lost, it is important that the two governments, having learnt a lesson from recent events, should apply themselves without delay to draw from present circumstances all the possibilities of which an energetic and daring conduct of the war still allows them to take advantage. [. . .] In the actual field of action of the Allies and of their collaboration, a revision of the methods of directing the war is certainly required, the procedure of discussion, in the course of which the necessary speed of decision is lost, must be modified, conception, preparation and execution of our plans must be assured so as to develop in such circumstances that they no longer expose us to discomfiture to which abstention would have been preferable.' After which Reynaud proposed – in the same rather tortuous English – not only to interrupt German shipping in Norwegian territorial waters, but also to launch a 'decisive operation' in the Caspian and the Black Sea area, with the aim of cutting Germany's petroleum supplies and 'paralysing the whole Soviet economy'![16]

In London, on 26 March, this note burst like a bombshell. 'Mr Reynaud', General Ironside noted in his diary, 'has issued the most extraordinary paper stating how he proposes to win the war. He says that so far nobody has done anything and he proposes to do it. I understand that when the PM read the paper he went through the ceiling. For it includes him amongst those who have so far failed. The leading sentence of the (very badly) translated French paper [. . .] made the Prime Minister very angry. [. . .] It gave him the impression of a man who was rattled and who wished to make a splash to justify his position.'[17]

At the War Cabinet on 27 March, Reynaud's note still rankled as the ministers went over the notes to be debated at the Supreme War Council the next day. According to Sir Alexander Cadogan, consensus was reached on at least one definite objective: 'Cross-examine French on their ridiculous "Black Sea" idea (if it can be dignified by that name) and discourage Balkan adventure.'[18] Actually, the subject was tackled at a preliminary meeting with the French Chiefs of Staff that very afternoon, and General Ironside's account of the session was even gloomier than usual: 'A very tedious conference. [. . .] I must say that I got terribly bored. We [. . .] discussed all the things like blocking the iron ore from Narvik to sending submarines into the Black Sea and bombing Baku. The French had thought out nothing and put up the very vaguest things. All of them to be executed by us with a little vague help from the French. The thing which emerged was that the French had not grasped the question of baiting Russia and Italy into war unnecessarily. I tackled Gamelin afterwards and he said rather bitterly that the "politicians" had not studied the results and consequences of any act.'[19]

They also had very little interest in secrecy, as Sir Alexander Cadogan found out that evening with considerable dismay: 'C. Peake tells me French press (Havas, therefore official) have put out that "Allies" "have decided" to police neutral waters! These French!!'[20] Besides, the news was quite untrue: on the evening of 27 March, in London as in Paris, nothing had changed, nothing was ready, the units earmarked for Scandinavia were dissolved or on leave, the ships redeployed, nothing was decided, and nothing seemed about to be decided. In Berlin, on the other hand, the decision had been taken long ago, the troops and ships were ready, and the attack date firmly settled: 9 April 1940.

When the Supreme War Council met in London on 28 March, it was abundantly clear that precious little had changed since the previous gathering of 5 February. Granted, there was now a new French government, but even that was hardly perceptible, since the delegates to the Council were practically the same – including of course Daladier, who was still not on speaking terms with Reynaud. There was, however, a new Air Minister, Laurent-Eynac, but that made little difference, since both he and his service chief were soon fast asleep. To make things equal perhaps, Winston Churchill and Lord Halifax also dozed off on occasion . . .

Chamberlain opened the proceedings with a ninety-minute monologue – which may explain the somnolence on both sides – and began by strongly advocating the 'Royal Marine' operation to mine the Rhineland waterways.[21] Concerning the iron ore, Chamberlain alluded in fairly general terms to the 'vulnerability of the Narvik and Luleå sea routes', after which, carefully avoiding any mention of the infamous 'Black Sea' project, he asserted diplomatically that the possibility of cutting off petroleum supplies from Baku was 'tempting' – though whether he was himself tempted he characteristically failed to say, merely hinting that the matter 'should be studied'. Just in case his interlocutors had missed the note of caution, he concluded by saying that the blockade ought to remain the main weapon, and that 'we should be unwise to think that we could win the war by short cuts'.[22]

Paul Reynaud thereupon took the floor. Having reminded his British counterpart that 'French public opinion was demanding action without delay', he declared himself in favour of mining the Norwegian Leads as soon as possible, while expressing the hope that the British government would 'give its assent to the plan for an attack on the Caucasus'. In the affirmative, Paul Reynaud concluded, his government might also agree to 'Royal Marine' . . .[23] In other words, the British were being offered a bargain! Seeing that his discreet appeals for caution had been overlooked, Chamberlain proceeded to explain his real position on the 'Baku project': a decision to attack the Soviets might well be popular in France; in Britain, however, it most certainly would not. The real question was actually 'whether it was in our interest that the war should spread to Russia, and that Russia and Germany should be brought closer together'.[24]

There was no mistaking the Prime Minister's meaning: the British adamantly refused to be dragged into a war with Russia, thus effectively condemning any French plans for an attack on Germany's petroleum supplies. But as 'French public opinion was demanding action without delay' there remained the alternative of an operation against the iron ore mines. As we know, Chamberlain was not really taken with this project either, but before the French – and before his own public opinion – he could not assume responsibility for doing nothing at all. In the end, the two delegations agreed on the following course of action:

1 April: 'Admonition' to Norway and Sweden – in fact, a formal diplomatic warning that the Allies reserved the right to stop the German iron ore traffic.

4–5 April: Mines in Norwegian territorial waters to stop the ore traffic from Narvik, coupled with 'operations against German shipping'; the mining of Luleå to be undertaken later on.

4–5 April: Mines in the Rhine (subject to agreement by the French War Council).

15 April: Magnetic mines to be dropped in all German rivers and waterways.[25]

Here, at long last, was a blueprint for action; indeed, by intervening in Norwegian territorial waters on 5 April, the Allies would even steal a march on Hitler – the latter, it will be recalled, only intending to attack Norway on 9 April. Should British naval units patrol Norwegian waters at that time, Hitler was most unlikely to give the green light for the operation; better still, should he decide to run the gauntlet of the Royal Navy, his landing forces would be opposed by substantial Allied contingents.

At the Supreme War Council, the eventuality of an Allied landing in Norway, or that of a German reaction to the minelaying in Norwegian territorial waters, had not even been mentioned by the French and British politicians. But the military had thought of it at once;[26] less than 48 hours later, the War Office planners were calling for an immediate reconstitution of both the 'Stratford' and 'Avonmouth' forces, and warned that 'they may be required at a very early date'.[27] Actually, quite a few personalities – very much including Winston Churchill – were hoping that the minelaying operation would trigger a German reaction, thus giving the Allies the best possible excuse for landing in Norway, while ruling out any possibility of German opposition. All in all, a more favourable situation could hardly be envisioned.

With that, the military undertook in all haste to build up the 'Stratford' and 'Avonmouth' forces. Naturally, five days was an unreasonably short time to reconstitute two expeditionary corps, whose formation had previously taken two months; of course, it seemed slightly hazardous to make use of operation plans that had been conceived to fight the Soviets in Finland, when the goal was now to take on the Germans in Norway; admittedly, the troops earmarked for the expedition, with already precious little training and equipment back in February, were even more destitute by early April: no more ski battalion, no anti-aircraft guns, and the men were to be equipped 'as lightly as possible'; to be sure, the Deputy Chief of the Imperial General Staff had been informed by his services as early as 2 April that 'Avonmouth and Stratford plans have been reconstituted hurriedly, without thorough consideration of the consequences which may follow through implementation. This immediately becomes apparent when we start drawing up instructions for the commanders of the various forces.'[28] No doubt, there also remained the thorny problem of the Swedish attitude to the operation; on 3 April, it was suddenly discovered at the Chiefs of Staff Committee that back in February, a third plan, 'Plymouth', had been conceived to 'support and reassure the Swedes' – and that it was now imperative to plan a force 'on the lines of Plymouth'![29] Granted, on 4 April, in the midst of all this agitation, General Ismay complained that 'a large number of entirely different projects have recently been referred to as "certain operations" ', which not unnaturally led to complete confusion. The General therefore proposed that 'index letters and numbers should be allotted so as to distinguish the various plans'[30] – and presumably ensure that henceforth, only the enemy be kept entirely in the dark.

All that was perfectly true; and yet on 4 April the British troops were set to embark, the ships were ready to sail, to lay the mines, to land the troops and beat Hitler to the post. Doubtless a considerable achievement . . . as considerable as it was useless; for there was to be no minelaying on 5 April.

It will be recalled that at the Supreme War Council on 28 March, the French had accepted 'Royal Marine', 'subject to agreement by the French War Committee'; two days later, however, the latter rejected 'Royal Marine', perhaps for fear of German reprisals, or perhaps because Daladier remained bent on torpedoing his rival Reynaud . . . Whatever the reason, 'Royal Marine' had been the price to pay for British acceptance of the Norwegian operation, and Sir Alexander Cadogan, disagreeably surprised, had no difficulty at all in persuading Neville Chamberlain to suspend that operation in retaliation. 'No mines, no Narvik!' the Prime Minister told French Ambassador Corbin on the evening of 31 March.[31]

Churchill was much distressed at this unexpected development; whatever the value of 'Royal Marine', he could not allow it to compromise 'Wilfred', his pet project of mining the Norwegian Leads. On the other hand, it was clearly desirable to carry out both operations if at all possible. With Chamberlain's blessing, Churchill therefore went to Paris on 4 April to persuade the French to reconsider their refusal, and also to engineer a reconciliation between Daladier and Reynaud, as he strongly suspected that their feud had something to do with the French War Committee's negative decision. Though he actually failed in both undertakings, Churchill quickly came to the conclusion that 'Wilfred' could no longer be postponed: 'I reported by telephone to the War Cabinet, who were agreed that Wilfred should go forward notwithstanding the French refusal of Royal Marine, but wished this to be the subject of a formal communication. At their meeting of 5 April, the Foreign

Secretary was instructed to inform the French government that not-withstanding the great importance we had throughout attached to carrying out the Royal Marine operation at an early date, and simultaneously with the proposed operation in Norwegian territorial waters, we were nevertheless prepared as a concession to their wishes to proceed with the latter alone. The date was thus finally fixed for 8 April.'[32]

In both London and Paris, the decision was greeted with obvious relief: at long last, words would be matched by deeds. To 'prepare the ground', Lord Halifax instructed his ministers in Oslo and Stockholm to deliver the formal 'admonition' prepared at the Supreme War Council. Even Chamberlain was in a buoyant mood; 'Hitler missed the bus!' he imprudently assured a Conservative gathering.[33] On 6 April, the four minelaying destroyers hoisted anchor, escorted by the battle-cruiser *Renown* and the cruiser *Birmingham* and eight destroyers, commanded by Admiral Whitworth. On the morning of 7 April, at Rosyth, the four battalions bound for Stavanger and Bergen embarked in two cruisers, while in the Clyde, troops earmarked for Trondheim and Narvik boarded a transport and the cruiser *Devonshire*. Under what was now known as 'Plan R4', these troops were poised to set sail as soon as Germany reacted – or appeared to react – to the British minelaying operation of 8 April. It was taken for granted that the Germans would do nothing but react to an Allied operation. That they might *act* instead of reacting had not been seriously considered.

And yet during the night of 5 April, a rather disturbing piece of news had been relayed by the British minister in Copenhagen: 'According to information from a "well placed" neutral source, Hitler had ordered on the previous night a division in ten ships to move unostentatiously at night in order to land at Narvik. Jutland would be occupied on the same day, but Sweden would be left alone.'[34] Although this information was corroborated by several others, it was not given proper consideration. On the morning of 7 April, an RAF plane spotted one German cruiser and six destroyers 130 miles south of Cape Lindesnes, sailing due north.[35] Here again, no conclusions were drawn from this information; all plans were based on the assumption that the initiative rested with the Allies.

On 2 April 1940, Norwegian Foreign Minister Halvdan Koht gave an interview to the Conservative newspaper *Aftenposten*: 'Of course, as long as two naval powers neighbouring Norway are at war, the peace we are now enjoying will remain threatened. But I cannot see why Norway should be dragged into the war for that reason.'[36] And yet there was no lack of distinctly preoccupying information: On 4 April, the *Daily Telegraph* announced that troop concentrations had been sighted in several German ports.[37] The next day, the Norwegian Foreign Ministry received a telegram from its minister in Berlin, Scheel, stating that according to the military attaché 'of a neutral country', a German attack against Denmark was imminent. That same evening, the Norwegian minister in Berlin was able to send additional information: 'Danish legation here has heard same rumours as those mentioned in my previous dispatch no. 638, and other ones mentioning occupation of certain parts of south Norwegian coast. The aim [. . .] would be to quicken the pace of war and steal a march on the Allies.' That same day, Colonel Adlercreutz, of Swedish Intelligence, gave his Norwegian counterpart a message that was strikingly similar in content: Denmark was indeed the target, 'and Norway as well in a second stage'.

On 7 April, a new telegram arrived from the Berlin legation: 'We are informed from a reliable source [. . .] that 15 to 20 ships, 150,000 tons in all, left Stettin with a western course on the night of 5 April.' On the afternoon of the next day, 8 April, a representative of the Danish Chiefs of Staff handed a note stamped 'urgent' to the Norwegian minister in Copenhagen, who immediately forwarded it to Oslo: 'Early this morning, two battle cruisers, an armoured cruiser, three destroyers, as well as a great number of torpedo boats and armed transport ships passed the Great Belt, following a northward course.'[38] By then, it was thus quite clear that the operation was not limited to Denmark. Indeed, less than half an hour after receipt of this message, the Norwegian Minister of Defence, while attending a special session of Parliament, was handed a message from the naval staff, which he immediately read to the deputies: 'A German merchant ship has just been sunk [. . .] off the coast of Kristiansand. The ship, named *Rio de Janeiro*, was quite probably torpedoed by a British submarine. [. . .] German soldiers were on board. [. . .] They stated that the ship had also carried horses and cannons. [. . .] They had been told that they were bound for Bergen, where they were to assist the Norwegians, at the request of the Norwegian government.'[39]

As curious as it may seem, the Norwegian government, even in the face of such alarming news, did not see fit to order a mobilization of the country's defences. That Prime Minister Nygaardsvold failed to react is hardly surprising: he never dabbled in foreign policy, less still in defence matters; but the abstention of Foreign Minister Koht is not so easily explained. Besides, several personalities in the Norwegian government, including the new Minister of Supply, Trygve Lie, normally displayed a keen interest in defence matters; even King Haakon VII, who was both highly vigilant and perfectly aware of his country's vulnerability, later confessed that he had not really paid attention to the warnings coming from Berlin and Copenhagen.[40] The reason for this general incredulity is that the attention of the Norwegian authorities was being monopolized at the time by a far more conspicuous threat coming from the west . . . from Great Britain to be precise.

Immediately after the Supreme War Council of 28 March, both the British and French press had hinted at possible operations to be undertaken by the Allies in Scandinavia; indeed, various public statements by both Churchill and Chamberlain on 31 March[41] and 2 April[42] sounded ominously like sabre-rattling, and by 3 April the Norwegian minister in London, Colban, was sending the following telegram to Oslo: 'Noel Baker, one of the Labour leaders in the Commons, gave me clearly to understand that British government were preparing to carry out a direct action against ore traffic in Norwegian territorial waters in the very near future.'[43] Two days later, as if to underline this threat, the French and British ministers in Oslo handed Mr Koht an ominous diplomatic note – the 'admonition' prepared at the Supreme War Council of 28 March. There was no mistaking the meaning of its last two sentences: 'The Allies, seeing that they are waging war for aims which are as much in the interests of the smaller States as in their own, cannot allow the course of the war to be influenced against them by advantages derived by Germany from Sweden or from Norway. They therefore give notice that they reserve the right to take such measures as they may think necessary to hinder or prevent Germany from obtaining in these countries resources or facilities which, for the purpose of the war, would be to her advantage or to the disadvantage of the Allies.'[44]

From then on, the Norwegians were all but hypnotized by the likelihood of a British operation. That same evening, Colonel Adlercreutz, of Swedish Intelligence, was visiting his Norwegian counterpart to inform him of the latest news he had received on German preparations. 'During our talk,' he recalled, 'my Norwegian colleague did not appear [. . .] particularly concerned; on the other hand, he seemed to be wondering what might come from the west.'[45] On 8 April, likewise, the Soviet ambassador in London, Maisky, noted the following confidential statement by his Norwegian interlocutor, minister Eric Colban: 'Germany has given us the most categorical assurances that she will respect our neutrality. [. . .] If there is something I am afraid of right now, it is rather some rash action by our British friends.'[46]

The minister's fears were well founded; that same day at 5 a.m., four British destroyers had laid a minefield at the entrance of the Vestfjord, north of Bodø. Shortly after 6 a.m., the British and French ministers had delivered yet another diplomatic note to the Norwegian Foreign Minister; it served notice that the Allies had decided to interrupt the passage through Norwegian territorial waters of all ships 'carrying war contraband'.[47]

That day, the minelaying operation and the diplomatic note were the object of lively discussion in the Norwegian government and in parliament. The possibility of a German attack was mentioned, but many thought it impossible, others still believed it could only come in the form of a limited reaction to the British operation.[48] The only firm decision taken that day was to send a solemn protest note to the British and French governments; it was, however, couched in the most moderate terms,[49] for, as Deputy Mowinckel had just stated at a meeting of the Storting's Foreign Affairs Committee, 'Whatever happens, a war against England is entirely ruled out.'[50]

All this seemed to have pushed the news of German activity entirely into the background. On 8 April, the German naval attaché in Oslo had remained in permanent contact with the Norwegian Admiralty. 'The British minelaying operation', he reported, 'had caused a certain nervousness both in the government and at the Admiralty. At the Admiralty [. . .] I was told that information had been received about the passage through Danish waters of several hundred German warships headed north. I was discreetly asked what it meant. [. . .] I answered that I was not informed, but that I supposed the fleet had sailed to protect the German coast. [. . .] Until late in the evening of 8 April, both the government and the General Staff at the Admiralty remained entirely ignorant of the whole operation. Actually, no one expected it.'[51]

Almost no one . . . Since 5 April, the army Chief of Staff, Colonel Hatledal, alarmed by the information received from Berlin and Copenhagen, had requested repeatedly that the four army brigades stationed in southern Norway be mobilized without delay. At noon on 8 April, the Minister of Defence, Colonel Ljungberg, told him once again that the Cabinet had as yet taken no decision on the matter, but Colonel Hatledal was asked to submit a detailed report on . . . the estimated cost of such a mobilization![52] Around 9 p.m., however, the Cabinet reconvened, and considered the mobilization request anew. Eventually, on the proposal of the Minister of Defence, it was agreed to mobilize . . . two battalions. Hardly a mass mobilization, of course, but even then the decision was not relayed to the General Staff that evening; at 9 p.m., the Minister of Defence had informed the General Staff officers that they would be notified the next morning of any decision taken by the government, and that in the meantime 'they could all go home'.[53] Completely discouraged, Colonel Hatledal told the duty officer that 'all his efforts to obtain a decision on mobilization [. . .] had come to naught', and that 'he was now so worn out that he asked not to be disturbed'. But the Colonel added: 'Unless hostilities break out . . .'[54]

## 7 APRIL, 8 P.M.

The seventeen naval units of Groups I and II ('Narvik' and 'Trondheim') were sailing at top speed towards Trondheim. At the British Admiralty, no one believed that Norway was the target: the German ships were expected to slip into the Atlantic in order to attack Allied convoys. At 8.15 p.m., five cruisers and nine destroyers, commanded by Admiral Sir Charles Forbes, left Scapa Flow to intercept them. A second squadron, with two cruisers and twelve destroyers, left Rosyth immediately afterwards. Further north, two cruisers and twelve destroyers, commanded by Admiral Whitworth, were heading for the Vestfjord to participate in the minelaying operation.

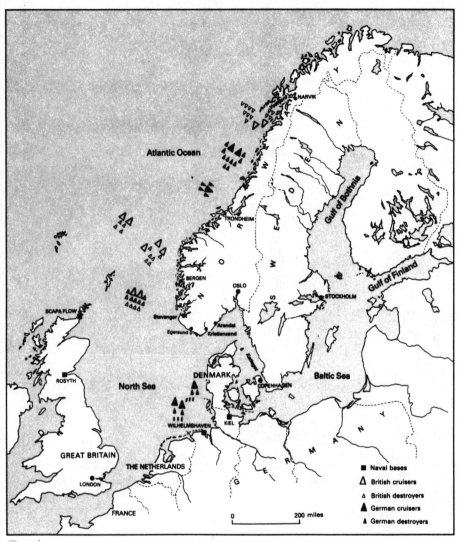

## 8 APRIL, NOON

The German Naval Groups 'Narvik' and 'Trondheim' had already passed Trondheim. The two Home Fleet squadrons were still north-west and south of Bergen, whereas further south, unbeknown to the British, Groups 'Kristiansand', 'Bergen' and 'Egersund' were fast approaching the southern tip of Norway.

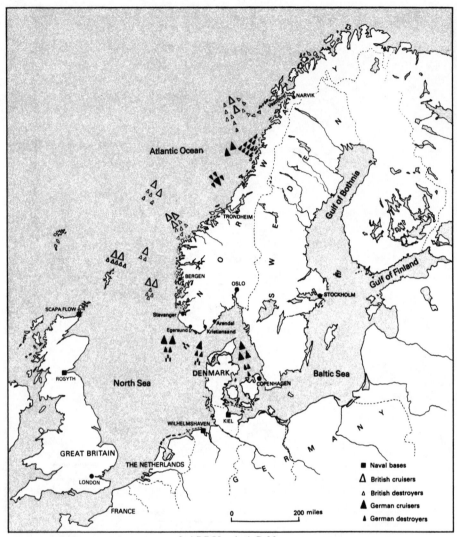

**8 APRIL, 4-6 P.M.**

Group II ('Trondheim'), having reached the area of its objective, changed courses several times as it lay in wait for the hour of the attack. A British plane spotted it as it was heading west, and radioed the message back to its base. As a result, Admiral Whitworth, who was guarding the approaches to Narvik, headed west with his squadron to intercept Group II, thus enabling Group I to slip into the Vestfjord and head for Narvik. Upon receiving the same message, Admiral Forbes, 120 miles south of Trondheim, also veered westwards, thus losing any chance of intercepting Group II. Further south, Groups 'Kristiansand', 'Egersund' and 'Bergen' were within reach of their objectives, and remained undetected owing to heavy fog. Group 'Oslo' was emerging from the Kattegat, heading north at full speed.

# CHAPTER FOUR

# The Longest Day

Shortly before 11.30 p.m. on 8 April, two coastal batteries reported that several ships of unknown nationality were entering the Oslo fjord. The army Chief of Staff immediately alerted the Commander-in-Chief, General Laake, as well as Prime Minister Nygaardsvold.

At 1.30 a.m., the members of the government, somewhat dazed for lack of sleep, gathered at Victoria Terrasse, the Foreign Ministry, where they were given the latest news: four large naval units and a dozen smaller ones were sailing up the fjord. A short while later, the ministers learned that five large ships were cruising before Bergen, another one in front of Stavanger, and that all these ships were German.[1]

At that, the Minister of Supply, Trygve Lie, proposed that an official call for help be sent forthwith to Britain and France. But Foreign Minister Halvdan Koht refused: in September 1939, he said, Norway had chosen to ignore a British offer to consider an attack against Norway as tantamount to an attack against Great Britain; therefore, it was impossible to ask the British for help at this juncture.[2] Questionable logic, no doubt, but then Halvdan Koht had a highly personal conception of foreign affairs ... At any rate, he was eventually prevailed upon to call the British minister and inform him of the German attack. The first attempt was fruitless, His Majesty's minister Sir Cecil Dormer being fast asleep, whereupon Prime Minister Nygaardsvold fairly lost his temper.[3] But Mr Koht eventually reached the British minister and, having summed up the situation, he added: 'Well, we are now at war!' Sir Cecil asked whether the government intended to remain in Oslo, to which Mr Koht replied in the affirmative, as 'he reckoned that the city's defences were strong enough'[4] – no doubt a highly optimistic statement. Naturally, King Haakon was also informed shortly before 1.30 a.m., and his first reaction was an interesting one; his aide-de-camp having told him, 'Majesty, we are at war!', the King immediately enquired: 'Against whom?'[5]

As soon as the members of the government heard that Bergen was threatened – and that the attackers were German[6] – they decided to order an immediate mobilization. But from then on, the administrative machinery began to falter; for one thing, the ministers of the Norwegian government knew nothing about the mechanism of mobilization, and they left the matter entirely to the Minister of Defence.[7] Unfortunately, the latter, having spent barely three months in office, was just as incompetent as his government colleagues; he was therefore inclined to heed the advice of the army Commander-in-Chief.

General Laake, 65, had been appointed Commander-in-Chief of the Norwegian army eight years earlier, less for his outstanding military capacities than for his readiness to accept further cuts in the military budget. On that morning of 9 April, however, the General obstinately refused to take the alert seriously, and it was only with the greatest difficulty that the officer on duty at headquarters could prevail upon him to leave his country home and return to Oslo.[8] But once in Oslo, the General called the Minister of Defence, and advised him . . . to mobilize the four brigades stationed in southern Norway, as the General Staff had been recommending since 5 April.

By the morning of 9 April, of course, such a step was entirely meaningless; under the Norwegian military code, the mobilization of four brigades was known as a 'partial and secret mobilization'. There was nothing wrong with this, except that, according to the self-same military code, such a mobilization could only be implemented by calling on the soldiers *through the mail* to assemble 48 hours later! The alternative would have been a 'general and open mobilization', that is, announced by all possible means including the radio, and with orders to assemble right away – clearly a more sensible proposition at this stage of events, yet it must be borne in mind that General Laake still could not bring himself to believe that anything serious was happening. At 2.45 a.m., Defence Minister Ljungberg accordingly submitted to his colleagues a proposal to mobilize the four brigades, and the latter – 'not having a code of mobilization at their disposal', as Trygve Lie later explained[9] – readily accepted the proposal, in the belief that they were thereby ordering a general and immediate mobilization. Minister Ljungberg then

informed General Laake by telephone of the Government's decision: mobilization of four brigades, in other words partial and
'secret' mobilization; convocations to be sent by mail, and the men
to assemble on 11 April . . .

At General Staff headquarters, the order was greeted with some
incredulity. Shortly after 3.30 a.m., in the course of a meeting
with Ljungberg and Laake, army Chief of Staff Colonel Hatledal
raised the most strenuous objections, but Ljungberg remained
adamant: the order had come from the Government, it was to be
obeyed. General Laake was even further removed from reality: 'A
little exercise should do these units no harm!' he told his startled
officers.[10]

In Oslo, a black-out was in force, and the ministers gathered at
Victoria Terrasse went on conferring by candlelight. Around 2 a.m.,
the Swedish legation informed them that Stavanger was now
directly threatened.[11] At 3.25, news arrived that two large ships had
also forced the entrance to the Trondheim fjord.[12] Meanwhile, the
ministers were anxiously following the progression of the formidable armada sailing up the Oslo fjord; between the German ships
and the city, there only lay the ancient fortress of Oscarsborg, with
its two nineteenth-century cannons, 'Moses' and 'Aaron' . . .

Shortly after 4 a.m., the cruiser *Blücher*, one of the newest and
most powerful units in the German navy, duly came in view of the
fortress. Colonel Eriksen, the fortress commander, being well
aware that his vintage cannons took a considerable time to reload
and that their servants had very little training, gave the order to open
fire only at the very last moment, when the cruiser was only 500
metres away. A surprisingly devastating salvo it was: one shell hit the
cruiser's anti-aircraft control centre, a second crashed into a starboard storeroom containing aviation fuel, and a huge flame shot
skywards, instantly illuminating the snowy banks of the fjord.[13]

Meanwhile, at the Foreign Ministry in Oslo, Mr Koht was conferring by candlelight with the German diplomat Kurt Bräuer, who
had just brought him a document prepared long beforehand in Berlin: nineteen closely typewritten pages, with promises, threats,
admonitions and one imperative demand: total and unconditional
capitulation. 'The sole aim of the German military operations is to
protect the North against the intended occupation of bases in Norway by Anglo-French forces. The German government is convinced

that in taking this action they are at the same time serving the interests of Norway. [. . .] The German government therefore expect that the Royal Norwegian government and people will regard the German action with comprehension, and will offer no resistance to it. Any resistance would have to be, and would be, broken by the German occupying forces with all the means at their command, and would therefore result in entirely useless bloodshed.' There followed a long list of practical steps demanded of the Norwegian government to bring all resistance to a stop, and effectively deliver the country to the invaders.

As Mr Koht perused the document, Bräuer repeated that the German government had engaged considerable forces in the operation, and that any resistance by the Norwegians would be 'completely senseless'.[14] Koht was not exactly a realist, as he had just proved three times during the last three hours, and on innumerable occasions during the last five years. However, when confronted with a direct attempt at intimidation, he lacked neither courage nor common sense: 'It appeared to me', he later wrote, 'absolutely impossible to surrender my country to German domination. I knew too much about Nazi methods to wish them to prevail in Norway, and I detested an alliance with such a regime. I had heard the German minister assuring me that his government would respect the political independence of the country. But I recalled too vividly all the broken pledges of Hitler to other nations, to Austria, to Czechoslovakia, to Poland; I could have no confidence in such assurances. I felt inwardly sure that, in spite of all dangers and menaces, the German demands must be refused, and the fight against the invaders taken up.'[15]

Such was Koht's state of mind as Bräuer concluded his admonition. Having reminded the German diplomat of Hitler's crushing indictment of the Czechs – 'The nation that bowed meekly to an aggressor without offering resistance was not worthy of living'[16] – Koht returned to his office and placed the German note before his colleagues; the ultimatum provoked a unanimous, almost instinctive rejection.[17] Shortly before 5.30 a.m., Koht rejoined Bräuer, and informed him of his government's decision.

'By our policy of neutrality, we have demonstrated that we did not wish to have enemies on any side. But we will maintain our independence as long as possible.'

'Then, there will be fighting,' Bräuer answered, 'and nothing can save you.'

'The fight is already in progress,' Koht replied.[18]

That was beyond dispute; less than two miles away, enveloped in the blinding glow of tracer bullets and exploding flares, a blazing, rudderless hulk was slowly drifting in the middle of Oslo fjord. Her engines flooded, her ammunition stores exploding below decks, *Blücher*, listing heavily to starboard, was being evacuated in all haste.* Behind the crippled cruiser, *Emden*, *Lützow* and three torpedo boats had just turned around. But the Luftwaffe was now above Oslo, and several heavy troop-transports were seeking to land at Fornebu airport, which was still shrouded in dense fog.

At 5.30 a.m., the President of the Storting, Carl Hambro, arrived at Victoria Terrasse. With considerably more foresight than his colleagues in the government, he had just given orders for a special train to leave at 7 a.m. for Hamar, eighty miles north of Oslo, with all the members of Parliament; he now endeavoured to persuade the ministers to do likewise, failing which, he assured them, they would inevitably be captured.[19] Koht and Nygaardsvold were initially reluctant, but the other ministers eventually agreed that evacuation could not be avoided. The King was informed, and he declared himself ready to join the group at the station, together with Crown Prince Olav. It was decided that in the short time that remained, the most important archives would be packed or destroyed, and the ministers of France and Great Britain notified of the evacuation.[20] Although the radio remained at the government's disposal, the haste of departure was such that no one thought of broadcasting a proclamation to the country.

This was to be rectified purely by chance a short while later. At 7 a.m., with the deputies and ministers all gathered at the Eastern railway station, a journalist from the NTB Press Agency managed to interview Mr Koht, who gave him a brief account of the latest developments. He expressed the hope that 'this state of affairs would not last too long', and mentioned in passing that 'a general mobilization had been ordered'.[21] This, as we know, was not correct, and besides, Mr Koht did not really know what a general mobilization was; but many Norwegians did, and when the interview was broadcast

---

* 1,000 men perished; there were 1,400 survivors.

shortly after 7.30 a.m., a mad scramble ensued throughout the country. Some divisional headquarters had issued a general mobilization order immediately after receiving news of the German attack; at 6 a.m., upon learning of the government's decision on partial and secret mobilization, they had countermanded their initial order. Now, after 7.30, mobilization in Oslo proceeded with a vengeance a few hours only before the arrival of the Germans; in some cities that were already occupied, like Halden, Kristiansand, Bergen or Trondheim, the Norwegians mobilized right in front of the Germans![22] General confusion had set in, and this was only the beginning.

Around 10 a.m., the army Commander-in-Chief, General Laake, reached Slemdal, in the northern suburbs of Oslo, where his headquarters had moved some hours earlier. Alas, he quickly found out that his whole staff had already moved on with all hands, vehicles, maps, and the General's aide-de-camp – not to mention his uniform. General Laake, who had no service car, undertook to pursue them, first taking a tram car, then vainly trying to hitch-hike, later proceeding on foot, and finally boarding a train,[23] in the forlorn hope of catching up. The retreat was quickly turning into a débâcle.

There was no disputing the fact that the Germans had achieved almost complete surprise, and yet their plan had failed in one crucial respect: Oslo was not to be occupied before noon that day. By the time German airborne troops coming from Fornebu airport finally reached the city, both king and government were well out of reach. Admittedly, Minister Bräuer had received imperative instructions to detain them all, in co-operation with the German military commander; but the latter, General Engelbrecht, had failed to show up at the appointed time, and with good reason: he was on board *Blücher*, and had to be fished out of the fjord by a small Norwegian detachment, which not unnaturally proceeded to detain him. General von Falkenhorst's whole campaign staff was also on board *Blücher*; the General himself was still in Hamburg, and would arrive in Oslo only the next morning.[24] In the afternoon of 9 April, therefore, a complete vacuum of power reigned in occupied Oslo; a vacuum, as we shall see, with especially dire consequences.

At Hamar, shortly after 1 p.m., forty-six dazed and depressed deputies slowly gathered in the so-called 'Festivity Hall'. Foreign Minister Koht first gave them a detailed report on the occurrences of the last twelve hours, which included the statement that 'the government had ordered the general mobilization of the 1st, 2nd, 3rd and 4th Brigades' – further proof that Koht had still not grasped the rules of mobilization ... yet none of the deputies present pointed out that this was pure nonsense: military affairs had never been popular in Norway. Koht went on to read several hastily translated excerpts from the German ultimatum, and concluded on a rather emphatic, if not entirely relevant note: 'So we are now at war; before the whole world, we may claim with no fear of being contradicted that we bear not the slightest responsibility for this war.'

Storting President Carl Hambro thereupon took the floor to announce that, according to a special broadcast of the Danish radio, Copenhagen was now occupied, and all of Denmark had capitulated to the Germans. After that, Prime Minister Nygaardsvold, who appeared quite shaken, briefly interjected that he had nothing to say for the time being, whereupon President Hambro adjourned the meeting.[25] A new parliamentary session was set for 6.30 p.m.

Shortly thereafter, Mr Nygaardsvold went to see the King, and offered him the government's resignation, 'in order to make way for a government of national unity'. But King Haakon refused to accept it, and referred the question to a meeting of the government council, to be held two hours later.[26] In the meantime, Koht had been informed by the Foreign Ministry in Oslo that Bräuer had returned to offer new negotiations, and left a note reaffirming that 'Germany does not intend by her measures to infringe the territorial integrity and the political independence of the Kingdom of Norway, either now or in the future.'[27]

Both questions were heatedly debated during the government council that opened at 4.30 p.m. Storting President Carl Hambro, speaking in the name of the Right, the Liberal Left and the Agrarian Party, flatly opposed Mr Nygaardsvold's offer of resignation. 'The Government', he asserted, 'has no right to resign at a moment such as this.' It was eventually decided to propose that the Labour government remain in office, but be broadened to include representatives of all three opposition parties.[28] But the most important question was naturally that of negotiations with the Germans. Mr Mowinckel, representing the Left Liberal Party, was resolutely in favour of establishing contact with the German minister without delay; Prime Minister Nygaardsvold and several ministers immediately approved. But Supply Minister Trygve Lie just as force-fully disagreed, and he was backed by Justice Minister Wold and Social Affairs Minister Støstad. How could one give in now, after having unanimously rejected the German ultimatum just twelve hours earlier?[29] A rather confused discussion ensued, but Lie soon found powerful support: King Haakon and Prince Olav both spoke up categorically in favour of the most determined resistance: 'If Denmark had surrendered,' the King declared, 'this did not mean that King Christian had given his assent. [. . .] Given the same possibilities as the Norwegians to avoid submission, he would quite certainly have followed the same course as Norway. [. . .] On no account was that course to be abandoned at the present time.'

Defence Minister Ljungberg and Finance Minister Oscar Torp thereupon joined the meeting. Torp announced that he had managed a few hours earlier to have the Bank of Norway's entire gold reserve evacuated towards Lillehammer. As for the military developments in the rest of the country, both ministers were just as ill-informed as their Cabinet colleagues; no one knew whether the Germans had already launched an offensive towards Hamar. Some ministers asked whether it would not be a good idea to cut the roads and blow up the bridges, in order to delay the German advance. Deputy Sundby, of the Agrarian Party, was opposed to the idea, on grounds that 'this would mean destroying valuable architectural works'. Mowinckel agreed, as 'this was no way of reaching an agreement with the Germans. [. . .] One cannot negotiate and fight at the same time.'[30]

The German invader, for one, did not seem to find it impossible, and several ministers, backed by Prince Olav, discreetly voiced some doubts about Mowinckel's distinctly unmilitary arguments. In the end, no decision was taken, but it was unanimously agreed that the question of negotiations with the Germans be referred to the Storting.[31]

The Government Council ended at 6.30 p.m., and the ministers proceeded to join the Storting session – their seventh major meeting in less than thirty hours . . . At this stage, it is interesting to note that one issue at least had not been debated since the departure from Oslo: that of British assistance. Only Prime Minister Nygaardsvold had mentioned Great Britain a few times, and even then in parti-cularly unflattering terms.[32] And yet the British Minister, Cecil

Dormer, who had followed the government to Hamar, remained in touch with London by means of a wireless transmitter carried by members of the British legation. That afternoon, Sir Cecil was visited by Colonel Gulliksen, Air Force Chief of Staff, who told him – on whose instructions remains unknown – that Norway 'imperatively had to receive immediate and powerful help to save the situation'.[33] That seemed fairly obvious, and Dormer undertook to communicate with London immediately. Shortly thereafter, in fact, he received the following cable, dispatched by the Foreign Office five hours earlier: 'You should at once assure Norwegian government that in view of German invasion of their country, His Majesty's Government have decided forthwith to extend full aid to Norway, and will fight now in full association with them. [. . .] HM's Government are taking immediate steps to deal with German invasion of Bergen and Trondheim. [. . .] Glad to learn what Norwegian government's plans are. [. . .] Destroy Stavanger aerodrome if unable to hold it.'[34]

Dormer handed this encouraging telegram to Koht just before the beginning of the second Storting session. By the time the latter opened shortly after 6.30 p.m., 84 out of the 90 Storting deputies had found their way to the 'Festivity Hall'. The first communication they had from President Hambro was a profoundly depressing one: 'Narvik is in German hands. The whole province of Trøndelag is occupied by the Germans. An offensive against Hamar, along the road or the railway line, is to be expected, as there are no explosives on the spot to blow up the bridges. [. . .] 5,000 men have landed in Bergen, and they are now progressing along the railway line, compelling the Norwegian troops just mobilized to withdraw gradually. [. . .] Two warships have entered the Hardanger fjord. [. . .] Information from various parts of the southern areas is incomplete and difficult to obtain. Kristiansand and Horten have been bombed; Sola airfield [near Stavanger] can no longer be defended. In Oslo, reinforcements are constantly being landed at Fornebu airport.'[35]

At this stage, Koht informed the deputies of the new offers of negotiation made by Bräuer, after which he proceeded to read the telegram just received from London. 'The British government', he concluded, 'have added that they wish to co-operate with the Norwegian government in order to organize the resistance.' But Nygaardsvold interrupted him:

'That is not likely to happen any time soon!'

'Did not the French War Council announce something as well?' asked President Hambro.

'Well,' Koht answered, 'the British minister told me orally that he had been informed by the minister of France that the French Council of Ministers had gathered, and that it had decided to dispatch assistance to Norway as soon as possible. But perhaps I ought to add that the British minister, Dormer, told me in confidence that "as soon as possible" did not mean "without any delay", "on the dot", only that they would do their best.'

Hambro then raised the question of negotiations with the German minister. He summed up the Prime Minister's arguments on the issue, then those of the King, which were far more categorical: Hitler was on no account to be trusted. Finally, Hambro mentioned Nygaardsvold's offer to resign, which the Storting members unanimously rejected by passing the following motion: 'The Storting has unanimously asked its president to request that the government remain in place, and that His Majesty confirm the members of the government in their functions.'

Nygaardsvold accepted with conspicuously little enthusiasm, then proceeded to paint a decidedly gloomy picture of the military situation, thus justifying his advocacy of negotiations with the Germans . . . He then broached the subject of Britain: 'I am aware of the fact that we can expect some help from Britain, but Dormer himself has stressed that England would be unable to dispatch assistance right away. Immediate help could not be expected, but they would do their best. Well, I have no wish to speak ill of England, but one might have expected from those who had laid mines – and written the following day: "England acts instead of talking" – that they would at least take steps to protect Narvik. [. . .] I cannot say that I am favourably impressed by England's assistance or by her present promises. [. . .] I therefore feel obliged to recommend that the government and the presidency of the Storting appoint a committee of three to negotiate with the German minister the conditions whereby Norway would be allowed to keep on exercising her sovereignty.'

After these remarkably defeatist utterances, Defence Minister Ljungberg rose to give the latest account of the military situation: 'We have now lost control of four of our largest cities. [. . .] I dare say that without an immediate and powerful intervention by the Western powers our prospects of success are hardly encouraging.'[36]

Suddenly, at 7.40 p.m., President Hambro interrupted the debate to announce that 'a special train for Elverum [. . .] will depart in five minutes. German forces are on their way to capture the Storting, and they have just passed Jessheim.'[37] As the deputies and ministers left the 'Festivity Hall' and headed for the railway station, dire events were indeed unfolding in various parts of the country.

Along the whole western Norwegian coast, from Narvik to Kristiansand, Operation Weserübung had proved a complete success: all the objectives had fallen to the invader without a hitch. But further east, in Oslo, the sinking of *Blücher* had completely upset the seemingly implacable mechanism of the German onslaught. The city was occupied at noon by a few hundred paratroopers, but the absence of both General Engelbrecht and the 'specialists' embarked in *Blücher*, as well as the escape of the legal Norwegian authorities, gave rise to a complete political vacuum in the capital. Having failed to prevent their escape by force, the German diplomat Kurt Bräuer was left with only diplomatic means to obtain a return to Oslo of the Norwegian king and government – which explains the conciliatory note he had sent to Koht through the Foreign Ministry.

At this juncture, however, there were two Germans in Oslo who were to carry out specific tasks in connection with the naval landing, and had been left unemployed by the failure of that operation: Captain Schreiber, the Naval Attaché, and Gruppenleiter Scheidt, Alfred Rosenberg's henchman. In fact, Scheidt had remained in contact with Vidkun Quisling since the latter's December interview with Hitler; on the morning of 9 April, Scheidt visited Quisling at the Continental Hotel. It would appear that the latter, pointing to the conspicuous political vacuum then prevailing in Oslo, reminded Scheidt of what had been agreed with Hitler on 18 December: 'The Nasjonal Samling would be entrusted with domestic policy, in case it became necessary to pre-empt a British occupation.' Was it really Quisling who persuaded Scheidt, as the Gruppenleiter was later to state,[38] or was it the reverse? Quisling, after all, was a dreamer, extremely hesitant and devoid of any practical sense, whereas Scheidt was the very prototype of the National Socialist 'man of action', careerist, assertive and opportunist. When the two men separated around noon, at any rate, they were in full agreement: in order to fill the political vacuum in Oslo, Quisling would take it upon himself to appoint a cabinet and exercise power, in collaboration with the German occupation troops. Scheidt would endeavour to secure the Führer's agreement by calling Berlin through the Naval Attaché's wireless transmitter.

In the afternoon of 9 April, the situation in Oslo remained extremely confused; the German paratroopers had occupied all strategic points, the Royal Air Force had bombed the city suburbs and in the resulting panic, numerous Norwegians had left Oslo without hindrance to heed the mobilization order. The first shipwrecked sailors and soldiers from *Blücher* had just reached the capital, where the German legation was trying to set up a first-aid station. Also at the legation, a group of paratroopers collected around 5 p.m., and soon left for Hamar by bus to capture the king and his government.[39]

By late afternoon, Scheidt had received an answer from Berlin: the Führer accepted Quisling's offer to step in, and 'wished him good luck in his undertaking'.[40] After that, Bräuer, who took a dim view of Quisling's project, had no choice but to co-operate.[41] Less than four hours later, at 7.30 p.m., Vidkun Quisling thus entered Broadcasting House, and delivered the speech that was to earn him world-wide fame – though not of the kind he was seeking.

'Fellow Norwegians!' he declared. 'By laying mines in Norwegian territorial waters, England has violated the neutrality of Norway, without calling forth more than a feeble protest from the Nygaardsvold government. The German government have offered their assistance to the government of Norway, together with solemn assurances that our national independence would be respected. [. . .] In reply to this offer [. . .] the Nygaardsvold government have called a general mobilization and given all Norwegian military forces the senseless order to oppose German assistance by force of arms. This government then fled, after having rashly imperilled the destiny of the country and its inhabitants. Under the circumstances, the Nasjonal Samling has both the right and the duty to assume the responsibilities of power. [. . .] The Nygaardsvold government having withdrawn, a national government has grasped the reins of power. [. . .] It is headed by Vidkun Quisling, who is also Foreign Minister, and by a cabinet composed as follows . . .'

Quisling went on to name the ministers of his 'government' – without mentioning that a number of them had not been consulted in advance – and he concluded: 'Under present circumstances, all resistance is not only senseless, but also criminal, for it imperils the life and property of our fellow countrymen. All civil servants, all municipal employees, all land, air, naval and coastal artillery officers are duty-bound to obey the orders of the new government. Any failure to do so would [. . .] expose the transgressor to the full rigours of justice.'[42]

At 9.40 p.m. that same day, the third and last session of the Storting opened in the little communal school of Elverum. Many years were to pass before this assembly reconvened, but this the exhausted deputies could not possibly know. President Hambro began by proposing the election of a three-man committee to negotiate with the German authorities, after which he put to the vote a motion that was to remain famous in Norwegian history: 'Until the Government and the Presidency of the Storting, after a common deliberation, call another ordinary session of the Storting, the latter hereby empowers the government to safeguard the interests of the Kingdom and to take, both in the name of the Storting and in their own, all decisions and dispositions they deem necessary to the security and the future of our country.'[43]

After lengthy deliberation, the motion was finally adopted, and the deputies proceeded to elect the members of the negotiation committee, as well as the ministers without portfolio who were to join the government.* But Hambro suddenly interrupted the proceedings: 'Mr Quisling has just formed what he calls a government of national unity, and he has broadcast an appeal for all civil servants and officers to collaborate loyally with that government.'

The debate was resumed, and Nygaardsvold was heard to say that 'having learned that we now have a Kuusinen government† in our country', he was in favour of 'trying to uphold the honour of the Norwegian government, in Sweden if necessary'.[44] The rest of the session was extremely confused; the deputies were mostly complaining about the lack of comfort that had attended the three

* Messrs Lykke (Conservative Party), Mowinckel (Liberal Left) and Sundby (Agrarian Party).

† Kuusinen was a Finnish Communist who had taken the side of the Soviet Union when the latter invaded Finland. His name had become a synonym of traitor in Northern Europe. It was soon eclipsed by that of Quisling.

meetings of the day, and expressed some anxiety for their personal security during the weeks to come. President Hambro, who was unquestionably the hero of that very long day, intervened once again in an attempt to restore some dignity to the debate: 'We have striven to take into account all foreseeable contingencies, but I fear that Mr Peersen may be right when he says that under certain circumstances, the members of the Storting may be imprisoned, merely because they are members of the Storting. [. . .] Should this happen, we can only hope that each and every one of us will act in such a way as to prove worthy of this country. [. . .] We hope and trust that our people will have the strength and the will to bear the heavy burden that awaits them, so that the future can be preserved for our children. [. . .] May God bless our beloved Fatherland.'[45]

At this, the whole gathering rose and began singing the national anthem. The session ended at 10.25 p.m., and the assembly dispersed. The King and the ministers drove to the little village of Nybergsund, considered safer than the town of Elverum. They were followed by Sir Cecil Dormer, who had been left behind at Hamar, but somehow managed to pick up their track during the evening. Thus ended the longest day in Norwegian history.

For some, it was far from over; at Midtskogen, half-way between Hamar and Elverum, four busloads of German paratroopers had just been stopped in front of an improvised road block hastily set up by a few Norwegian volunteers. The heavily armed Germans left the buses and opened fire, but most of the entrenched Norwegians were sharpshooters from a local rifle club, and the Germans were soon compelled to withdraw with heavy losses. The German Air Attaché, Captain Spiller, lay mortally wounded on the battlefield. In his pocket was found a list of the people to be arrested; at the head of the list: King Haakon, Nygaardsvold, Hambro . . .[46]

# CHAPTER FIVE

# The Awakening

'In the very early hours of 9 April,' wrote General Ismay, 'I was awakened out of a deep sleep by the telephone bell. It was the Duty Officer at the War Cabinet Office. I could not make head or tail of what he was saying, in spite of frequent requests for repetition; so, suspecting the trouble, I suggested that he should draw the black-out curtains, switch on the lights, find his false teeth and say it all over again. My diagnosis was evidently correct, because after a pause he started speaking again and was perfectly intelligible. His report was brutal in its simplicity. The Germans had seized Copenhagen, Oslo, and all the main ports of Norway. [. . .] As I hurried into my clothes I realized, for the first time in my life, the devastating and demoralizing effect of surprise.'[1]

A surprise it was . . . It will be recalled that the British were expecting a delayed reaction to their minelaying operation, not a simultaneous undertaking by the Wehrmacht. Besides, all information reaching London on 7 and 8 April about German naval movements in the North Sea had persuaded the Admiralty that the Kriegsmarine was attempting to break out into the Atlantic, and the counter-measures adopted by the Royal Navy considerably eased the Germans' task; thus the British naval units guarding the minefields since the early hours of 8 April might well have intercepted the German ships heading for Narvik, had they not been diverted westward a few hours later, in pursuit of an imaginary enemy.[2]

In London, at six o'clock that morning, it was a particularly sleepy and morose group that sat down for the hastily summoned Chiefs of Staff meeting. To make things worse, only fragmentary and unverifiable information was available; Bergen and Trondheim were reported to be occupied, and so was Oslo – although that was somewhat less certain. On the other hand, the Chiefs of Staff did not believe that the Germans had occupied Narvik, and they decided to dispatch a battalion there at once. However, they considered that the first objective of a major offensive operation ought to be Bergen and Trondheim – in that order.[3]

By the time the War Cabinet convened at 8.30 a.m., the situation appeared distinctly more complex. General Ironside first laid out the conclusions of the Chiefs of Staff Committee: the immediate action to be undertaken was to 'go ahead with the plan to seize Narvik', as 'our information was that the Germans were not in occupation there. One battalion could be at Narvik in three days.' The most important, however, was to 'prevent the Germans from establishing themselves at Bergen and Trondheim', so as to 'leave these two places open for the Norwegians to fall back upon, and preserve them as ports of entry for ourselves'. A rather startling cacophony followed these words. The First Lord of the Admiralty, Winston Churchill, was not opposed to operations against Bergen and Trondheim, but as 'no large forces would be required in the initial stages', he 'strongly advocated that we should proceed with operations against Narvik'; Lord Hankey, Minister without Portfolio, recommended 'that we should take immediate action at Oslo', while the Chief of the Air Staff, Sir Cyril Newall, preferred operations against Stavanger, and the Chief of the Naval Staff observed that an 'exploratory' naval action was being undertaken off Bergen.[4]

In the end, the War Cabinet decided that 'the Norwegians should be encouraged as much as possible, and told that the Allies would come to their assistance'. Besides, the Chiefs of Staff were to make all preparations for 'a military expedition to recapture Trondheim and Bergen, and to occupy Narvik'. Finally, the French ought to be informed, and 'asked whether it would not be suitable to carry out Royal Marine forthwith'. Thus, the Cabinet's decision to concentrate the brunt of their offensive capacity on the recapture of Bergen and Trondheim rested on two main considerations: as Narvik was apparently not in German hands, there was no need for an all-out attack in northern Norway; besides, it was felt that the recapture of Bergen and Trondheim would be the best means of encouraging Norwegian resistance – should there be any, which at that early hour was by no means a foregone conclusion.

By the time the War Cabinet reconvened at noon, at least one of the postulates of their strategy was already being seriously called in question, for the Chiefs of Staff had informed the ministers that 'according to a broadcast from Oslo, a small German force had landed at Narvik'. They therefore recommended the dispatch of several destroyers in the Vestfjord 'to ascertain the situation', and that of a battalion 'to support the destroyers' action'.[5] In addition, they informed the ministers that seven other battalions would be ready to sail on 12 April, but they had no recommendations to make as to their destination. Bergen? Trondheim? Narvik? The German occupation of Narvik was clearly making British strategy far more difficult, though this was not immediately realized at the War Cabinet, where the mood was resolutely optimistic. Thus, for Winston Churchill, the situation was now far more favourable: 'Our hands were now free, and we could apply our overwhelming sea power on the Norwegian coast. We could liquidate their landings in a week or two.' Even Lord Halifax seemed to agree: 'It would seem', he asserted, 'that our chance of getting to Gällivare was better now than at any time since the beginning of the war.'[6]

In the end, the First Lord of the Admiralty, who was evidently the driving force at this stage on account of his personality, his notions of strategy, the information he received,* and the predominant role of the Navy in the whole affair, told his colleagues that 'orders had been given to the naval forces to force their way into Narvik and Bergen'.[7] Naturally, these orders had been given by Churchill himself. Thus, when at 12.55 Lord Halifax had sent Sir Cecil Dormer the aforementioned telegram, informing him that 'HM's Government are taking immediate steps to deal with the German invasion of Bergen and Trondheim', the War Cabinet, under Churchill's impulsion, had already begun to move away from Trondheim and concentrate on Narvik . . .

In the afternoon of 9 April, two new developments considerably reinforced this trend. The First Sea Lord, Admiral Pound, upon being informed that there were two German cruisers in Bergen and that the coastal batteries were in German hands,[8] called back the seven cruisers and four destroyers that were to 'force their way into Bergen'. Second and most important, the French allies had just given their own views on the strategic situation in the north.

In Paris, on the morning of 9 April, the surprise was just as com-

---

* Churchill had arranged for the Admiralty to deliver the latest telegrams on the situation in Norway directly to him. He was thus informed of new developments long before his colleagues, a fact from which he naturally drew the maximum advantage during deliberations.

plete as in London. The latest sessions of the French Cabinet had mainly revolved around the possibility of opening an 'Eastern Front'. At the session of 8 April, Premier Reynaud had announced the British minelaying operation, but beyond that, as Under-Secretary of State Paul Baudouin later recalled, 'Generals Gamelin and Georges, who attended the conference, had given no hint of any military repercussion'.[9] Baudouin was also to give a colourful description of the meeting in Paul Reynaud's office on the morning of 9 April: 'The German reaction burst like a thunderclap. [. . .] General Gamelin arrived at 8.20 a.m., and found us, despatches in hand, trying to locate on an atlas map the names which appeared in the telegrams. For the last five minutes, the Prime Minister and I had been vainly seeking another Narvik on the Norwegian coast, as we were sure that the Narvik where the presence of German troops had been reported could not be the iron ore port in the north.'[10]

The Alpine Division previously earmarked for Finland was still in its peace-time quarters in the Jura, and Paul Reynaud was growing more nervous by the minute. The Commander-in-Chief, General Gamelin, was by contrast quite unmoved; the British, he remarked, were responsible for operations in Norway, and there was nothing to do but wait on events: 'There is no point in getting agitated. [. . .] We are witnessing a mere incident of war. War, after all, is made of unexpected news.'[11] Paul Reynaud was most unfavourably impressed – so much so, in fact, that he decided that very day to get rid of the Commander-in-Chief.[12] This, however, was not the easiest decision to implement, in view of Reynaud's persistent feud with his Minister of War, Daladier. For now, at any rate, the War Committee was summoned,* with the object of finding a fitting answer to the latest German outrage. After some rather stormy discussions, it was decided: (1) To ask the Belgian government for permission to enter Belgium. If the latter agreed, the movement would be carried out simultaneously with Royal Marine, the mining of the Rhine; (2) To promise all possible assistance to the Norwegian government; (3) That Reynaud, Daladier and Admiral Darlan would fly to London immediately for a meeting of the Supreme War Council.[13]

* The War Committee was made up of President Lebrun, Premier Reynaud, Ministers Campinchi (Navy), Laurent-Eynac (Air), Daladier (War), Mandel (Interior), as well as Generals Gamelin, Georges, Vuillemin and Admiral Darlan.

A session of the Supreme War Council duly opened at 10 Downing Street shortly after 4.20 p.m. Needless to say, Norway – or rather, Scandinavia – was at the centre of the debate, since for all the French participants and most of their British counterparts, Northern Europe was of interest only in so far as it enabled the Allies to deprive Germany of its iron ore. To anyone who might have forgotten this elementary fact, Paul Reynaud was quick to deliver a reminder: 'It must be borne in mind that one of the Allies' main objectives is to cut off Germany's ore supplies. It is therefore indispensable to undertake a quick and powerful action in Scandinavia.' Chamberlain fully agreed, stating that he hoped to recapture Bergen, Trondheim and Narvik. But that seemed a tall order, and the Secretary of State for War, Oliver Stanley, effectively damped the prevailing optimism by reminding the participants that there were only seven battalions left in Britain. Two of them would sail that evening from Scapa Flow, and the five remaining ones three days later. But the British military authorities, according to Stanley, had earmarked these troops for Bergen and Trondheim.

That, of course, was not to his French counterpart's liking; 'the Allies', he interjected, 'ought to concentrate their forces, so as to bring them to bear fully on a point considered vital, and that point is Narvik'. Churchill was quick to reassure him: 'The actual operation of clearing any Germans out of Narvik should not present great difficulty. What had to be decided was what was to happen subsequently, when the Allied forces reached the Swedish border.'[14] But Daladier was not so easily fobbed off; he proceeded to remind his interlocutors that 'the Allies had always given top priority to the acquisition of Narvik, considered as the key to the Swedish iron ore mines. [. . .] Besides, the Alpine Division, which was France's contribution to the common undertaking, was to be employed at Narvik.' At this, Oliver Stanley retorted that 'it would be a mistake to throw away an opportunity of capturing Trondheim and Bergen.' Indeed, without the occupation of Bergen, 'it was difficult to see how Norwegian resistance could continue'.

This dialogue of the deaf continued for quite some time, in spite of a diplomatic intervention by Chamberlain, who pointed out that there was no real disagreement, only a difference of emphasis, due mainly to the fact that there was no reliable information as to whether or not the Germans were in Narvik. But Paul Reynaud pretended not to hear: 'One must not lose sight of the extreme importance of Narvik,' he muttered.[15]

This delicate situation was further complicated by the fact that several other pressing problems were to be dealt with at that conference: the plan to enter Belgium, Operation 'Royal Marine', and also the threat of an Italian declaration of war. In the end, no definite decision was taken as to the employment of forces in Norway. The final resolution only mentioned rather irrelevantly that the forces were to be sent to 'ports on the Norwegian seaboard'. To please the French, it was, however, decided to stress the 'particular importance' of occupying Narvik.[16]

That evening, at 9.30, the Military Co-ordination Committee gathered under the chairmanship of Winston Churchill; the latter thus effectively succeeded Lord Chatfield, whose function as Minister for the Co-ordination of Defence had been abolished on 3 April. This time, Churchill proposed without ambiguity 'that no action be taken at Trondheim'. General Ironside agreed: 'We must [. . .] concentrate our attack on Narvik.' This was accepted by everyone present, 'having regard', the conclusions stated, 'to the strategic importance of Narvik in relation to the Gällivare ore fields'. The Chiefs of Staff were therefore instructed to 'put in hand' a plan for the capture of Narvik, but a rather startling proviso was added: 'This plan should take into consideration the possibility of establishing a foothold by Allied forces at Namsos and Aandalsnes.'[17]

Thus, by the evening of 9 April, as the Germans were reinforcing their positions in Norway, and the Norwegians were still vacillating between resistance and submission, the Allies, after six major gatherings in seventeen hours, had covered considerable ground – on paper at least: at 6.30 a.m., top priority given to Bergen and Trondheim, with a progressive drift towards Narvik in the course of the morning; confirmation of Narvik's new-found predominance during the afternoon, under insistent pressure from the French; 'definitive' shelving of Trondheim in the evening, with the surprise appearance in the late-evening conclusions of the Military Co-ordination Committee of the small ports of Namsos and Aandalsnes . . . some 500 miles south of Narvik.

In the early morning of 10 April, several depressing facts began to dawn on the British authorities. The first was laconically expressed by Winston Churchill himself: 'We have been completely outwitted.'[18] The second was that London had no accurate or reliable information on the latest developments in Norway: all contact had been lost with Sir Cecil Dormer,[19] and no one knew the intentions – or even the whereabouts – of the Norwegian government. In addition, owing to the interruption of telephone communications between Norway and Sweden, the British naval attaché in Stockholm reported to Naval Intelligence that 'no information as to German forces in various ports is obtainable'.[20] That may be the reason why Lord Halifax was compelled to ask the Belgian ambassador in London if he had any news from Norway . . .[21]

The third fact that dawned on the British planners in the course of the day was the extraordinary difficulty of improvising in all haste an opposed landing on the Norwegian coast. For one thing, the strength of enemy opposition was unknown; thus, in Narvik, the number of German defenders was estimated at 'between 400 and 4,000'.[22] Besides, topographical information on the landing-places in Norway was almost entirely missing; in the course of the day, a number of officers were sent to travel agencies and navigation bureaux in order to 'requisition' posters and photographs of the quays and ports of various towns along the Norwegian coast.[23] By early afternoon, the planners also found out that the forces available for the Narvik operation – one regular brigade and one territorial battalion – were neither trained nor equipped to carry out an opposed landing at such short notice.[24] At 3 p.m., they therefore wrote the following terse note to General Ironside: 'If object is immediate recapture of Narvik, it is not considered that this is a feasible operation with the forces that are available.'[25]

Such was the information available to the War Cabinet in the afternoon of 10 April – to which must be added the latest reports on naval operations along the Norwegian coast, and they were anything but encouraging; the evening before, Vice-Admiral Layton's squadron had been attacked outside Bergen by German bombers that sank a destroyer and damaged two cruisers. In the early morning of 10 April, five destroyers commanded by Captain Warburton-Lee, having entered the Narvik fjord, managed to sink two German destroyers and seven transport ships, but two British destroyers were lost in the operation, and Captain Warburton-Lee himself was killed.

These tragedies, uncertainties and insufficiencies must have weighed heavily on the ministers gathered for that day's War Cabinet session. But this time, the priority to be given the Narvik operation was reaffirmed by Chamberlain, Churchill, Halifax and even Oliver Stanley, and it was quite clear that the mirage of the Swedish iron mines continued to haunt everyone's imagination. 'If we could gain possession of Narvik,' the conclusions stressed, 'it might still prove possible to press on toward Gällivare, or, at any rate, to take effective action against Luleå from the air.'[26] Yet the ministers were also beset by other grave preoccupations; for one thing, they had just heard unconfirmed rumours that the Norwegians were negotiating with the Germans; in addition, the British press, parliament and public opinion were beginning to realize that the lightning operation carried out by the Germans represented a crushing defeat for Britain, and as usual in such cases, they were casting about for someone to blame. This was naturally reflected in the deliberations of the War Cabinet; the Lord Privy Seal thus argued that it was 'necessary to counter criticism of our Navy', and the First Lord of the Admiralty added that 'it should be made clear that blame attached not to us but to the neutrals, and we should take every opportunity of bringing this point up.'[27]

The next day, indeed, Winston Churchill made in the Commons a long and passionate speech that was clearly intended to defuse criticism levelled at the government: 'It is not the slightest use blaming the Allies for not being able to give substantial help and protection to neutral countries if we are held at arm's length until these neutrals are actually attacked on a scientifically prepared plan by Germany. The strict observance of neutrality by Norway has been a contributory cause to the sufferings to which she is now exposed and to the limits of the aid which we can give her.'[28] These limits were admittedly considerable; thus the six battalions earmarked for the Narvik operation – now code-named 'Rupert' – were still at the Dunfermline camp, trying to find and sort out their equipment which had been rather roughly handled during a precipitate disembarkation five days earlier. Their commander, General Mackesy, was to leave Scapa Flow on 11 April with an advance force of 200 men, in order to 'establish contact with and encourage local Norwegian forces'.[29] But the General was only in charge of land operations, as the command of naval operations at Narvik had just been entrusted by Winston Churchill to Admiral Lord Cork and Orrery.

Alas! the Admiral and the General did not know each other, they had not conferred before departure, they were not even to travel to Norway together – and to make things worse, the instructions given to each of them were highly contradictory and mutually exclusive. But this they were only to find out upon arrival at Narvik . . .

Admiral of the Fleet Lord Cork and Orrery was known throughout the Royal Navy for his boundless energy, resolutely offensive spirit and devastating fits of temper; a retired First Sea Lord, he had sprung back into active service at the very beginning of the war. On 10 April, in Whitehall, Lord Cork had been given no written instructions, but having attended the session of the Military Co-ordination Committee that evening, he understood perfectly well what was expected of him: he was to expel the Germans from Narvik with the least possible delay.[30] As for General Mackesy, he received written instructions from the War Office at Scapa Flow on the morning of 11 April. They did specify that he was to 'eject the Germans from the Narvik area, and establish control of Narvik itself', but did not instruct him to attack right away. On the contrary, he was to 'establish his force at Harstad', 'ensure the co-operation of any Norwegian forces that may be in the area', and 'obtain the information necessary to enable him to plan future operations'.[31] The impression that the War Office wished caution to prevail over celerity was reinforced by several significant features of the instruction: for one thing, prescribing a landing at Harstad, 35 miles north-east of Narvik,[32] was to accept the necessity of a long and arduous approach over mountainous terrain before reaching the objective. For another, the War Office had added a significant passage to General Mackesy's instructions: 'It is not intended that you should land in the face of opposition.'[33] Finally, should Mackesy decide to take a bold step and land directly at Narvik, he would be entirely unable to do so. Indeed, the five transport ships that were to leave Scapa Flow between 12 April and 14 April had embarked both troops and equipment as they arrived; in other words, the equipment was stacked on the ships with no method whatsoever – and there was no inventory.

For all that, Lord Cork's impression was fully justified: the Admiralty and its forceful First Lord wanted speed to prevail over caution. At 0.15 on the morning of 11 April, Captain Maund was urgently summoned to Admiral Pound's office in Whitehall: 'It was a sadly overworked and tired group of officers that sat around the table,'

Captain Maund recalled. 'I was told that I was to go as Chief of Staff to the naval commander for the attack on Narvik, and that I was to join the army commander, who was in ship at Scapa, at once. I asked for information about the enemy forces and what the plan for the operations was to be. I was told it was no time to talk of these things.'[34] All in all, it was hardly an auspicious beginning.

Upon returning from the Supreme War Council in the evening of 9 April, Paul Reynaud, with only limited confidence in the martial prowess of his British allies and the ability of his own commanders to land French troops in Norway in the foreseeable future, began casting about for some other means of settling the question of Swedish iron ore – an issue that continued to obsess him for reasons that were both strategic and political – and decidedly less strategic than political.

The answer to Reynaud's preoccupations presented itself in the guise of a plan submitted by one of his advisers, Colonel de Villelume. Villelume's idea was to send a diplomatic mission to Sweden, headed by General Mittelhauser and by Robert Coulondre, a former ambassador to Berlin. These men would tell the Swedes that their country and its iron ore were 'Germany's main objective', and that Sweden 'could count on receiving all the assistance it was in our power to grant her'; they would also state that 'we were ready to hold military conversations with Sweden'.[35] Why expend so much eloquence? The real purpose was of course to encourage Sweden to declare war on Germany, which would result in an immediate interruption of Germany's iron ore supply. But as this was a diplomatic mission, and the Swedes were known to cherish their neutrality, an excessively blunt approach was considered inadvisable. However, it was hoped that the Swedes would understand what was expected of them.

Neville Chamberlain was immediately seduced by the idea. He had been stung to the quick by increasingly harsh attacks in the press and in parliament against the man who had been saying only a week earlier that Hitler had 'missed the bus'. Now, like his French counterpart, Chamberlain wanted to show public opinion that he could be depended on to prosecute the war with relentless energy. Thus, when on the morning of 11 April, Coulondre and Mittelhauser stopped off in London en route to Stockholm, they were immediately received by Chamberlain, who proposed to send a British delegation with them to Stockholm. Besides, the Prime Minister thought aloud, if the Swedish government 'could be induced to send forces overland to assist the Allies at Narvik', the town might be recaptured 'very much sooner'.[36] The British delegation was soon set up; it was composed of Admiral Evans, General Lewin, and Wing Commander Thornton, British Air Attaché in Stockholm.[37] Yet, by the end of the morning, Chamberlain was already beginning to have second thoughts: should the Swedes declare war on Germany, they would require assistance, which would necessarily weaken Allied defensive positions on the Western Front, where the Germans might attack at any time. Would it not be a better idea after all to encourage the Swedes to remain neutral?[38]

Actually, Chamberlain had nothing to fear, for the Swedes needed no encouragement at all to remain neutral – as the Franco-British mission was to discover in Stockholm after its very first interviews with King Gustav V and Foreign Minister Günther. The Swedish Commander-in-Chief, General Thörnell, was even less forthcoming, as evidenced by his own notes of the interview: 'Mittelhauser told me that the British and French intended to land in northern Norway, and represented that the expulsion of the Germans from Norway would be very much in Sweden's interest. He added that a Swedish contribution to that end would be most desirable. It was clear that he was asking for my support to persuade the Swedish government to intervene actively in the war. [. . .] I answered that Sweden would remain neutral in all eventualities, and would meet any incursion on its territory, from whatever quarter, with armed opposition.'[39]

The Franco-British mission to Stockholm had thus proved useless, and though the Swedish Foreign Minister tactfully told British Ambassador Mallet that 'he was very grateful for the Allied mission' he added pointedly that he 'thought it wiser that they should not stay too long'.[40] But, although the Swedes firmly intended to remain spectators in the conflict that was raging just across their border, they had no inhibition about expressing their sympathies – or dispensing advice; thus, on 13 April, Ambassador Coulondre sent the following telegram to Paris: 'The Allied missions here, and also the Swedes, are unanimous in their opinion that the most effective Allied help would be the capture of Trondheim.'[41] That same day, the members of the British delegation sent an almost identical telegram to the Foreign Office.[42] It fully confirmed the opinion expressed two days earlier by Erik Boheman, General Secretary of the Swedish Foreign Ministry, according to whom 'Trondheim was the key to the situation'.[43] Finally, on 12 April, Sir Cecil Dormer, who had managed to rejoin the Norwegian government near the Swedish border, sent the following telegram to the British Legation in Stockholm, for immediate transmission to the Foreign Office: 'King and government more determined than when I last saw them at Elverum midnight 9 April. [. . .] Government are anxious to establish themselves at Trondheim as soon as Germans expelled from there. [. . .] The Norwegian government definitely do not feel capable of coping with the situation if British support is confined to naval operation only.' The end of the telegram was quite unambiguous: 'I venture to urge that military assistance at Trondheim is first necessity. Seizure of Narvik of little assistance to Norwegian government.'[44] All this was to exercise considerable influence on the strategic debate in London.

Ever since 9 April, there had been some supporters of an attack on Trondheim within the Military Co-ordination Committee; Sir Cyril Newall, Chief of the Air Staff, was one of them. Admittedly, that was the initial strategy, but to return to it now would mean going back on all the decisions that had been so laboriously reached in the course of the last 48 hours. At the Military Co-ordination Committee session of 11 April, when Newall again brought up the idea of an operation 'against either Trondheim or Bergen', it seemed to exercise a certain attraction on his colleagues, but Winston Churchill was quick to see the danger behind the idea; though he agreed that the study of the Trondheim operation – and even that of an 'exploratory' landing at Namsos – should be allowed to proceed, he also warned that 'no action should be taken' until it was known what would be involved in the Narvik operation ('Rupert').[45]

Not only was Churchill the chairman of the Committee, he was also better informed, more forceful and more eloquent than his colleagues; besides, the Military Co-ordination Committee met in the evening, and both ministers and Chiefs of Staff were worn out by 72 hours of almost uninterrupted work and meetings – except Churchill, whose powers of recuperation were quite amazing. At any rate, the First Lord carried the day: the target was to remain Narvik, and there would be no side-shows . . . for the time being.[46]

Alas! The process of British strategic decision-making was a three-stage mechanism that was slow to start and prompt to stall; at the top of the pyramid was the War Cabinet, where the strategic debate was repeated the very next morning, under the added influence of information coming from both Norway and Sweden. Churchill acknowledged that there was some pressure in favour of an operation to occupy Namsos, but repeated that 'it was not thought right to interrupt in any way the progress of operations against Narvik'. But Chamberlain, who was inclined to dabble in strategy that day, asserted that 'he also had intended to suggest that we should put a force ashore at Namsos. The Swedes were emphasizing the vital importance of recapturing Trondheim, which was the key to the routes of communication into Norway and Sweden, and it looked as if Namsos might be a useful jumping-off place.'

'The recapture of Trondheim', Churchill answered with commendable patience, 'was an operation the difficulty of which should not be underrated. [. . .] However, if we could recapture Narvik rapidly, then it might be possible to make use of the Chasseurs Alpins against Trondheim. We had as yet no information of what troops the Germans had at Trondheim. The need for information about the situation throughout Norway was vital.'[47] That of course was perfectly true; thus, at the MCC (Military Co-ordination Committee) meeting the previous evening, no one knew whether the town of Tromsø was occupied by the Germans or not.[48] In addition, the War Office estimate of the number of German troops in Norway at this juncture was still in the order of two divisions; there was little or no information on the strength – or even the existence – of Norwegian troops in any particular area; finally, the War Office and the Admiralty knew practically nothing about the land and sea defences of either Trondheim or Narvik. In many cases, it was clear that the ministers, and even the military planners, were depending on the press for their information; yet, as the press was often carrying accounts that were either impossible to check or downright improbable, absurd situations were bound to result; thus, on the evening of 11 April, the Foreign Office cabled the British minister in Stockholm to request confirmation of a Reuter report according to which British forces had retaken Bergen and Trondheim![49]

The War Cabinet reconvened in the afternoon of 12 April, and this time it was Lord Halifax who spearheaded the drive in favour of

Trondheim; he drew his colleagues' attention to the telegrams just received from the British legation in Stockholm, remarking that 'operations in Narvik, however sound from a military point of view, would have very much less political effect than an attempt to clear the Germans out of the southern part of Norway.' Unperturbed, Churchill pointed out once again that 'an opposed landing at Trondheim would be a very difficult operation, and if mounted without proper preparation, might only lead to a bloody repulse. Preparations for an expedition to Narvik were well advanced, and the landing would be made within a few days.' At this point, Secretary of State for War Oliver Stanley unexpectedly bolstered Churchill's position by observing that 'the assistance of French troops would be required for a landing at Trondheim, and the French had insisted that the Narvik operation should be carried out first'.

Stanley's intervention, the abstention of the Prime Minister and the uncertainty as to French reactions finally proved decisive, and by late afternoon, Churchill had won the day when the Cabinet concluded that 'it was generally agreed that landings on the Norwegian coast even on a small scale would have an important political effect and from that point of view were desirable, but that they should not be carried out at the cost of a diversion of effort from the Narvik expedition now in course of preparation.'[50]

That sounded definitive . . . It was not; for over and above the aforementioned three levels of decision – Chiefs of Staff Committee, Military Co-ordination Committee and War Cabinet, there was a fourth level of decision, which could even overturn the decisions of the War Cabinet: that all-powerful body was of course the War Cabinet of the following day.

Indeed, on the morning of 13 April, everything was called back into question; Lord Halifax reiterated his arguments in favour of an immediate expedition towards Trondheim, General Ironside objected that this might require additional troops which would have to be withdrawn from France, and Churchill repeated his arguments of the previous day. But this time, Chamberlain intervened in the debate and, mentioning the telegram just received from Ambassador Coulondre in Stockholm, he confessed that he 'was impressed with the urgency of obtaining a firm foothold at Trondheim, particularly from the political point of view. If at that moment we merely concentrated on Narvik, there was a danger lest the Norwegians and Swedes should feel that our only interest was the iron ore. In that event, they might become disheartened and give up the struggle.'[51]

It was a little difficult to understand how the Swedes could give up the fight, considering that they had not even taken it up – and clearly had not the slightest intention of doing so. Neither was there much danger in making the Norwegians and Swedes feel that the Allies' only interest was the iron ore: they had been perfectly aware of it for the last seven months at least; indeed, it would have been all but impossible to miss the point . . . At any rate, Lord Halifax immediately backed up the Prime Minister, repeating that 'early action against Trondheim was imperative from the political point of view, while it seemed that if necessary, the operation at Narvik could wait.'

Chamberlain went on to suggest that 'the French division of Chasseurs Alpins might be more usefully employed in operations at Trondheim than at Narvik, and that the French should be pressed to give us a free hand as regards the employment of these troops.'[52] This led Churchill to urge 'that no alterations should be made in the present plans for the capture of Narvik, which were, in fact, already in process of being carried out'. But Chamberlain seemed hypnotized by the telegrams received from Stockholm, which he proceeded to read at length. After that, Churchill warned that if anything else were undertaken before the capture of Narvik 'there was a grave danger that we should find ourselves committed to a number of ineffectual operations along the Norwegian coast, none of which would succeed', but Chamberlain's words clearly carried the greatest weight with his ministers. Lord Halifax reiterated that 'there was a very important political factor which must be taken into account', Oliver Stanley hesitated between Narvik and Trondheim, and General Ironside assured them that there were good chances of taking Narvik – provided the town were defended by not more than 4,000 Germans; but he effectively switched sides when he added that 'a diversion would not impair the plan'. Finally, Sir John Simon, Chancellor of the Exchequer, also spoke in favour of Trondheim, even though his knowledge of strategic matters lay somewhere between that of Chamberlain and Lord Halifax . . .

By the end of the afternoon, it was all over, and the Cabinet's conclusions were the exact opposite of those reached the day before: the Stockholm embassy would be told that it was intended to take *both Trondheim and Narvik*; as for the French, they would be asked for permission to use the Chasseurs Alpins for operations 'elsewhere than at Narvik'.[53]

That evening, shortly before the meeting of the Military Co-ordination Committee, information of the greatest importance reached the Admiralty: at noon that day, a British squadron with the pre-1914 battleship *Warspite* and nine destroyers had entered Narvik fjord; by 5.45 p.m., its commander, Admiral Whitworth, could cable the Admiralty that his ships had sunk the seven German destroyers remaining in Narvik fjord since the first engagement of 10 April.[54] The news was received with relief and jubilation at the Military Co-ordination Committee, whose members, encouraged by the latest conclusions of the War Cabinet and convinced that Narvik would now fall in a matter of hours, resolutely turned their attention to other objectives along the Norwegian coast. The following plan eventually emerged:

– A 'reconnaissance' landing at Namsos, 80 miles north of Trondheim, with a small detachment of 300 men (code-name 'Henry'), to be carried out the very next day.

– A second, 'diversionary' landing to be made on the 16th at Aalesund, 150 miles south of Trondheim, by a force of about 600 men (Operation 'Primrose').

– At the same time, a landing at Namsos of 5,000 men, who would march on to Trondheim (Operation 'Maurice').

The possibility of a direct naval attack on Trondheim (code-named 'Boots') was also considered. Last but not least, it was agreed that one of the two brigades then sailing for Narvik, the 146th Territorial Brigade, should be diverted at sea to join in Operation 'Maurice' at Namsos.[55]

For the first time in this campaign – though by no means the last – Churchill abruptly gave in on the Trondheim plan, and proceeded to implement it with exemplary zeal and energy. He may have estimated that any initiative that had the approval of a majority of the Cabinet was preferable to the deplorable vacillation that had hitherto characterized the Allies' Norwegian strategy. A few hours later, at any rate, Churchill, accompanied by Admiral Tom Phillips, Deputy Chief of the Naval Staff, went to see General Ironside at the War Office; it was by then two o'clock on the morning of 14 April.

'Tiny,' said Churchill, 'we are going for the wrong place. We should go for Trondheim. The Navy will make a direct attack on it and I want a small force of good troops, well led, to follow up the naval attack. I also want landings made north and south of Trondheim, one at Namsos and the other at Aandalsnes, to co-operate with the assault when it comes off by a pincer movement on Trondheim.'[56] General Ironside protested that no troops would be available for Trondheim until Narvik had been taken, but Churchill brushed aside the objection: all it would take was the diversion of the 146th Brigade from Narvik to Namsos, as had just been decided a few hours before. General Ironside strenuously objected, but in the end had to give in, the plan having been approved by the Military Co-ordination Committee.[57]

At the War Cabinet session of 14 April, Winston Churchill and Admiral Pound were duly congratulated for the 'brilliant operation' carried out at Narvik the day before; Churchill was now quite confident of success at Narvik, and he announced that the landing of the 24th Brigade that day 'might possibly be made in the town itself'. 'The altered situation at Narvik,' he added, 'permitted a more hopeful view to be taken with regard to operations in the Trondheim area.' Indeed, his naval staff had even suggested that 'it might be possible to effect a landing at Trondheim itself'.[58] The War Cabinet thereupon approved the various plans recommended by the Military Co-ordination Committee – including the diversion of the 146th Brigade to Namsos. Finally, the French, consulted by telephone, had agreed to send their mountain troops to Trondheim rather than to Narvik. At the War Cabinet, the situation was thus being viewed with increasing optimism: in the course of the next 48 hours, the great offensive would be unleashed all along the Norwegian coast.

On a closer look, however, it must be admitted that there was little justification for such euphoria. The 'Rupert' Force sailing towards Narvik was left with only the 24th Brigade, equipped for a peaceful landing under the former 'Avonmouth' plan ... and even deprived of part of that equipment, as it had been loaded in the ships of the 146th Brigade now being diverted to Namsos. It will also be recalled that the naval commander, Lord Cork, and the army commander, General Mackesy, had been issued different and even contradictory instructions, the former being expected to take Narvik by a bold *coup de main*, the latter only to establish a base at Harstad, then reconnoitre the ground in anticipation of subsequent action that might eventually result in an offensive on the town itself. Granted, no one expected much opposition from the German defenders of Narvik after the successful operation of the day before, but Churchill had confessed that morning at the War Cabinet that there was 'no news on the strength or location of the German forces at Narvik'.[59]

In the case of Operation 'Maurice' at Trondheim, there was hardly more reason to be optimistic: the 146th Brigade that had just been diverted to Namsos was a territorial unit with very little training; its equipment had been embarked, then partially disembarked (in a rather chaotic way) on the morning of 7 April; re-embarked on 12 April, it had been partially amputated two days later when the convoy split in two on its way to Narvik. Thus, the men of the 146th Brigade, now bound for Namsos, only had maps of Narvik and part of the 24th Brigade's armament, while their own vehicles, some of their armament – and their commander – were still sailing towards Narvik.[60] As for the men of the 148th Brigade, they were equipped with maps of Namsos, but had precious little use for them: they were to land at Aandalsnes . . .

It will also be observed that the plans about to be implemented, having all been elaborated in less than five days, could hardly be expected to prove flawless. Thus, the 'Maurice' plan failed to address the highly relevant question of whether the port of Namsos was equipped to allow the disembarkation of several thousand men with all their equipment. Besides, none of the plans drawn up since 9 April seemed to mention the thickness of the snow in the various theatres of operations, and the troops had not been equipped accordingly: no snow-shoes, no skis either – though in fact the soldiers would have had little use for such implements, since most of them had never seen a mountain in their lives . . .

The plans included various other baffling deficiencies. Thus, it was nowhere mentioned that after having landed at Namsos, the 'Maurice' Force would have to march 134 miles before reaching Trondheim – provided they used the roads, of course, which was hardly advisable for troops without air cover or anti-aircraft guns. In addition, neither the 'Maurice', 'Rupert', 'Henry' nor 'Primrose' Forces could hope to catch the enemy by surprise: ever since 10 April, the whole British press had been announcing imminent landings at Trondheim, Narvik, Namsos, Aalesund, Aandalsnes and Molde, with learned estimates of their chances of success. The plans also included practically no instructions on collaboration with Norwegian forces at Narvik, and in fact, as late as 14 April, no one really knew where they were, or even if they were still resisting.[61] As for southern Norway, nothing was known, either, of the whereabouts of King Haakon and his government, and the first messages from Norwegian field headquarters were only received in the afternoon of 13 April; transmitted by highly rudimentary means, they were brief, difficult to decipher, and they bore the signature of a certain General Ruge, of whom no one in London seemed to have heard. All other information about the Norwegians remained very much in the nature of guesswork; thus, at the War Cabinet session of 14 April, Winston Churchill had stated that 'it seemed possible [that] the railway to Trondheim was still in Norwegian hands.'[62] In other words, it seemed just as possible that it was not.

It has been said quite rightly that the British government was no better informed about developments in Norway than the average newspaper reader.[63] The problem was that British, Swedish and American newspapers still carried highly confused and conflicting reports on the military operations, partly because the journalists were far more interested in the 'Archtraitor' Quisling and his 'Fifth Column', on whom hundreds of wildly improbable articles were appearing almost daily. Eventually, London had decided to send the Military Attaché in Helsinki, Lieutenant-Colonel E. J. C. King-Salter, to try to make contact with Norwegian headquarters; Admiral Evans had also been dispatched to try to find the King and his government. But, for the time being, there was no news from either the Lieutenant-Colonel or the Admiral, and the fact remained that five days after 9 April, the British and the Norwegians were still fighting an entirely separate war.

# CHAPTER SIX

# The Fighting Neutrals

By the morning of 10 April, the situation in Norway was still highly confused; it was obvious that the country was no longer at peace, since several thousand German soldiers were occupying its main cities, ports and airfields; yet it was not quite at war either, since negotiations were still in progress between the Norwegian government and the representative of a power that had come allegedly to 'protect the neutrality of Norway'. In fact, apart from a few skirmishes and intensive aerial bombardments, there had as yet been no fighting on land: first, because the Germans were still in the process of consolidating their positions around Oslo, Kristiansand, Bergen, Stavanger, Trondheim and Narvik; second, because the Norwegian army had been instructed to defend itself, but not to counter-attack; for the last thirty hours, actually, it had received no orders at all, its commander-in-chief, General Laake, having been effectively struck dumb by the suddenness of the German onslaught. As for the government, it was still hesitating between the alternative of fighting and that of negotiating, mainly for fear that the former might jeopardize the latter.[1]

On the morning of 10 April, in fact, no one could say whether or not the Norwegian army was mobilized. It will be recalled that as a result of an almost farcical combination of confusion and incompetence, a partial mobilization had been ordered for 11 April, with all soldiers to be called up by mail. However, Foreign Minister Koht having mentioned by mistake to a press correspondent that a general mobilization had been ordered, a mad scramble to arms followed throughout the country. As the main towns and weapons depots were already in German hands, the mobilization was carried out in the greatest confusion. French Minister Robert de Dampierre, who had left Oslo on 9 April to follow the government to Hamar, occasionally met on the road 'isolated individuals who had learned by chance of the general mobilization order. They were wandering about the countryside with their little suitcase in hand, not knowing what to do or where to go, and in most cases they were sent home in the end.'[2] Mr Rowland Kenney, of the British legation, likewise recalled having seen 'reservists and volunteers leaving the recruiting stations in tears when told that there were no arms for them'.[3]

That same morning of 10 April, the Norwegian army had evacuated its headquarters to Rena, half-way between Lillehammer and Nybergsund. There, early in the afternoon, Minister of Justice Terje Wold had a rather stormy meeting with General Laake. The latter began by saying that 'given the military situation, we have no other choice than to pursue the negotiations or capitulate unconditionally'.[4] He then proceeded to complain bitterly about the absence of any contact with the government, whereupon Wold asked if anyone had thought of contacting the Prime Minister, who was still at Nybergsund, less than 25 miles away . . . No one seemed to have thought of that, and Wold was fast losing patience:

'What have you done until now, General? Where are your orders to the troops? And what is this I hear: our country has been at war since yesterday, and the first day of mobilization is to be tomorrow? Was there really no other way of handling this matter?'

'Well, actually . . . Yes, there was,' answered Lieutenant-Colonel Wrede-Holm.* 'We could have ordered an open mobilization.'

'And why was this not done?' asked Mr Wold.

'The government ordered otherwise,' replied General Laake.[5]

Wold then pointed out that the government had ordered a general mobilization, and that it was General Laake's responsibility to 'settle technical details'. The Minister of Justice evidently did not realize that this was no 'technical detail', and that his colleagues and himself had ordered a partial mobilization in the belief that it was a general mobilization. Naturally, General Laake forgot to mention that it was on his own advice that the government had ordered a partial mobilization.

The misunderstanding persisted when the three men left the past to dwell on the sad realities of the present. Mr Wold, though admitting that he was not competent to discuss strategic matters, evoked

---

* Harald Wrede-Holm, Chief of Section IV (Intelligence-Security) at the General Staff.

the possibility of a fighting retreat up the Gudbrandsdal, coupled with a determined effort to contain the Germans until British assistance could reach central Norway, as had been promised the day before. But General Laake obstinately repeated that there were only two solutions left: negotiation or capitulation. As for British assistance, he considered that it would be useless unless it arrived within the next two days – something the General obviously did not believe. 'My plan fell on stony ground,' Wold recalled. 'I had the feeling that [. . .] the whole General Staff considered it impracticable.'[6]

Wold left headquarters deeply struck by the almost palpable defeatism pervading the General Staff, and quite shocked by the attitude of the Commander-in-Chief, as he confided by telephone later that afternoon to his colleague Trygve Lie. The latter promised to inform the rest of the government as soon as possible; for the time being, both the King and the Foreign Minister were in Elverum, negotiating with the German minister.

Actually, what went on that afternoon in the little communal school of Elverum could hardly be called a negotiation; having first insisted on talking to the King alone, Minister Bräuer launched into a long tirade that was not appreciably different from his ultimatum of the day before: Great Britain bore full responsibility for what had happened, the sovereignty and integrity of Norway were by no means threatened, and any resistance would be mercilessly crushed.[7] Yet there was now an additional demand of some importance: 'We can no longer trust this government [. . .] that refused our generous offer for incomprehensible reasons. [. . .] It is therefore important for us to have in Norway a government [. . .] that would show understanding for [. . .] the German position. Now, a government was set up yesterday in Oslo under Minister Quisling, and we consider it only right that this man, whose patriotism and understanding for our cause are well known, be entrusted at present with the responsibilities of government.'[8]

Bräuer later reported to Berlin that the King 'had been visibly impressed' by his arguments. That was most unlikely; King Haakon, who was very ill at ease, had merely answered in broken German that he could take no decision without consulting his government, after which he had asked his Foreign Minister to join him. From then on, the account of the conversation on the Norwegian side becomes far more accurate. Bräuer repeated his previous arguments for the benefit of Koht, though the tone this time was much harsher: 'The German government demanded that the King appoint Major Quisling as Chief of Government, and as ministers the men he had named in his proclamation, to whom some other personalities might be added.' Having consulted with his Foreign Minister, King Haakon answered that 'he could not appoint a government that did not enjoy the confidence of the Norwegian people, and several elections had shown that Major Quisling did not enjoy such confidence to a sufficient degree. His government would be nothing more than a Kuusinen government.'

Koht then intervened to say that the Nygaardsvold government had expressed their readiness to resign, and he asked Bräuer 'whether the German government might agree to the formation of a government ready to co-operate with Germany, but composed of other personalities than the ones just mentioned'. Bräuer answered that the appointment of various ministers could be negotiated, but that 'the Führer had decided that the head of that government could be no other than Quisling himself.' The King thereupon answered that he would submit the matter 'to his legal government',[9] and it was agreed that Bräuer would be informed by telephone of the government's decision.[10] With that, the meeting ended shortly after 4.25 p.m., and Bräuer immediately set out for Oslo, while the King and his Foreign Minister drove back to Nybergsund.

At the Government Council in Nybergsund that evening, King Haakon, after having summed up his interview with the German diplomat, was the first to express his views on the situation. That was highly unusual, but then, so was the situation. The King of Norway had very limited powers, but according to the constitution, he alone could appoint the Prime Minister. In peacetime, that was a symbolic privilege at best: the King would of course appoint the head of the party that had won the election. But on that evening of 10 April, the situation was quite different: King Haakon was to follow the dictate of his own conscience, and for the very first time, he held in his hands the entire future of his adopted country. An almost impossible choice it was, between probable destruction and certain damnation ... With a quivering voice that betrayed deep inner conflict, the old King finally spoke up: 'I am profoundly moved at the idea of having to assume personal responsibility for the woes that will befall our country and our people if German demands are rejected.

It is such a heavy responsibility that I shudder to bear it. The government is free to decide, but I shall make my own position clear: I cannot accept the German demands. This would conflict with everything I have considered to be my duty as a king ever since I came to Norway almost thirty-five years ago. [. . .] I have endeavoured to embody a constitutional monarchy that was entirely loyal to the people who elected me in 1905. [. . .] I cannot name Quisling Prime Minister, because he has neither the confidence of the people nor that of their deputies. As a result, should the government choose to bow before the German demands, I would understand their motivations perfectly, in view of the imminent peril now threatening, and the prospect of seeing so many young Norwegians sacrifice their lives in this war; yet I would then have no other alternative than to abdicate [. . .] to renounce the throne of Norway for myself and my family.'[11]

'That instant burnt itself into my memory,' Trygve Lie later recalled. 'Having said these words, the King gazed intently at Prince Olav. For a long while, he was unable to resume, then he bent over the table and burst into tears. Prince Olav also had tears in his eyes.'[12] But the King raised his head, and with considerable effort managed to carry on: 'The Government must now take its decision. It is not bound by my position. [. . .] Yet I felt it was my duty to make it known.'[13]

If, according to the Norwegian constitution, the King had the power to name – or not to name – the Prime Minister, he could only exercise that prerogative 'upon the government's proposal' and, whatever the gravity of the hour, there was no question of abandoning the usual constitutional formalism. The ministers had been strongly impressed by the King's intervention, and during the debate that ensued, there was no trace left of the defeatism prevailing the day before.[14] In the end, Prime Minister Nygaardsvold himself, after having spoken in favour of continuing the struggle, proposed that his colleagues vote the following formal motion: 'The Council of Ministers proposes that the King reject the ultimatum presented by Germany [. . .] that Major Quisling be named Prime Minister.'[15] Constitutional formalities were to be observed to the very last: 'The King hereby approves the Government's proposal.'[16]

That evening at 8 p.m. Bräuer reached Eidsvold, from where he called Koht on the telephone. The ensuing conversation was to be a brief one; Koht immediately told the diplomat that King Haakon would not appoint a Quisling cabinet, whereupon the diplomat asked 'whether that meant that the Norwegian resistance would continue'.

'Yes, as long as possible,' answered Koht.[17]

The Norwegian authorities had burnt their boats; there were to be no more negotiations with the Germans . . . Neither at Oslo nor at Nybergsund had the ministers taken their decision after careful consideration of the possibilities of Allied help, or even of the chances of a successful resistance to the German invaders.[18] Perhaps they simply felt that such evaluations were outside their field of competence. But from a political, constitutional, juridical and even moral point of view, the answer had seemed perfectly obvious: the German demands were unacceptable, and even more so since they had crystallized around the nomination of a Quisling government. As for the strategic aspect of the question . . . well, that was a problem to be dealt with by the military.

But during that same afternoon of 10 April, two ministers, Terje Wold and Trygve Lie, were having grave doubts as to the competence of the military in general, and of General Laake in particular. As he had promised the Minister of Justice, Trygve Lie duly informed his colleagues of the impressions gathered by Wold during his interview with General Laake earlier in the afternoon. Actually, Lie went one step further, and proposed that the Commander-in-Chief be replaced without delay.[19]

A difficult undertaking it was – the Minister of Defence, for one, would not hear of General Laake's replacement – but Trygve Lie proved highly persuasive, and he scored a decisive point that evening, when both Prime Minister Nygaardsvold and Prince Olav came down on his side. Admittedly, Colonel Otto Ruge, the man Trygve Lie was proposing as a successor to General Laake, commanded the greatest respect in both civilian and military circles; Army Chief of Staff between 1933 and 1938, then Inspector-General of the Infantry, he personally led the small detachment that had stopped the Germans at Midtskogen the day before. On the morning of 10 April, he had also told Lie that he saw no alternative to the most determined resistance to the German invader. Towards the end of the Council of Ministers, the question of General Laake's replacement was raised anew, and agreement was finally reached: Minister Ljungberg was asked to call the General to Nybergsund immediately.

Late that night, General Laake arrived at Nybergsund, where he was received by Ministers Lie and Ljungberg. After he had repeated his view that he had no faith in the success of an armed resistance to Germany, the General was tactfully appraised of the government's decision; by a fortunate coincidence, he had reached retirement age just the day before, and the ministers had no difficulty at all in getting him to sign a letter of resignation. Lieutenant-Colonel Roscher-Nielsen, who was waiting in the next room, later recalled that Laake emerged from the meeting very depressed, but also 'somewhat relieved'.[20] It was almost midnight when Colonel Ruge received a phone call from Trygve Lie, informing him that he had just been appointed Commander-in-Chief; he was to assume command the very next day. Admittedly, the next day was to begin in only a few minutes' time, but that was just as well: there was obviously not a moment to lose . . .

In the early morning of 11 April, the sun was shining frostily over the little snow-covered village of Nybergsund. Inside the village's only inn, King Haakon and Prince Olav were conferring with their ministers, while several children played in the immediate vicinity. Suddenly, a man ran towards a parked car and hooted several times. At that signal, everyone rushed out of the inn and ran across a snowy field towards the nearest wood. Almost simultaneously, six Heinkel bombers passed overhead and raked the village, then the wood with heavy machine-gun fire. Explosive bullets pelted the snow, ricocheted from stones and cliffs, mowed down the trees and branches; then there was a loud explosion, and a fir tree collapsed. The planes veered and made a second pass over the village, dropping clusters of incendiary bombs, and the little wood was again bombed and strafed. Several more trees crashed down, with twigs and splinters shooting out in all directions. Finally, after almost an hour, the planes departed; one of them was to be shot down a few days later, and the following entry was found in the pilot's diary: 'The King, the Government, all annihilated . . .'

The devastated village slowly returned to life as the inhabitants trickled back, carefully picking their way among the huge bomb craters and the smouldering ruins. It was something of a miracle:

no one had been hit. The ministers were clearly rattled by the ordeal, but Prince Olav was perfectly calm. King Haakon was both shaken and indignant, and he later explained why: 'Seeing all these bombs fall so near my friends, my ministers and my son was a terrible shock for me. But, above all, I could not bear to see these children crouching in the snow as bullets mowed down the trees, and branches rained down on them.' The King added that he regretted having stopped in this place, and that never again, for the duration of the war, would he stop to rest when children were in the vicinity. The Prime Minister, the Minister of Culture and the King's Aide-de-Camp were just as indignant, though for reasons that were rather more down to earth: as the planes swooped down on them, they had all thrown themselves face down . . . and landed in a pigsty.

There was a lengthy debate that evening as to which course to follow. The Prime Minister had had enough, and was in favour of seeking refuge in Sweden. Trygve Lie, on the contrary, wanted to head north and rejoin army headquarters at Lillehammer. The other ministers appeared to vacillate, but King Haakon, having recovered both his composure and his determination, declared flatly that he would on no account seek refuge in Sweden; Prince Olav agreed. The time was long past when the King's views on such matters could be conveniently ignored: Lillehammer it would be.

On that same 11 April, at 6 a.m., General Ruge had issued his first order of the day to the Norwegian troops. The first order to emanate from headquarters since the German landings 48 hours earlier, it was brief and to the point: 'Contain the German onslaught with all available means. Isolate Oslo completely, by setting up roadblocks as close as possible to the capital.'[21] The new Commander-in-Chief had already devised a general strategy: to contain the enemy along the southern coast long enough to allow an orderly mobilization in the interior of the country, and a gradual retreat towards the north – or, rather, the north-west, as General Ruge, for one, was firmly counting on British assistance; it was even the *conditio sine qua non* of his entire strategy.[22] He would therefore endeavour to 'trade space for time'.[23]

As could be expected, the next few days were to prove very difficult indeed. The Germans, having received a steady stream of reinforcements by sea and air since 9 April, took the offensive on 13 April along three different axes, east, north and west of Oslo. In execution of General Ruge's orders, roadblocks had been set up on the approaches to the city, but they were perforce only makeshift stacks of timber defended by a few companies of ill-trained, lightly armed and worn-out soldiers and volunteers – a far cry from what the BBC was calling the 'circle of steel thrown around Oslo'.[24] The German troops, with powerful air support, quickly swept away such improvised obstacles, and scored some lightning successes: between 13 and 14 April, a whole Norwegian regiment capitulated before Tønsberg, south-west of Oslo; at Kongsvinger, in the north-east, 3,000 Norwegian soldiers, threatened with encirclement, were compelled to cross into Sweden. After that, four columns of motorized infantry, supported by tanks and planes, converged on a broad front towards General Ruge's front line of defence between the Randsfjord and the eastern shores of Lake Mjøsa.

Aerial bombardments were a permanent threat to the Norwegian army's communication and supply lines. Its two transmitters, at Hamar and Vigra, were almost immediately bombed, so that for long spells at a time, General Ruge's headquarters were entirely isolated from the world at large. Besides, both the bombings and the German advance compelled the High Command to remain constantly on the move; on 11 April, headquarters were shifted from Rena to Øyer, north of Lillehammer, at which time they had lost contact with the King and the government, who were themselves under intense bombardment at the time. In addition, the High Command was having the greatest difficulty remaining in contact with its own troops facing the enemy: the telegraph cables had been cut, the telephone lines were being monitored by the Germans, and there were no field radios; liaison officers therefore had to be dispatched by car, on skis – or on foot. Contact had also been lost with whole regions of the country: the south-west, the centre, and the whole of northern Norway. To make things even worse, the news of Quisling's treason had caused a violent outbreak of spymania throughout the country; any stranger to the area – or to the village – was apt to be detained by suspicious country folk and volunteers as a member of the Fifth Column; that included refugees, foreign diplomats, members of the government, and also, unfortunately, some of General Ruge's liaison officers.[25]

This should give an idea of the extraordinary difficulties encountered by the Commander-in-Chief in his attempt to mobilize troops and stabilize the front north of Oslo, around Trondheim and in the mountains east of Bergen. The mobilization centres were under constant bombardment, most weapons depots and the lists of the men to be mobilized were already in German hands, and yet young men by the hundred kept streaming out of occupied towns in trains, buses, trucks, cars, on bicycles, on skis, and even on foot, to join General Ruge's highly improvised fighting forces. 'These forces', the General later wrote, 'included makeshift companies and battalions, badly equipped, made up of both veterans and raw recruits, young and old, a motley crowd of infantrymen, dragoons, artillerymen, pilots and sailors, commanded by officers belonging to various units and even various service branches, either retired or on active service, cadets or junior officers fresh from military schools. [. . .] These troops could hardly manoeuvre, they were almost useless for offensive operations, and had never been exposed to the fire of artillery, planes or tanks.' And Ruge concluded with the following admirable understatement: 'I trust that all our readers, even the civilians, will understand that such units have their limitations.'[26]

There were nevertheless some grounds for cautious optimism: the rough and wooded terrain on both sides of Lake Mjøsa would make it somewhat easier to delay the Germans' northward progression; furthermore, the new Commander-in-Chief, General Ruge, was a peerless organizer and an officer of whom it was said that 'he had a unique ability to inspire confidence'.[27] Finally, as the General himself later pointed out, the mobilization having been carried out in the greatest confusion, nothing was easier than to avoid it. Thus the roughly 40,000 men who had joined his army were all genuine volunteers, with a firm resolve to fight.[28] Among them, in fact, was a certain Major Hvoslef, whom Quisling had appointed Defence Minister five days earlier – without bothering to consult him beforehand.[29]

For Ruge, however, the only hope of Norwegian resistance lay in the speedy arrival of an Allied expeditionary corps. Yet, ever since his government had received the encouraging but vague telegram from the Foreign Office on the afternoon of 9 April, Norwegian authorities had been kept entirely in the dark as to future British intentions. On 12 April, however, Ruge was informed that Captain Francis Foley, First Secretary of the British Legation in Oslo – and an officer in MI6 – had reached Aandalsnes with part of the Legation staff, and managed to contact London thanks to a secret code. The

Captain was accordingly called to Øyer, where he arrived on the morning of 13 April. At Norwegian headquarters, Ruge himself greeted him with the following words: 'Mr Foley, I have asked you to come because I was told that you were in contact with England. I am entirely cut off from the outside world. [. . .] I must tell you quite frankly that if Great Britain does not come to our assistance immediately with all the forces and equipment she can muster, we shall be incapable of carrying out the fight. [. . .] At present, the country is mobilizing, but once the men are assembled they have neither uniforms to wear nor weapons to fight with. Without any help from Great Britain either today or tomorrow, we shall have to surrender before having really begun to fight for the defence of our motherland.'[30]

Captain Foley promised to help, and thanks to his secret code, several telegrams were sent to London that morning. The numerous relays through Lillehammer, the oft-bombed transmitter at Vigra, and the Scottish station of Wick, added to the fairly primitive character of the code being used,* made communication extremely difficult, yet the messages duly got through, and the first real Anglo-Norwegian contacts were thus established in the early afternoon of 13 April. The first telegram to be received in London was an appeal by General Ruge to the Prime Minister: 'We began this war in the belief that the British government would act at once. We were surprised before we had time to mobilize and lost all our aircraft, supplies and stores. I am now rallying a [?few] infantry battalions and two or three batteries, who have had to fight during mobilization. We are prepared to receive troops at once and to act immediately from our side. My King, Crown Prince and government are being hunted by German bombers and were bombed last night. The people are all for fighting but they cannot fight without assistance. Details of assistance required follow at once.'[31] Owing to a cipher error, the details of the assistance required did not arrive that day.[32] Several hours later, however, the following telegram arrived, probably dictated by Captain Foley himself: 'The Commander-in-Chief wants the British to send a division to take Trondheim. He will co-operate with one infantry battalion, two motorized companies

---

* The cipher key was based on a book known only to the decoder and the encoder. The system was fairly secure, but encoding took a long time, and any mistake could make the whole message unintelligible.

from the north and two to four infantry battalions and two or three field batteries which he hopes to concentrate from the south.'[33]

Captain Foley quickly developed a genuine admiration for General Ruge, which found expression on several occasions in his telegrams to London. The Captain was joined on the morning of 15 April by Lieutenant-Colonel King-Salter, Military Attaché in Helsinki, who was henceforth to send all available information on the defences of Trondheim[34] – and who also became almost immediately an ardent advocate of Ruge's cause in his dealings with London. Another highly interesting testimony in this respect is that of an American, Captain Robert M. Losey, Assistant Air Attaché in Stockholm, who visited Ruge that same 15 April. In his own report, he described the General as an extremely shrewd and energetic officer, but also as one who was growing increasingly critical of the Allies' lack of preparedness, and of the incomprehensible delays in their assistance.[35]

General Ruge was indeed becoming highly impatient. The replies from London to his telegrams of 13 April had been extremely vague, and betrayed complete ignorance of the strategic realities in Norway. Thus, the War Office had asked him to 'prevent the Germans from capturing Bardufoss airfield near Narvik',[36] without realizing that he was completely cut off from Norwegian forces operating in northern Norway, and had no control over developments in the Narvik sector. Furthermore, apart from a few vague – and highly exaggerated* – promises, the British were careful not to give their newfound ally the slightest indication as to their general strategy. Anyone having read the previous chapter might object that this was perhaps because they did not have one . . . but this General Ruge could not possibly know, and in the afternoon of 14 April, he sent the following telegram to Mr Chamberlain: '(1) British action in some form is necessary both to make further resistance possible and to make the Norwegian people and army understand that England really means business. (2) The critical point is [?eastern] part of Norway north of Oslo, where Norwegian army is trying to rally, pressed by German forces. We cannot hold on many days without help, which must be given by bombing Fornebo. (3) Trondheim must be taken at a time when I am able to help you, and I shall not be able to do so unless you attack at once.'[37]

* Thus, in a telegram received on 14 April, Neville Chamberlain promised to send five divisions at once . . .

It was the first time General Ruge had stressed the crucial importance of the capture of Trondheim for Norwegian resistance further south. Indeed, should the Germans manage to force their way up the Gudbrandsdal, Norwegian or Allied troops attacking Trondheim by land would be directly threatened from the rear, and all would be lost. On 15 April, Ruge therefore issued the following directive to his officers:

> Our task in south-eastern Norway will be to play for time. Operations to be conducted in the immediate future will therefore aim at:
> - Holding up the enemy by blocking the access routes with defences in depth, which can be manned with reduced forces.
> - Holding such positions until the enemy manages to bring up vastly superior forces, and meanwhile prepare massive demolitions in the rear.
> - Retreating swiftly from one position to another, preferably at night, making use of all available means of transportation, and simultaneously carrying out demolitions on a massive scale.[38]

Such was the strategy to be implemented during the next fortnight. The initial results were quite satisfactory; until 17 April, Norwegian troops succeeded in containing the Germans south of a line running roughly from Røa to Tangen and Sørma. Between 14 and 17 April, admittedly, the Luftwaffe had been considerably hampered in its operations by snow and heavy fog; but when the weather lifted, the four German motorized columns resumed their northward progression. East of Lake Mjøsa, Elverum and Hamar fell on 18 April, while further west, Gjøvik and Raufoss, with its large ammunition plant, were in imminent danger of being overrun by two tank columns surging forward along the Randsfjord. To block the offensive, which threatened his whole defensive apparatus, Ruge summoned his last reserves: some 5,000 men of the Bergen division. Norwegian defences were thus increasingly thinning out, in the face of an enemy that was constantly being reinforced, and had even dropped 200 paratroopers far behind the front on Dombås, halfway between Lillehammer and Aandalsnes.*

* These men succeeded for a time in cutting the Norwegian lines of communication, but being themselves badly mauled, surrounded and shelled, they finally surrendered to the Norwegians on 20 April.

German diplomat Bräuer in front of the Elverum Communal School: 'Any resistance will be mercilessly crushed.'

His interlocutor, King Haakon VII of Norway: 'Resistance will continue as long as possible.'

King Haakon and Prince Olav rushing for cover during the German air attack on Nybergsund, April 11, 1940.

Norwegian troops manning a roadblock, April 1940: 'Makeshift companies and battalions, badly equipped, made up of both veterans and raw recruits, young and old, a motley crowd of infantrymen, dragoons, artillerymen, pilots and sailors, commanded by officers belonging to various units and even various service branches.'

But in the midst of this increasingly desperate situation, Ruge was informed that the 148th British Brigade under Brigadier Morgan had just landed at Aandalsnes. True, its orders were only to occupy Dombås, then head northward to take part in the capture of Trondheim; but for Ruge, a consolidation of the front south of Lille-hammer was far more important. Captain Foley and Lieutenant-Colonel King-Salter entirely agreed with him, and the very next day, the latter set off for Dombås to make contact with the commander of the 148th Brigade. And so it was that on 19 April, the man who presented himself to Brigadier Morgan was less the British Military Attaché than the personal emissary of the Norwegian Commander-in-Chief.

In theory, of course, Brigadier Morgan was bound by the orders of the War Office. But for the last two weeks, these orders had undergone so many alterations as to become practically worthless: on 6 April, within the framework of a (hastily) resurrected 'Stratford' plan, the 148th Brigade, aboard two cruisers, was to carry out an unopposed landing at Stavanger;[39] a counter-order arrived the next day, and the brigade was put ashore in the greatest confusion, with much loss and destruction of equipment; on 13 April, a new order arrived: the brigade was to land at Namsos; but that order, too, was rescinded three days later: the 146th Brigade having just been diverted from Narvik to Namsos, the 148th Brigade was now to land at Aandalsnes rather than at Namsos.[40] That order reached Rosyth on the evening of 16 April, as the whole brigade had already embarked in the Namsos-bound transport *Orion*. That night, in the pitch darkness of the blackout, the men were accordingly taken off *Orion* and reloaded in five warships, not without additional damage to the already battered equipment. Colonel Dudley Clarke, a member of the expedition, later described the scene: 'The hatches were off now and the scene below decks had become a sort of storeman's inferno, with shadowy figures burrowing in the semi-darkness of shaded lamps and torches. In the original haste to get off to a quick start, goods of every kind had been stowed in the holds in the order in which they arrived, with each following consignment piled in on top. Now reserves of food and ammunition were mixed with unit equipment and skis for the Norwegians; bicycles and sappers' tools lay with medical provisions, while such things as the long-range wireless equipment as often as not was split between two holds.

There was never a chance of sorting this out in the dark and getting it into the right ships in time, so the plan was being adopted of skimming the top layers from every hold and loading them in turn into each warship as she came alongside.'[41]

Only mid-way across the North Sea did the full scope of the disaster begin to sink in: for lack of space in the ships, half a battalion had remained behind, together with the greater part of the communications gear, the range-finders and searchlights for the anti-aircraft guns, all the mortar shells and most of the vehicles; the brigade was thus to land at Aandalsnes with one truck and three motorcycles![42] Besides, the officers soon found out that they had full sets of maps for Namsos, but absolutely nothing on Aandalsnes.[43] In fact, only two of these officers apart from Brigadier Morgan had ever seen action,[44] and most of their men had received rather cursory training: thirty hours of evening courses . . .[45]

For all that, the orders issued a few hours before its departure to the 148th Territorial Brigade – now renamed 'Sickle' Force – were nothing if not ambitious: it was to land in the Aandalsnes area, secure Dombås (60 miles inland), then 'demonstrate northwards and take offensive action against the Germans in the Trondheim area'.[46] While at sea, however, Brigadier Morgan received two additional instructions from General Ironside, which further complicated matters: 'When you have secured Dombås, you are to prevent the Germans from using the railway to reinforce Trondheim'; and: 'You should make touch with Norwegian GHQ, believed to be in area Lillehammer, and avoid isolating Norwegian forces operating towards Oslo.'[47]

These orders were as obscure as they were contradictory: how could Brigadier Morgan, once in Dombås, 'avoid isolating Norwegian forces operating towards Oslo', and at the same time 'demonstrate' towards Trondheim, 250 miles further north – i.e., in exactly the opposite direction? What, in any case, could he hope to do in Trondheim with 1,000 ill-armed, under-equipped and untrained men with no means of transportation, further considering that part of that force was also to stay behind in order to 'secure Dombås' and 'prevent the Germans from using the railway'? Granted, the War Office had promised reinforcements, but no one knew when they were to arrive, and in the meantime 'Sickle' Force, with its port of landing and lines of communication, would remain

114

entirely at the mercy of the Luftwaffe. Finally, apart from the rather mysterious last instruction, it was not said to what extent the Brigade ought to co-operate with the Norwegians, whom many British officers, having read too many newspapers, already viewed with considerable suspicion.

It was therefore an extremely perplexed Brigade Commander who greeted Lieutenant-Colonel King-Salter at Dombås on 19 April. But the Military Attaché was categorical: marching towards Trondheim with the forces at Brigadier Morgan's disposal would be suicide pure and simple; besides, his brigade would soon be attacked in the rear by the German forces sweeping northward from Oslo. Far better to heed General Ruge's advice, and reinforce the Norwegian troops trying to contain the Germans south of Lillehammer.[48] In the end, Morgan agreed to come down to Øyer and meet General Ruge; this was to be the very first meeting between the commanders of two newly allied forces, in great danger of fighting two separate campaigns in the same country against the same enemy.

'After midnight, on the morning of the 20th,' Colonel Clarke recalled, 'we found ourselves face to face with General Ruge, and any doubts we may have had before of Norway's determination to fight on disappeared for good, leaving behind some shame that we should ever have voiced them at all.' General Ruge appeared to the British officers as 'an erect, spare figure, with keen, blue eyes. A kindly, friendly man with something of the appearance of a Master of foxhounds'. The conversation was brief and to the point; Ruge 'made it clear that he was staking everything on help from Britain'. He asked Brigadier Morgan about his instructions, and 'added dryly that for some reason he had never been informed of the strength of the British troops nor of their intended plan of campaign'.

Brigadier Morgan having informed the Norwegian Commander-in-Chief of his plan of attack against Trondheim, Ruge tactfully but firmly stressed that he 'expected all troops in the country, of whatever nationality, to conform to his own strategy'. That strategy was to 'concentrate every available man on the decisive front below Lillehammer [. . .] until British reinforcements could redress the inferiority in numbers'. After that, he could counter-attack towards Oslo. As for Trondheim, it 'could wait [. . .] the major British assault [by sea]'.

Brigadier Morgan finally replied that as 'he had been sent to help Norway', he would give General Ruge 'maximum assistance wherever he needed it the most'. Colonel Clarke recalled that Ruge responded 'with a warmth of feeling that was deeply moving'. After that, the Colonel concluded, 'we knew that we had made a firm friend'.[49]

The die was cast; Brigadier Morgan, bypassing War Office orders, was to send his men south towards Lillehammer. At 2.50 a.m. on 20 April, General Ruge came to meet the British troops at the Lillehammer railway station. One of his officers, Lieutenant-Colonel Roscher-Nielsen, recalled that 'his disappointment upon seeing the British troops that marched past was easy to read on his face. [. . .] These were not regular troops [. . .] and we were alarmed to see that they were only armed with rifles and light machine-guns. [. . .] No anti-aircraft guns, no heavy anti-tank weapons, no artillery, no vehicles . . .'[50]

It was indeed a highly vulnerable force that had come to join the Norwegian troops south of Lillehammer. Positioned at the end of a deep valley, waist-deep in snow, without a single map of the area, no transport, no transmitters, rudimentary training, incomplete equipment, minimal armament and a 150-mile supply-line to Aandalsnes, the men of the Forester and Leicester Regiments awaited the enemy onslaught. Worse still, they were not even awaiting it together: to raise the morale of his own troops, General Ruge had dispersed the British soldiers throughout the Norwegian defensive positions on both sides of Lake Mjøsa. There was thus a half-battalion of Foresters at Biri under Norwegian Colonel Dahl, a half-battalion of Leicesters with the 2nd Norwegian Dragoons at Åsmarka, and another half-battalion of Foresters at Lunderhøgda, with the Torkildsen Battalion.[51]

For all these men, the next three days were to bring unmitigated disaster. On 21 April, three German battalions, supported by heavy mortars, tanks and dive-bombers, struck east of Lake Mjøsa, and almost immediately, the two British half-battalions at Åsmarka and Lunderhøgda suffered very heavy losses. The next day, after a difficult retreat through the snow, on foot and in open trucks, they regrouped north of Lillehammer, at the Balbergkamp. But as the German offensive rolled forward, they narrowly escaped encirclement by Bavarian ski companies that had moved behind their

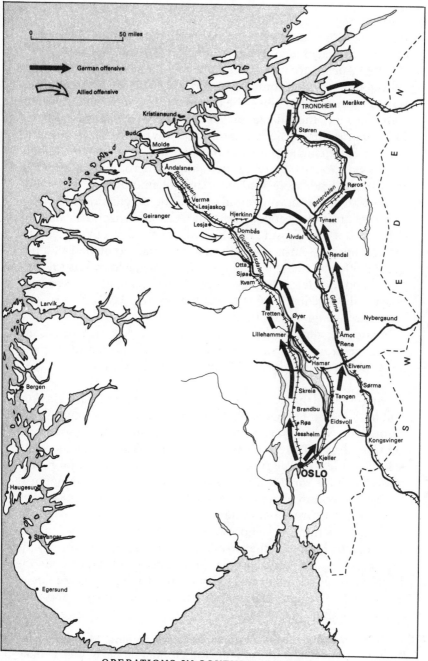

OPERATIONS IN SOUTHERN NORWAY
APRIL 1940

positions. More than a hundred men were captured, and a large part of the light machine-guns and anti-tank weapons were lost.

On 23 April, survivors from these two battalions, joined by the Foresters retreating from the western side of Lake Mjøsa and supported by three companies of Norwegian Dragoons, made another stand around the village of Tretten, some 19 miles north of Lillehammer. The position was undoubtedly of great strategic value, since it commanded access to the Gudbrandsdal, where General Ruge's worn-out troops were attempting to regroup. But the men of the 148th Brigade were dead tired, short of ammunition, and utterly demoralized after having found out that their light anti-tank weapons were quite ineffective against the German Panzer. That day, the defenders of Tretten were annihilated, captured or put to flight. By the evening of 23 April, the badly mauled remnants of the 148th Brigade, 9 officers and 300 men, had been evacuated by bus towards Kvam and the Heidal.[52] A few dozen others managed to reach the coast or the Swedish border during the next few days, after exhausting treks through the mountains.

In London, meanwhile, no news of all this had been received, and Brigadier Morgan's 'Sickle Force' was still expected to 'demonstrate' towards Trondheim, 170 miles further north.

Having escaped the German bombing at Nybergsund, King Haakon and his government had embarked on a long and perilous journey through the snow-bound valleys and mountain passes of south and central Norway. To keep ahead of the Germans, they remained constantly on the move, disguising their identity and avoiding large population centres. On 12 April, however, they reached Drevsjø, near the Swedish border, and Foreign Minister Koht called his Swedish counterpart Christian Günther to request assurances that if the King and his ministers chose to spend one night in Sweden safe from enemy bombing, they would be free to return to Norway the next morning. The reply given an hour later by Mr Günther in the name of his government was to bring about a drastic worsening of Swedish–Norwegian relations for the next four years – and even some time after that.*

* Günther had replied that 'he could promise nothing'. More generally, the Swedes, evidently fearful of complications with Germany, were to show during the whole campaign a distinct lack of understanding towards their Norwegian neighbours.

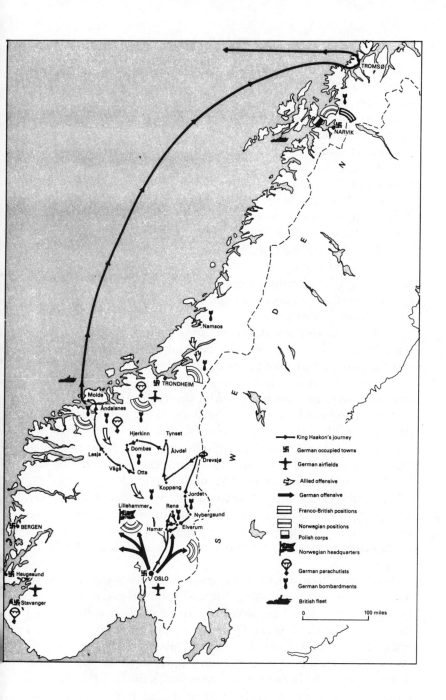

TROMSØ

NARVIK

N

E

D

Namsos

TRONDHEIM

Molde

Åndalsnes

Hjerkinn    Tynset

Lesja    Dombås    Ålvdal

Vågå    Otta    Drevsjø

Koppang

Jordet

Lillehammer    Rena

Nybergsund

Hamar    Elverum

BERGEN

Haugesund

Stavanger

OSLO

W

E

S

→ King Haakon's journey

卐  German occupied towns

✚  German airfields

⇨  Allied offensive

➡  German offensive

▭  Franco-British positions

▭  Norwegian positions

▭  Polish corps

⚑  Norwegian headquarters

☔  German parachutists

⚜  German bombardments

⛴  British fleet

0                100 miles

In the end, the convoy did stop half an hour in Sweden to escape attack by a flight of German bombers. During a short stop at a border village, the travellers met several Swedish and foreign journalists, who noticed that although the King looked tired, he had lost neither his resolve nor his sense of humour. There are indeed exceptional circumstances when a strong will can repulse the combined assaults of weariness, old age and adversity . . . On 13 April, the five cars, painted white for camouflage from the air, passed through Koppang, Rendal, Tynset and Hjerkinn; edging cautiously along narrow and slippery mountain roads overhanging bottomless abysses, they reached Otta on the 14th, then Dovre in the Gudbrandsdal. On the 15th, they returned to Otta, after having narrowly escaped capture by the German paratroopers dropped on Dombås. On the 17th, they stopped at Vågå, which opened the way to the Romsdal, and six days later, at last, they safely reached the coastal town of Molde.

The Østerdal, Gudbrandsdal and Romsdal were by then one large battlefield, so that the King, his aides and his ministers were constantly moving, resting and conferring under a deluge of bombs. All sources are at one in reporting that both King Haakon and Prince Olav seemed to treat such perils with sovereign contempt;[53] in this, they were followed by Foreign Minister Koht, who would stroll peaceably in the midst of the worse bombardments – though one witness at least was moved to write that he 'had always suspected that at the root of that courage lay a firm conviction that he was invulnerable by virtue of International Public Law'.[54] Not all the other ministers displayed similar mettle, yet it would have taken uncommon courage to admit one's fear in the company of men such as these . . . Councils therefore proceeded as usual, in the most unexpected places, with bombs crashing and fires raging all around.

Once in the Romsdal, the government had been joined by several foreign diplomats, including Sir Cecil Dormer and Count de Dampierre. Contact had also been re-established with General Ruge's headquarters. Naturally, the government members carefully avoided any interference in strategic planning, being perfectly aware of the abilities of the new Commander-in-Chief – and of their own limitations in the field of military science. Besides, there was no lack of work in other fields: administration had to be entirely reorganized in non-occupied areas, the government was to be enlarged, the latest developments in Oslo required close scrutiny, production and supply were to be controlled, taxes collected, a moratorium enacted on debt payments, not to mention countless decrees to be drafted on criminal procedure in wartime, civil defence, military tribunals, expropriation, war damages, conscription, etc.[55] In addition, all the Bank of Norway's gold reserves that had been spirited out of Oslo now had to be brought to safety; for the time being, they were stacked in a railway tunnel above Aandalsnes. Finally, the government had requisitioned the whole Norwegian merchant fleet, which was placed at the disposal of the Allied war effort on 18 April. Minister Trygve Lie was later to describe in colourful terms his visit to Aandalsnes that day, when he entered British headquarters and 'offered' Captain Vian 1,000 ships and 35 tons of gold . . .

After 19 April, the King and his ministers followed with understandable interest the southward progression of Brigadier Morgan's 148th Brigade. Moreover, Sir Cecil Dormer had just informed them of the imminence of the capture of Narvik and of the naval attack against Trondheim. Yet the Norwegian leaders, for all their incompetence in military matters, could not fail to notice that a great deal of confusion seemed to prevail among Allied strategic planners.

# CHAPTER SEVEN

# Confusion

It will be recalled that since mid-April, the planners in London had devised six different operational plans: 'Primrose', the 'diversionary' landing at Aalesund, that became rather more than a diversion when on 16 April it was somewhat haphazardly complemented by 'Sickle', a landing at Aandalsnes by Brigadier Morgan and his 148th Brigade, who were to secure Dombås and (all going well) proceed to Trondheim; there was also 'Henry', the reconnaissance landing at Namsos, to be complemented two days later by Operation 'Maurice', the northern prong of the land attack against Trondheim; and also 'Boots', the naval attack on Trondheim, considerably enlarged after 15 April under the new code name of 'Hammer'. Last but not least, there was of course 'Rupert', the operation to recapture Narvik . . .

## 'RUPERT'

By 14 April, the capture of Narvik appeared imminent – seen from London at least. But on the spot, nothing seemed to be going according to plan. Having entered the Vestfjord that morning on board the cruiser *Aurora*, Admiral of the Fleet Lord Cork sent the following signal to General Mackesy: 'In view of successful naval action at Narvik yesterday, 13th April, and as enemy appear thoroughly frightened, suggest we take every advantage of this before enemy has recovered. If you concur and subject to information we shall receive tonight, 14th April, from *Warspite*, I should be most willing to land military force in *Southampton* at Narvik at daylight to-morrow, Monday, from *Aurora* and destroyers. Supporting fire could be provided by cruisers and destroyers, and I could assist with a naval and marine landing party of 200 if you wish.'[1]

Following the tradition of Nelson and the wishes of the Admiralty,

Lord Cork was therefore preparing to attack boldly and without delay. Unfortunately, the above signal only reached General Mackesy in the afternoon of 14 April, as he was supervising the landing of his 350 Scots Guards at Sjøvegan, some 140 miles to the north-east. Admittedly, the Admiral and the General were separated not only by distance and faulty communications, but also by an obvious difference in character . . . and the complete incompatibility of their instructions. By training and by temperament, General Mackesy, who belonged to the Sappers, was not inclined towards lightning offensive actions – which at any rate were well outside his instructions; in accordance with the latter, Mackesy therefore set up headquarters at Harstad, on the island of Hinnøy. He then proceeded to land his advance units on the Continent, about 37 miles north of Narvik, in the vicinity of (suspected) Norwegian positions between Bardufoss and Fossbakken. Even after receipt of Lord Cork's signal, the General decided to continue his operation without any change. Lord Cork was therefore compelled to give up his plan for immediate attack, especially since he received shortly before midnight a message from the Admiralty instructing him to 'act together' with General Mackesy.[2]

The two commanders were only to meet on the following day, 15 April, when the cruiser *Aurora* entered the Andfjord, north of Harstad: 'I met General Mackesy for the first time when he boarded the *Aurora*,' Lord Cork later wrote, 'and was astonished to hear that not only was his force embarked as for a peaceful landing, and consequently was unready for immediate operations, but that the orders he had received [. . .] just prior to sailing ruled out any idea of attempting an opposed landing. Even the reserve ammunition had still to arrive. Thus the General and myself left the UK with diametrically opposite views as to what was required.'[3]

For all that, the two commanders had met, and they were now aware of the fact that they disagreed – a significant progress. At any rate, Lord Cork's advocacy of immediate action seemed a bit rash, in view of the extraordinary difficulties that were already to be encountered when carrying out a much simpler landing at Harstad during the next few days. After all, Harstad, a fishing town of 4,000 inhabitants, had nothing in common with Southampton: two small wharfs, no cranes, and no anchorage for large ships that had to lie at anchor at three different places around the Vaagsfjord, one of which was 15

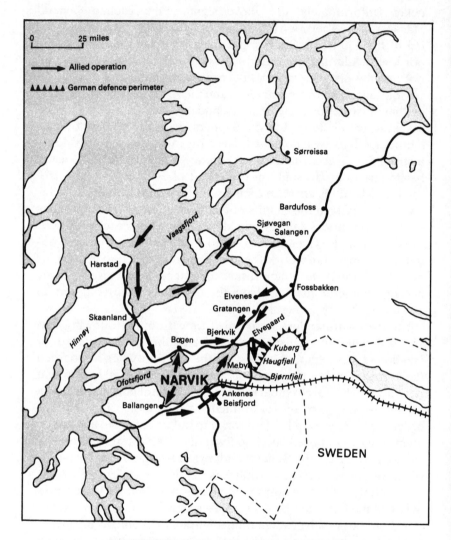

OPERATIONS IN NORTHERN NORWAY
UNTIL 27 MAY 1940

miles away from Harstad. The ships were therefore unloaded with the help of some 120 unreliable Norwegian fishing craft known as 'Puffers', usually in the midst of a violent snowstorm or under one of the furious German bombings that occurred daily after 16 April. Under such conditions, the average rate of discharge was two ships in five days.[4] Yet twenty ships arrived on the very first day with most of the 24th Brigade and its equipment, followed without warning during the next five days by several convoys bringing such additions as an entire railway operating battalion,[5] the complete personnel of the 203rd Field Battery – without a single cannon[6] – 1,000 administrators, office clerks and accountants, together with huge amounts of office furniture[7] and . . . the greater part of the equipment of the 146th Brigade, diverted to Namsos two days earlier. All this was discharged at random on the shore, naturally creating a huge congestion in the whole dock area; 'and permeating everything', added one military observer, 'was the smell of rotting cod'.[8]

None of this prevented General Mackesy from discovering that his brigade had practically no mortar shells, very few grenades, no spare ammunition, no artillery, no anti-aircraft guns, no skis, no snow rackets, no trucks, no tanks, no landing craft[9] . . . and no news from the two brigades that were to arrive as reinforcements. To top it all, it was soon learned that the Germans in Narvik – whose exact strength was still unknown – had considerably reinforced their defence installations.[10] After all that, General Mackesy's reluctance to order an immediate attack became somewhat more understandable.

On 16 April, after almost 24 hours of palaver, the two commanders finally agreed on the text of a common telegram to be sent to the Admiralty and the War Office. Perhaps because Lord Cork had just spent two days observing the deplorable conditions prevailing at Harstad, this common telegram very much reflected the views of General Mackesy: 'German defences are known to be strong and possibility of assault is ruled out. Until snow melts at the end of April, operations on any scale across country cannot take place. [. . .] On arrival of Chasseurs Alpins [. . .] intend to operate against Germans about Gratangen.'[11]

At the War Cabinet, where Narvik was expected to fall in a matter of days – if not hours – the telegram caused complete consternation. The most disappointed was no doubt Winston Churchill, who immediately drafted the following reply: 'Your proposals involve damaging deadlock at Narvik and the neutralization of one of our best brigades. We cannot send you the Chasseurs Alpins. The *Warspite* will be needed elsewhere, in two or three days. Full consideration should therefore be given by you to an assault upon Narvik covered by the *Warspite* and the destroyers, which might also operate at Römbaksfjord. The capture of the port and town would be an important success. We should like to receive from you the reasons why this is not possible, and your estimate of the degree of resistance to be expected on the water-front. Matter most urgent.'[12]

This energetic telegram, which obviously made light of local difficulties, effectively rekindled the argument between Lord Cork and General Mackesy; each commander thereupon sent a new set of conclusions to his superiors. Mackesy thus wrote to the War Office: 'All my plans which are already in execution were of course based upon arrival of these troops.* Without them I am inferior to the enemy, and have no troops capable of fighting under snow and mountainous conditions. Norwegian troops are almost entirely untrained and I have, I am afraid, not much confidence in them.'[13]†

Lord Cork, for one, preferred to consider matters from a purely naval standpoint; on 17 April, he therefore sent the following cable to the Admiralty: 'My view is that under the overwhelming gun power a force of one battleship, 2 cruisers and 8 destroyers could bring to bear, the troops could be landed with slight loss. [. . .] Enemy defences are stronger now than they were, but my belief is [that] such an attack would succeed.'[14] On the morning of 18 April, Lord Cork received an unambiguous reply from Churchill personally: 'Should you consider situation is being mishandled, it is your duty to report to me personally or to Admiralty upon it, and stating what you would do yourself.'[15] To which Lord Cork answered with the requisite blend of logic, diplomacy and irony: 'Situation cannot

---

* The Chasseurs Alpins, and no doubt another brigade in replacement of the 146th, re-directed towards Namsos.

† The latter comment clearly lacked indulgence, especially coming from a general whose troops were unable to move on snowy terrain; it was also quite unfair: the men of the 6th Norwegian Division were in fact remarkably well trained, as they were to demonstrate shortly thereafter.

be described mishandled, being in strict accordance with War Office orders.'[16]

That afternoon, at Harstad, the two commanders held a new conference to try to resolve their differences. The perils of an opposed landing were quite obvious, and General Mackesy did not mince words: 'It is not a justifiable operation of war for a numerically inferior force, scarcely able to move owing to the snow, to attack an enemy who enjoys all the advantages of the defensive. When the difficulties of landing from open boats on very limited beaches are added, the operation becomes sheer bloody murder.'[17]

With great reticence, the two commanders eventually agreed on a common plan, which they submitted to London that same evening: after close-range bombardment of Narvik by one battleship, two cruisers and eight destroyers, reconnaissance parties would be landed from destroyers. Should German opposition no longer be effective, two battalions would be landed in fishing boats. In case of further opposition, bombardment would resume, then a new reconnaissance party would be landed. D-Day was put at 22 April.[18]

During the next two days, General Mackesy went to conduct a reconnaissance of the landing beaches, but upon returning to Harstad he learned that at the instigation of Winston Churchill, the command of all forces in the Narvik area had been transferred to Lord Cork.[19] However, the Admiral himself had just conducted a personal reconnaissance of the Narvik beaches. To test the going on land, he even went ashore accompanied by a section of Royal Marines, with decidedly inauspicious results: the Marines were soon knee-deep in snow, but Lord Cork, being a small man, had to be extricated 'snowed up to the waist and very angry'; he also lost his monocle in the process . . .[20] The Earl eventually returned to his ship with considerably more respect for the difficulties of the terrain, as evidenced by the telegram he sent to the Admiralty that evening: 'I personally tested [the snow] and found it easy to sink to one's waist. To make any progress was exhausting.'[21]

All of which clearly demonstrates the value of personal experience.* Naturally, Lord Cork, who was now sole Commander-in-Chief, could not cancel the whole operation on that account; he did,

* Besides lending some substance to the old saying that sailors are at sea on land.

however, alter it the next day on one very important point: after the naval bombardment, a landing would only be carried out if the defenders of Narvik hoisted the white flag.[22] An assault therefore seemed to be ruled out.

Finally, the operation began on 24 April, just like the landing at Gallipoli a quarter of a century earlier. There the resemblance ended, however, for after a three-hour bombardment of the town's defences, in the midst of a raging snowstorm, it was utterly impossible to assess the destruction; visibility was practically reduced to zero, and, in the words of Lord Cork, 'nothing indicated any intention to surrender'.[23] The noble Earl failed to explain how one could have distinguished a white flag in the middle of a snowstorm, but at any rate the attack was called off. In spite of Winston Churchill's fulminations, it would now be necessary to return to a more gradual and cautious approach – and to co-operate with the Norwegian troops of the 6th Division operating north of Narvik. Whatever General Mackesy might have said, they were well trained, they knew the area perfectly, and besides, they could move through snowy terrain.

In London, the news of the aborted attack of 24 April was naturally greeted with much dismay. But the fact that the dispatch of reinforcements had been refused would seem to indicate that the planners' attention had shifted to another theatre. Indeed, already on 17 April, Churchill had written to Admiral Forbes, Commander-in-Chief of the Home Fleet: 'Whatever happens at Narvik, all now centres upon the assault and capture of Trondheim.'[24]

## 'MAURICE'

According to the plans approved on 14 April by the Military Co-ordination Committee, the direct naval attack against Trondheim (Operation 'Boots') was to be preceded by the landing at Namsos of a substantial force that would proceed to attack Trondheim from the north (Operation 'Maurice'). Such were indeed the instructions received that evening by General Carton de Wiart, an illustrious officer of the First World War who had just been appointed to command 'Maurice'.

The General had been promised a very substantial force: the

Namsos before the German air raid of April 20 . . .

. . . and after.

German armoured column forcing a roadblock north of Lillehammer.
'The whole history of warfare teaches that carefully prepared operations
usually succeed with relatively insignificant losses.' (Adolf Hitler)

146th Brigade was to arrive at Namsos on 15 April, the 148th two days later, two battalions of French Chasseurs Alpins on 18 April, and the 147th Brigade with artillery two or three days later.[25] Admittedly, the 146th Brigade, diverted from Namsos on 14 April, had lost much of its equipment; granted, the 148th Brigade was itself diverted from Namsos to Aandalsnes two days later; no doubt the 147th was never to arrive at Namsos either. But all this General Carton de Wiart could not yet know as he boarded a seaplane bound for Norway. On the other hand, he could not fail to notice that, although his mission was to attack Trondheim by land in conjunction with a great operation to be conducted simultaneously by sea ('Boots'), no one in London had been able to tell him when the latter operation would be set in motion.[26]

At Namsos, where the 300 Marines of Operation 'Henry' had established a beach-head on 14 April, the men of the 146th Brigade landed with some difficulty between 15 and 17 April, in the midst of constant German air raids. The rather hazardous conditions of landing caused further loss of material – some being destroyed, some shipped back to England by mistake – and de Wiart's already poorly trained soldiers now found themselves with supplies for two days instead of two weeks, a serious shortage of munitions, and a complete lack of anti-aircraft guns, field artillery, vehicles, skis and snow-shoes, not to mention the conspicuous absence of air cover. Besides, even the equipment available only seemed to raise additional problems, as de Wiart later explained: 'The British troops had been issued with fur coats, special boots and socks to compete with the cold, but if they wore all these things, they were scarcely able to move at all, and looked like paralysed bears.'[27] Bringing in new supplies would also prove exceedingly difficult, for the town of Namsos presented numerous drawbacks, both as a port and as an operational base: there was only one stone wharf, no cranes, anchorage was reduced in the extreme, and large ships could not even enter the harbour; the town, with mostly wooden houses, was highly vulnerable to bombing, and there was a shortage of drinking water, which was not compensated by an overabundance of snow in the streets.

Not easily discouraged, General Carton de Wiart decided to send his force southward without delay. His task was made much easier by the co-operation of Norwegian military units in the area; there were indeed north of Steinkjer two battalions belonging to the 5th Norwegian Division. The latter, which had been unable to mobilize properly, only existed on paper, the soldiers lacked both training and ammunition,[28] and the Division Commander, General Lauraritzon, had been described somewhat euphemistically as 'out of touch with reality'.[29] Finally, the whole force was completely cut off from General Ruge's headquarters at Øyer. Amidst all these tales of woe, however, one man had stepped forward to organize resistance – and co-operation with the Allies: he was Colonel Getz, the commanding officer of the 5th Brigade.

Even with the very limited means at his disposal, Colonel Getz was to give his new allies invaluable assistance, notably in the form of tactical support by his detachments of ski troops, and also by supplying the trucks that enabled the British troops to advance rapidly toward Steinkjer, and even up to Verdal, which was reached on 18 April. The very next day, General Carton de Wiart received a substantial reinforcement: three battalions of the 5th Half-Brigade of French Chasseurs Alpins, diverted from Narvik two days earlier, arrived at Namsos on the night of 19–20 April. Trained to fight in the snow, these men were to give the British force a much needed increase in both mobility and efficiency – at least in theory, for unfortunately the embarkation and disembarkation of these Chasseurs Alpins had been carried out in the very worst conditions: almost half the equipment had been lost, and the other half, including the brigade's skis, mules, light trucks, transmitters and anti-aircraft artillery, had not yet materialized.[30] When all that eventually arrived on board the liner *Ville d'Alger*, nothing could be unloaded except two crates of food and the skis – which the lack of one small strap rendered entirely useless.[31] Finally, the arrival of the Chasseurs Alpins triggered the next day a massive bombing, which almost entirely eradicated the town of Namsos, sent up in smoke the greater part of the remaining French supplies and ammunitions,[32] and effectively decimated the staff of the French commander, General Audet.

The advance towards Trondheim therefore proceeded perforce without the French. But by 18 April, the Commander of 146th Brigade, Brigadier Phillips (who had succeeded at long last in extracting himself from Narvik), received an urgent warning from Colonel Getz: Norwegian troops had just withdrawn north of Steinkjer,

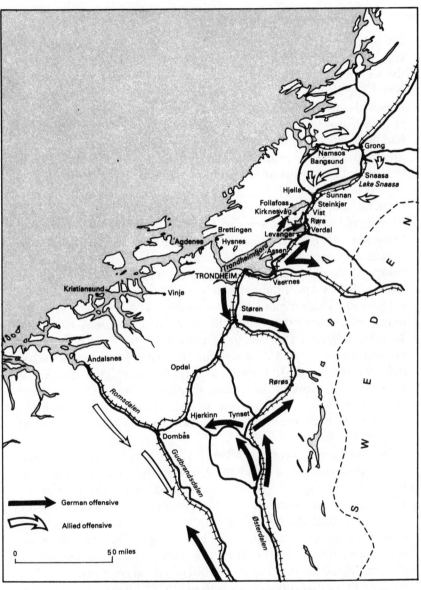

Grong
Namsos
Bangsund
Snaasa
Lake Snaasa
Hjella
Sunnan
Follafoss
Steinkjer
Kirknesvåg
Vist
Brettingen
Røra
Verdal
L'Agdenes
Hysnes
Levanger
Assen
Trondheimfjord
TRONDHEIM
Vaernes
Kristiansund
Vinje
Støren
Åndalsnes
Opdal
Rørøs
Romsdalen
Hjerkinn
Tynset
Dombås
Gudbrandsdalen
Østerdalen

S W E D E N

German offensive

Allied offensive

0          50 miles

**OPERATIONS IN CENTRAL NORWAY**
**APRIL 1940**

because the Steinkjer–Verdal road, bordering the Trondheimfjord, would become highly vulnerable to German naval attack as soon as the ice melted in the fjord – which was already beginning to happen.[33] The British chose to ignore that particular warning, because they had only limited confidence in the competence and reliability of their Norwegian allies, but also because General Carton de Wiart had been informed that same day of the imminence of 'Boots', the great naval attack against Trondheim;[34] his troops therefore had to be brought within striking distance of Trondheim with the least possible delay.

On the morning of 21 April, as two forward battalions of the British brigade were still dispersed between Steinkjer, Vist, Røra and Stiklestad, the fears expressed by Colonel Getz suddenly materialized: a destroyer and a troop transport landed German mountain troops at Verdal and Kirknesvåg, thus effectively outflanking the British. By 23 April, the extremely mobile German force, closely supported by naval gunfire, dive-bombers and light artillery, had managed to expel the British from all their positions along the Trondheimfjord.[35] This was to be a black day for de Wiart's forces around Steinkjer, just as it was for Brigadier Morgan's men 200 miles further south. In the end, assisted by Norwegian ski detachments and by those of the Chasseurs Alpins who had managed to requisition Norwegian skis, the British succeeded in extricating themselves and regrouping around Hjelle, safely north of Trondheimfjord.

The overland advance of Allied forces towards Trondheim had thus been brought to a standstill. Although the losses incurred had been relatively light (19 dead, 42 wounded, 96 missing), 'Maurice Force' was now definitely on the defensive, and would probably remain so until the arrival of reinforcements, air cover, and of course precise information on the launching of 'Boots', as de Wiart later reported: 'Still I waited for news of our naval attack, which was to be my signal to take Trondheim, but still it did not come. Hourly it became more and more obvious to me that with my lack of equipment I was quite incapable of advancing on Trondheim, and could see very little point in remaining in that part of Norway sitting out like rabbits in the snow. I wired to the War Office to tell them my conclusions, only to get back the reply that for political reasons they would be glad if I would maintain my positions. I agreed, but said it was about all I could do. They were so relieved that they actually wired me their thanks.'[36]

It was clear that complete confusion continued to prevail in London, as de Wiart was explicitly told soon thereafter: 'Now that my chances of taking Trondheim had gone, I sent Peter Fleming* to the War Office to find out their future plans. He came back after a couple of days and told me that plans and ideas about Norway were somewhat confused, [. . .] adding: "You can really do what you like, for they don't know what they want done." '[37]

## 'BOOTS'/'HAMMER'

'For myself,' wrote Churchill to Sir Charles Forbes on 17 April, 'I regard the operations from Namsos and Aandalsnes in the light of feints to confuse and distract the enemy in order that the blow may be delivered with full surprise and force at the centre.'[38] The centre was Trondheim, and the blow was of course the direct naval attack known as 'Boots', now renamed 'Hammer'; the Joint Planners, the Chiefs of Staff, the Military Co-ordination Committee and the War Cabinet had been lavishing considerable attention on that plan since 14 April.

Apart from the planners, who had estimated from the outset that such an operation would be both costly and unlikely to succeed,[39] everyone in London appeared to be in favour of a naval attack on Trondheim; thus, on 14 April, Churchill was writing to the Commander-in-Chief of the Home Fleet: 'Intention up to present has been to land at Namsos for the Trondheim area. For many reasons it would be advantageous to land the force inside Trondheimfjord. Do you consider that the shore batteries could be either destroyed or dominated to such an extent as to permit transports to enter? And, if so, how many ships and of what type would you propose to use? Request early reply, as any plan must depend on the above.'[40]

The reply sent by Sir Charles Forbes was hardly encouraging: 'Shore batteries could no doubt be either destroyed or dominated by battleship in daylight, [. . .] if she had high-explosive bombardment shells for main armament, but none of Home Fleet have. This, however, is only the minor part of the task. The main difficulties are,

* Captain Peter Fleming, the General's Chief of Staff.

(1) Surprise having been lost, to protect troopships from a heavy-scale air attack for over 30 miles in narrow waters, and (2) then to carry out an opposed landing of which ample warning has been given, under continuous air attack. [. . .] For foregoing reasons, I do not consider operation feasible, unless you are prepared to face very heavy losses in troops and transports.'[41]

As could be expected, neither the Admiralty nor Churchill were satisfied with these arguments, and they replied the very next morning that both Stavanger and Trondheim airfields could be bombed immediately before the attack. As for the high-explosive shells, they would be dispatched forthwith. The message, though unsigned, ended with the following characteristic Churchillism: 'Pray, therefore, consider this important project further.' Sir Charles Forbes finally capitulated, and cabled that his previous answer had been misinterpreted; actually, he was not really opposed to the operation, provided the assault troops be carried in warships.[42] Armed with this 'endorsement', and with the agreement of the Chiefs of Staff, Churchill then proceeded to lay the plan before the Military Co-ordination Committee.

At this stage, further complications arose; Churchill's rather unorthodox methods having given rise to some discontent among members of the Military Co-ordination Committee and their advisers, Chamberlain was asked to chair the meeting of 16 April.[43] This seemed to ease matters somewhat, and plan 'Hammer' was finally accepted. The War Cabinet ratified it the very next day, and 22 April was selected as 'provisional date for landing'.[44] The forces available for the attack were to be: the 15th Brigade, 2,500 French Chasseurs Alpins, 1,000 Canadians, and the 147th Territorial Battalion as reserve. The operation was to be covered by 100 aeroplanes, and supported 'by the full strength of the Fleet'.[45]

This time, it seemed that nothing could get in the way of Operation 'Hammer', which had even received the Prime Minister's blessing on the evening of 17 April.[46] Of course, the French were still insisting that priority be given to Narvik[47] and that yet another expedition be landed at Molde in order to 'stop the enemy that had landed at Oslo and was progressing northward',[48] but the British strongly suspected that both Paul Reynaud and General Gamelin were dabbling in exercises of theoretical strategy, using maps without contour lines. Besides, they noted that General Gamelin was quite content to place troops at their disposal and saddle them with complete responsibility for the conduct of operations, as had been decided at the Supreme War Council back in February. Admittedly, the object of the plan at that time had been to assist the Finns against the Soviet Union, whereas it was now intended to help the Norwegians against the Germans, but no one was really interested in raising such petty details.

Still on 17 April, the Secretary of State for War appointed a military commander for Operation 'Hammer': Major-General Hotblack, who was duly briefed that afternoon at a meeting of the Chiefs of Staff; but, that same evening, the General had a stroke and was picked up unconscious. The attack was then postponed to 24 April,[49] and a new commander appointed: Brigadier Berney-Ficklin, who was immediately briefed and left for Edinburgh. Alas! The very next day, the plane carrying the Brigadier and his staff to Scapa Flow crashed on the airfield at Kirkwall, and all occupants were seriously injured. The attack was again postponed – to 25 April this time – and yet another successor appointed; this time, the choice fell on General Paget.[50] Yet in the meantime it appeared that high civilian and military authorities were having second thoughts about the operation. 'Up to this point,' Churchill later explained, 'all the Staffs and their Chiefs seemed resolved upon the central thrust at Trondheim. [. . .] Although Narvik was my pet, I threw myself with increasing confidence into this daring adventure, and was willing that the Fleet should risk the petty batteries at the entrance to the fjord, the possible minefields, and most serious, the air. [. . .] Left to myself, I would have stuck to my first love, Narvik; but serving as I did a loyal chief and friendly Cabinet, I now looked forward to this exciting enterprise to which so many staid and cautious Ministers had given their strong adherence, and which seemed to find much favour with the Naval Staff and indeed among all our experts.'[51] This was still true on 17 April; it was somewhat less true on 18 April . . . and had entirely ceased to be true the day after that.

What was happening? Quite simply, the Chiefs of Staff were having second thoughts: all things considered, a direct naval attack on Trondheim was far too risky an undertaking. The First Sea Lord, Admiral Pound, had initiated the about-face on the morning of 18 April. The day before, the cruiser *Suffolk*, after having been bombed for seven hours by German dive-bombers in front of

Stavanger, had returned to Scapa Flow with her prow almost entirely blown off. Admiral Pound had naturally reflected on what might happen if his fleet were subjected to similar treatment in the middle of Trondheimfjord, and that same evening he shared his doubts with General Ironside. Reckoning that what applied to ships protected by anti-aircraft guns would apply even more to unprotected landing troops, the General quickly sided with Admiral Pound; together, they had little trouble persuading the Chief of the Air Staff, who was not wildly enthusiastic himself at the idea of having to cover an operation of such dimensions with only 100 aircraft, less than half of which were fighters.[52]

As a result of all that, the Chiefs of Staff met again on the morning of 19 April, and drew up a new report categorically opposing Operation 'Hammer':[53] Owing to the urgency of the situation, there had been no time for detailed and meticulous preparation, and the plan would involve concentrating almost the whole of the Home Fleet in an area where it could be subjected to heavy attack from the air. Besides, there were reliable reports that the Germans were improving the defences at Trondheim, and reports of Allied intentions to make a direct landing at Trondheim had appeared in the press.* The Chiefs of Staff therefore opposed the direct frontal assault, and recommended instead that advantage be taken of the 'unexpected success in landing forces at Namsos and Aandalsnes' to develop a pincer movement on Trondheim from north and south.[54] Hardly a new strategy, but perhaps a less risky one . . .

To Winston Churchill, so recently converted to Operation 'Hammer', all this came as a most unpleasant surprise, as he later wrote in his memoirs: 'No more decisive stopper on a positive amphibious plan can be imagined. [. . .] When I became aware of this right-about-turn, I was indignant, and questioned searchingly the officers concerned. It was soon plain to me that all professional opinion was now adverse to the operation which only a few days before it had spontaneously espoused.' What, then, was to be done? Churchill had reluctantly agreed to de-emphasize 'Rupert' in favour of 'Hammer', provided action was taken without delay. Yet it now appeared

---

* That was quite true, but all prospective operations in Norway having been regularly announced and analysed in the press, it followed that no operation at all could be undertaken . . .

that objections to a direct assault against Trondheim were even more vehement than those holding up offensive action at Narvik. No doubt there was still at least one forceful proponent of the naval attack, in the person of Admiral of the Fleet Sir Roger Keyes, the hero of Zeebrugge, who was even offering to take personal command of the assault.[55] To Churchill, this must have seemed tempting, but the Dardanelles had taught him the political risks of forcing such issues in Cabinet; besides, there were grounds to fear that the adoption of Keyes's plan would have triggered a rash of resignations in the upper echelons of the Admiralty.[56] Churchill therefore discarded that alternative,[57] and with the same surprising swiftness he had displayed five days earlier in the opposite direction, he turned his guns round once again: 'I accordingly submitted to the abandonment of "Hammer". I reported the facts to the Prime Minister on the afternoon of the 18th, and though bitterly disappointed he, like me, had no choice but to accept the new position.'[58] There was a slight mistake here: all available documents, as well as simple considerations of chronology, point to 19 April as the date of that decision.

That same evening, at any rate, the Military Co-ordination Committee took note of this about-face and, on the morning of 20 April, Churchill told his Cabinet colleagues that 'the new plan was, broadly, to send the whole of the 1st Light Division of Chasseurs Alpins to General Carton de Wiart for his attack on the Trondheim area from the north, and to send the regular brigade from France to reinforce Brigadier Morgan, who had landed at Aandalsnes.'[59]

Thus presented, the change in strategy appeared both natural and justified; yet it was only attractive in theory, as the Secretary of State for War was quick to point out: 'The new plan', he stressed, 'was indeed little less hazardous than that of the direct assault on Trondheim.' Indeed, he explained, 'it was not altogether correct to say that the new plan was for a "pincer" movement against Trondheim, since [. . .] the first care of the southern force must be to secure themselves against a German attack from the south, for which purpose a considerable proportion of the force would have to be used.' General Ironside was quick to confirm that 'the troops now at Dombås had no guns or transport, and were therefore not in any condition to fight a serious action'.[60]

There was of course much force in these arguments, particularly in view of the situation in Norway at that time. But the members of the War Cabinet were clearly unwilling to risk a major naval disaster, which in their view would reinforce the likelihood of an Italian declaration of war. In addition, the First Lord of the Admiralty had just reminded his colleagues of the inadvisability of deviating from the main objective, which had always been . . . 'the control of the Gällivare ore fields'![61] The War Cabinet eventually approved the new strategy and, by the evening of 20 April, Operation 'Hammer' was officially declared defunct.

During the next three days, no decisions of any consequence were taken by the War Cabinet. The minutes of their debates showed that the ministers and Chiefs of Staff were informed of the difficult situations of both General Carton de Wiart north of Trondheim and Brigadier Morgan in the south; but they also indicated that the information available was both vague and fragmentary, and that, voluntarily or not, the ministers avoided drawing any conclusions from it. Thus, between 21 and 23 April, vague, then increasingly accurate information was received in London on the German bombing of Namsos and its disastrous results;[62] a message was even received from General Carton de Wiart, mentioning the possible evacuation of his troops owing to their vulnerability to air attack.[63] Yet the War Cabinet continued to consider Namsos as the main supply base for an attack on Trondheim, in accordance with the 'new' plan adopted on 20 April. Likewise, General Dill, the new Vice-Chief of the Imperial General Staff, was still stating at the War Cabinet meeting of 23 April that 'it was curious that Carton de Wiart made no reference to the 3,000 French troops which had been landed at Namsos, and which were equipped for movement over the snow.'[64] In other words, General Dill did not appear to understand that no reference was made to the French troops precisely because they were *not* equipped for movement over the snow.

Information about the southern half of the pincer was clearly not getting through either; thus, nothing in the War Cabinet debates of 21, 22 or 23 April betrayed the slightest awareness that Brigadier Morgan's troops were being severely mauled south of Lillehammer. There was barely a passing reference to their presence at Dombås, then Øyer,[65] and only Lord Hankey – with some backing from Oliver Stanley – was heard to remark that, Brigadier Morgan's force having two entirely different missions, 'there were clearly not enough troops to take the offensive in both directions.'[66] Lord Hankey evidently did not realize that there were not even enough troops to ensure the *defensive* in any *one* direction.

What the British authorities could not understand – or refused to admit – was that the two arms of the pincer, 'Sickle' and 'Maurice', instead of closing in on Trondheim, were actually opening widely, and even falling apart, under the merciless blows of German artillery and aviation; in other words, there was very little left of the pincer . . . and nothing at all of the hammer, which had been discarded three days earlier. But precisely here lay perhaps the most extraordinary and disquieting element of all: neither the members of the War Cabinet nor the Chiefs of Staff had seen fit to apprise the commanders on the spot of this crucial change of plans!

That the Norwegians themselves had not been informed of the cancellation of 'Hammer' on 20 April was not really surprising; since the beginning of the campaign, after all, the War Office, the Admiralty and the Prime Minister himself had studiously avoided giving their new allies any indications as to their strategic plans. This was not only because they did not know themselves what these plans were, but also because they trusted neither the discretion nor the competence of the Norwegian military authorities. Indeed, the British officers present at General Ruge's headquarters often received from London various orders, the contents of which were not to be revealed to the Norwegian Commander-in-Chief, owing to 'suspected leaks within Norwegian headquarters'.[67] As London knew nothing of General Ruge, his staff officers, or even their exact whereabouts, it was difficult to understand what lay behind such suspicions . . . The British officers present at Norwegian headquarters probably thought so too, since they promptly showed all such orders to General Ruge – together with the instructions not to show them.[68] At any rate, Neville Chamberlain, for one, was still telling the War Cabinet on 18 April that he 'was sceptical about our placing any reliance on the Norwegians, who were offering no serious resistance'[69] – hardly a perceptive comment, considering that the Norwegians had by then been holding the line for nine days, whereas British troops had not yet fired a single rifle shot in Norway.

It was therefore highly regrettable, but by no means astonishing, that the Norwegian Commander-in-Chief was deliberately kept in ignorance of the decision to abandon the naval attack on Trondheim: in the same country, against the same enemy, British and Norwegian planners were still conducting an entirely separate war. But things become far more alarming when it emerges that neither the commander of 'Sickle' Force, nor that of 'Maurice', had been informed of the cancellation of Operation 'Hammer' on 20 April. As fantastic as it may seem, although the Namsos and Aandalsnes forces had since then advanced resolutely towards the enemy – and even taken up dangerously exposed positions in the front lines – it was not considered opportune to inform their commanders that they had been deprived of the support of a naval assault on Trondheim; yet ever since 14 April, that assault had been the very *raison d'être* of the Namsos and Aandalsnes expeditions. This being so, how could such crucial information possibly be withheld?

Neither historians nor witnesses, nor even Winston Churchill himself, have ever come up with a rational explanation of this intriguing fact.[70] A retired British general did supply the author with an explanation that was as concise as it was probable: 'Sheer damn negligence!'; yet it is tempting to follow a second lead – which does not by any means exclude the first: as is known, the British War Cabinet and Chiefs of Staff had since 20 April pinned all their hopes on the success of 'Sickle' and 'Maurice'. It will also be recalled that on 22 April, the War Office had received a cable from General Carton de Wiart mentioning the likelihood of an evacuation from Namsos, and that in their reply they had expressly entreated the General to maintain his positions; now, had Carton de Wiart learned of the cancellation of 'Hammer', he would most certainly have considered his own expedition from Namsos as entirely useless, and ordered an immediate evacuation. But why, then, did London continue to attach so much importance to the presence of 'Maurice' Force around Namsos? It will be remembered that when asking de Wiart to maintain his positions in Norway, the War Office had added: 'for political reasons'.[71] These reasons will soon become apparent; for the time being, de Wiart had called for reinforcements[72] without knowing exactly how they would be able to land, how they could be protected from the Luftwaffe once on shore . . . or even what purpose they would serve.

For London, it was also imperative to send reinforcements to Brigadier Morgan, who was admittedly not 'demonstrating' towards Trondheim as planned, but was still doing his best to delay the German troops from Oslo in their attempt to link up with those in Trondheim – an undertaking which, if successful, would deliver all south and central Norway to the Germans. So it was that General Paget, given command of Operation 'Hammer' on 19 April, and relieved of his command when the operation was cancelled on 20 April, was appointed Commander-in-Chief of Operation 'Sickle' on 21 April. At the head of the 15th Brigade, freshly brought back from France, he was to join the 148th Territorial Brigade somewhere between Aandalsnes, Dombås and Lillehammer, and, all going well, he would eventually proceed towards Trondheim. The latter part of the plan naturally rested on a degree of optimism that was hardly warranted at this juncture.

On 21 April, accordingly, General Paget arrived at the War Office and was formally given command of the operation. According to his Chief of Staff, Lieutenant-Colonel Nicholson, 'everything was in a state of improvisation. There were no maps; we had to tear them out of geography books and send the ADC out to the Norwegian travel agency to buy a Baedeker. From the Norwegian Embassy and a series of tourist agencies, we gathered an armful of travel advertisement folders. From amongst them we unearthed one showing a picture with a bit of Aandalsnes in the background, and other photographs of the valley between Aandalsnes and Dombås. These were our only clues as to what our prospective theatre of operations looked like.'[73]

On 23 April, with the 15th Brigade half-way across the North Sea, there were still no grounds for optimism: 'During the voyage to Aandalsnes, General Paget held a conference in the War Room. Opinion was universal: the expedition was ill-founded. The lack of air support, anti-aircraft defence, facilities for base expansion, artillery support and alternative means of communications were already apparent.' During the landing, however, Lieutenant-Colonel Nicholson was to notice several fishing rods and many sporting guns . . .[74]

Once at Aandalsnes, the Commander of the 15th Brigade met Colonel Dudley Clarke,[75] and thus learned at first hand what had happened to Brigadier Morgan's 148th Brigade in front of Tretten.

Yet there was probably even worse to come: in the Østerdal valley, which ran parallel to the Gudbrandsdal in the east, the Germans were fast advancing towards Trondheim, with little opposition from the increasingly worn-out Norwegian detachments. In other words, the British troops would now be threatened with attacks coming from the east and north as well as the south. General Paget's officers were quite right: the expedition was ill-founded.

# CHAPTER EIGHT

# Storms at the Reich Chancery

In Berlin, there was every reason to be satisfied with the latest news from Norway; but for the moment, it was anxiety rather than satisfaction that prevailed at the Reich Chancery, and the reason for that was first and foremost the strategic situation at Narvik; indeed, Hitler had considered the British naval attack of 13 April as a first-rate disaster, inasmuch as it effectively deprived the German defenders of any possibility of substantial reinforcement in the future. Now, the commander of the German garrison, General Dietl, was one of the Führer's oldest companions from the 'heroic' times in Munich, his men were mostly Austrian and, even more importantly, the defeat or surrender of the Narvik defenders would deal a severe blow to the Führer's personal prestige.

Admittedly, General Dietl's situation was not a very brilliant one; having occupied Narvik with very little difficulty on the morning of 9 April, he now found himself under siege with his 1,500 mountain troops, faced with the formidable power of the Royal Navy and the growing might of the Allied expeditionary force. Moreover, he had practically no artillery, very few means of transport, his communications were highly precarious, and he had to defend an extensive perimeter around the town under truly deplorable climatic conditions; besides, the British naval bombardment of 13 April had largely demoralized his soldiers – and compelled him to make room for some 2,500 sailors who had escaped from the ten German destroyers sunk in the fjord.

For all that, General Dietl's situation was far from desperate: his mountain troops from the 3rd Gebirgsdivision were superbly trained and equipped, there were abundant stocks of food in the town, and the very rough terrain afforded excellent defensive positions: Ankenes in the south, the whole length of the Rombaksfjord with the railway line to the north, and a vast crest line extending from Bjerkvik to Gratangen and Fossbakken in the north-east.

There were admittedly not enough soldiers to man such an extensive defence perimeter, but the 2,500 sailors from the sunk destroyers were hardy fellows who, once re-armed and re-equipped, more than doubled the garrison's defensive capacity. Indeed, there was no lack of weapons or equipment, as the Germans had seized a vast arsenal in the Norwegian military camp at Elvegårdsmoen: rifles, heavy machine-guns, mortars, together with tons of ammunition; besides, there was nothing to prevent the defenders of Narvik from receiving additional supplies by parachute. All in all, General Dietl, himself a seasoned veteran, was perfectly aware of the immense difficulties the Allies would experience in landing on such strongly defended shores; he was therefore definitely optimistic.[1]

No such thing could be said of the Führer; as early as 14 April, though Narvik itself had not yet been attacked, Hitler was about to order the evacuation of the town. That day, General Jodl, Chief of the Command Section at the OKW, wrote in his diary: 'Nervousness has now reached fever pitch. [. . .] Führer wants Dietl to make his way south. I come out against such an unthinkable project.'[2] The next day, 15 April, the Army Chief of Staff, General Halder, noted that 'Keitel told Army Commander-in-Chief[3] that Narvik was to be evacuated. Not something to be done.'[4] Perhaps not, but Hitler had already spent several sleepless nights,[5] and he was fast losing his self-control. General Warlimont, who was present at the Reich Chancery that day, recalled having seen the Führer 'sitting in a corner all by himself, staring vacuously as if immersed in some apathetic meditation; he appeared to be expecting his sole salvation from some phone call which he was anxious to receive without the slightest delay, at the same time as the chief of the Command Section'.[6]

The next day, all were bracing themselves for a powerful British attack against the Norwegian coast,[7] and in the night of 16–17 April, tension rose still further at the Reich Chancery. 'Stavanger is calling for help,' noted General Jodl. 'The Führer, beside himself, repeats that Dietl Group must make its way south or be evacuated. I repeat categorically that: a) A march southward is not feasible; b) An air operation could only evacuate an insignificant part of the troops, cause the loss of many planes, and break General Dietl's morale. You don't give up the game before it's actually lost.'[8]

But Hitler was not listening: '3.30 p.m., another battle over orders to be given to Narvik Group. Every bit of bad news gives rise to the worst fears'[9] (by the Führer).[10] Actually, the 'battle' must have been a short one, for that very afternoon a written order was received at the 'Territorial Defence' section of the OKW, for immediate transmission to General Dietl; written by General Keitel, it bore the Führer's signature, and instructed General Dietl to evacuate Narvik with his troops and cross the border into Sweden, where they would all be interned.[11] Owing to a last-minute intervention by a young OKW officer, Lieutenant-Colonel von Lossberg, the order was held up;[12] that same evening, after new reports had been received on the effects of German bombings and the vacillations of British strategy at both Narvik and Trondheim, Hitler calmed down and rescinded his order. To General Jodl's intense relief, he issued a new one, instructing Dietl to hang on as long as possible.[13] After that, the Führer relaxed somewhat, and at the OKW, everyone breathed a little more easily . . . for a short while at least.

The second reason for the anxiety prevailing in Berlin was clearly summed up after the war by General von Falkenhorst himself: 'Time was short, because the attack in the West was to be launched in May. Operations in central Norway were therefore to be concluded as fast as possible. [. . .] The Führer [. . .] insisted that the pace of operations be accelerated.'[14] Actually, it was not in May, but in April, only a few days after 'Weserübung', that the Führer had wanted to launch 'Gelb', the decisive attack in the West.[15] But it was quite true that von Falkenhorst was under intense pressure from Hitler and his staff to bring operations in Norway to an end as fast as possible – particularly as they were diverting part of the Luftwaffe necessary for the attack in the West.

Naturally, this was easier said than done. After all, the operational plans for 'Group 21' had not allowed for any serious opposition on the part of the Norwegians, yet by mid-April, Norwegian resistance was not only continuing, but intensifying. Hundreds of young men were still slipping away to join General Ruge's army, and after 11 April, the first acts of sabotage were registered in Oslo. Yet for Minister Bräuer as for General von Falkenhorst, this unexpected stiffening of Norwegian resistance had a very precise political cause: Major Vidkun Quisling's accession to power.

It will be recalled that Minister Bräuer had only half-heartedly agreed to let Quisling announce the formation of his 'government' on the evening of 9 April; but Bräuer had immediately undertaken to persuade his superior Ribbentrop, and beyond him the Führer himself, that the intervention of the mercurial leader of Nasjonal Samling could only harm the real interests of Germany. In Oslo, to be sure, Quisling's initiative had caused a wave of indignation in business circles, trade unions, the civil service, and even among the German community. During the next few days, countless personalities had thus called at the German Legation to register their protest against Quisling's coup, and his backing by Germany. To their amazement, all these men were received most cordially by the German diplomat; Victor Mogens, the leader of Fedrelandslaget – a right-wing nationalist group – was even told on 12 April by Legation Councillor von Neuhaus that 'the Legation would welcome any information that would help convince Berlin that he [Quisling] was unacceptable.'[16]

Actually, Minister Bräuer had already taken a few personal initiatives to that end; the day before, he had written to Berlin: 'As I have already reported by telephone, the adherents of the new Minister President, Quisling, are few. [. . .] As a man, Quisling is respected; only a few take him seriously as a politician. There is no doubt that the personality of Quisling renders the situation exceptionally difficult for Germany. The consensus of opinion is that the great majority of Norwegians would have accepted the German occupation, as in Denmark, but that they will not accept Quisling. [. . .] In the Norwegian view it would be quite possible to form a government from the Storting acceptable to the Germans, and possessing in sufficient measure the confidence of the Norwegian people. Although matters have already gone very far, it is still thought possible that everything can be put right without disowning Quisling. [. . .] There even seems to be some readiness to admit Quisling as a member of this government and to entrust him with the Ministry of Defence or of Foreign Affairs. It is said here that this arrangement, which is entirely acceptable to Quisling, will have a steadying effect. People are saying that in this way Germany will save at least two divisions and that the danger of the Western Allies "coming to Norway's assistance" would be automatically reduced. [. . .] Already the probability is becoming apparent that, under Quisling, the German occupying power will of its own accord have to take things more and more in hand if general anarchy is not to break out to the detriment of our armed forces.'[17]

An amazingly clever report, which was to be followed by quite a few similar ones during the next few days. Considering the extraordinary tension prevailing at the Reich Chancery at that time, and Hitler's growing exasperation with the stubborn resistance offered by the Norwegians, it is easy to understand why the Führer was likely to be influenced by Bräuer's arguments; after all, in exchange for Quisling's demotion, the German diplomat was promising nothing less than the complete pacification of Norway – and even the formation of a pro-German government that would supplant that of Nygaardsvold, while enjoying the confidence of the Norwegian people. Admittedly, the Führer felt that he had a debt of gratitude towards Quisling for the latter's warnings of December 1939, but then, the leader of a Thousand-Year Reich could hardly afford to be too sentimental... Bräuer accordingly received the green light from Berlin for his negotiations with Norwegian personalities opposed to Quisling.

Very delicate negotiations they would prove to be; for Bräuer's main interlocutors – Supreme Court President Paal Berg, Governor Christensen and Bishop Berggrav – were indeed interested in reestablishing normal conditions in the country and in getting rid of Quisling, but they had not the slightest intention of forming a new government to replace the legal one, or of calling on all Norwegians to lay down their arms and collaborate with the Germans. In fact, they were only interested in setting up a purely provisional body to ensure the economic and administrative management of all areas under German occupation, without in the least working against the Crown or the Nygaardsvold government. German and Norwegian conceptions were thus separated by a gaping chasm, made even wider by Hitler's insistence that Quisling be allowed 'an honourable exit',[18] whereas the latter was unwilling to make any exit at all.

But Bräuer, assisted by Under-Secretary of State Habicht who had just arrived from Berlin, was prepared to undertake the impossible – and he succeeded: by the morning of 15 April, Quisling had been eased out of power;[19] Paal Berg was persuaded to thank Quisling publicly 'for his dedication and patriotism', and to accept that the latter be 'put in charge of demobilization'.[20] A formula was even conjured up that appeared to conciliate Hitler's need for a new Norwegian government with the Norwegians' desire to set up a

147

temporary administration of occupied territories that was anything but a government!

Like all conjurers' tricks, this one rested on a clever piece of deceit that made good use of the intricacies of German and Norwegian terminologies. The following extract from Paal Berg's diary gives an excellent idea of what was afoot – as well as a graphic illustration of the harshness with which negotiations had been conducted: 'I said that I was personally willing to place before the Supreme Court a proposal for the nomination of an organ entrusted with the civil administration of the areas of the country under German occupation. The German side stressed that what was wanted was a real government. [. . .] I refused, and they gave in fairly quickly. But I was then told that Quisling would have to be included in the Council I intended to set up. I refused that, too, and they eventually climbed down. But they insisted that Quisling be allowed an "honourable exit", and they further wanted the Council to be called "Government Committee". I answered that this would be misinterpreted in Norway; it ought to be called "Administrative Council", or something of the sort. They accepted, but immediately added that the German translation of that title ought to be *'Regierungsausschuss'* as, according to them, that word was a perfect rendition of the Norwegian word *'Administrasjonsråd'*.* I answered that as the Norwegian title was to be the only official one, I was not concerned with the way they translated it in German. The title "Administrative Council" was thereupon adopted.'[21]

On the afternoon of 15 April, Supreme Court President Paal Berg and Governor Christensen were thus able to inform their countrymen that a seven-member Administrative Council had been formed 'to exercise civilian administration in areas of the country occupied by Germany'.[22] Bräuer swiftly proceeded to cable Berlin a slightly retouched version of their statements, naturally including his own translation of the new Council's title . . .

In Berlin, that particular piece of trickery seemed to work wonders – initially at least. The Führer fully expected the new Committee

---

* That was of course quite untrue: *Administrasjonsråd* means 'Administrative Council', whereas *Regierungsausschuss* means 'Government Committee'. No one was fooled in Oslo, but the idea was naturally to make the formula acceptable to the Reich Chancery.

to put an end to Norwegian resistance, and during the next few days, both Bräuer and von Falkenhorst sought to confirm him in this idea by producing lengthy reports on the considerable easing of tension in relations with the Norwegians, ever since the proclamation of the 'Administrative Council' – pardon, the 'Government Committee' – and of course since the departure of Vidkun Quisling.

All good things have an end, however; on 17 April, the Nygaardsvold government, meeting in a temporary refuge near Vågå, issued a statement expressing its position on the subject of the Administrative Council. That statement was broadcast the same evening, and printed the next morning in several newspapers appearing in the non-occupied areas of Norway: 'The so-called government formed in Oslo by Major Quisling [. . .] has been compelled to step down, and one can only express satisfaction that all attempts to set up a new government in opposition to the legal one [. . .] have now been given up. [. . .] The formation in Oslo during the last few days of an Administrative Council for those parts of the country occupied by Germany is to be considered as an emergency arrangement, which can in no way take over the role of the Norwegian government. This Council [. . .] does not represent the will of the country, and has no legal basis in Norwegian law. However, it may to some extent help to guarantee civil rights as long as enemy forces occupy certain parts of the country. But it goes without saying that this Council will be required to make way for the legal government in all areas coming back under the latter's control.'[23]

It was only on the morning of 19 April that Hitler received a copy of this statement. Now his translators, having little regard for diplomatic subtleties, had supplied the Führer with a translation that was both complete and strictly accurate; after a 24-hour lull, the halls of the Chancery therefore resounded with fresh outbursts, and General Jodl noted in his diary: 'Another crisis. Political action has failed.'[24] Four months later, indeed, Hitler himself told Quisling what had happened: 'All of a sudden, he [the Führer] had realized that what had been formed was not a government for Norway, but merely an "Administrative Council" for the occupied areas. He [. . .] had no use at all for such an "Administrative Council" in the areas occupied by his soldiers. What he wanted was a Norwegian government.'[25] Naturally, the full weight of Hitler's wrath fell on

Bräuer, who was summoned back to Berlin . . . and dispatched forthwith to the Western front.* Concerning Norway, Hitler also took sweeping decisions: he would place the country under the control of Gauleiter Terboven.[26]

Josef Terboven, Gauleiter of Essen, was Hitler's henchman in the Rhineland. A fanatical Nazi, a protégé of Hermann Goering, he was at once vain, cunning, brutal and entirely devoid of scruples. Such was the man appointed by the Führer to take direct administrative control of occupied Norway.

But Hitler's attention quickly reverted to strategic matters. The Luftwaffe, temporarily hampered by climatic conditions, had failed to detect the British landing at Namsos on 20 April. But the very next day, the BBC announced the landing:[27] Hitler, extremely restless and fearing an encirclement of Trondheim, personally ordered the 5th Luftflotte to carry out a massive bombing of both Namsos and Aandalsnes.[28] His orders, as we know, were faithfully executed.

During the next few days, Hitler, in an ever-increasing state of agitation, personally followed hour by hour the effects of bombings around Trondheim and the progress of the German columns north of Lillehammer. On 22 April, General Jodl again noted that 'the Führer is increasingly anxious over the British landings, and the resulting impossibility of quickly establishing overland communications with Trondheim.'[29] And the next day: 'Tension has risen yet another notch, as northward progression of 163rd and 196th Divisions is very slow, and new destructions of bridges are being reported.'[30]

On 24 April, tension suddenly dropped as reports of the British rout north of Lillehammer began to flow in: many British officers and men had been captured, as well as a considerable amount of equipment and even a complete set of British operational orders. The next day, General Jodl could write in his diary: 'The mood is now definitely optimistic. Führer quite satisfied with latest news. [. . .] Further operations to be prepared, taking into account orders found on British prisoners.'[31]

---

* An assignment that could hardly be considered a sinecure in April 1940.

# CHAPTER NINE

# The Spectre of Defeat

On 22 April, news of the British reverses around both Lillehammer and the Trondheimfjord had not yet reached London, but Winston Churchill, on his way to yet another meeting of the Supreme War Council, nevertheless noted: 'We arrived in Paris with our minds oppressed by the anxieties and confusion of the campaign in Norway.'[1]

In Paris, actually, it was not Norway itself that seemed to preoccupy the French leaders; the political atmosphere was still being poisoned by the rift between Reynaud and Daladier, as well as by the innumerable intrigues set up by Paul Reynaud's entourage to get rid of the Commander-in-Chief, General Gamelin. Political deliberations had not substantially evolved, either: any military initiative on the French north-eastern border being out of the question, there only remained the possibility of attacking the Reich's iron and petroleum supplies. That strategy was enthusiastically endorsed by both deputies and senators, inasmuch as it seemed to offer some hopes of victory while keeping the war well away from French borders. Naturally, such a strategy could only reinforce Reynaud's political position – provided of course he could show the country and its deputies that it was being pursued with the utmost vigour.

Admittedly, responsibility for the Norwegian theatre of operations lay with the British, but it took only moderate political skill to present their successes as the fruit of Allied co-operation – in other words, of Paul Reynaud's policy. On 11 April, the French Premier had done just that when he assured the deputies that 'the permanent route of Swedish iron ore to Germany has been severed, and will remain severed.'[2] Reynaud was only playing with words, of course, and he knew it; for there was another route used by the iron ore ships, that of the Baltic; and, though it was not permanent but seasonal, it would become accessible as soon as the ice began to melt, in less than three weeks. Yet the government's survival depended very much on parliamentary moods, and the latter could easily be swayed by ringing phrases; that one had earned Paul Reynaud thunderous applause, and given his embattled government a new lease of life.

Since then, the military situation in Norway had taken a turn for the worse, thus once again weakening the government's position in parliament. But Reynaud was not easily caught off balance: if the British were suffering setbacks in Norway, he pointed out, it was only because they were not waging war with the required determination. In other words, British successes were also Reynaud's successes, but British defeats could only be blamed on the British. After all, the French were doing their utmost to supply them with troops, advice and encouragement. What more could one ask?

Naturally, such arguments need not be limited to a domestic audience; they were in fact used with equal skill in a letter which Reynaud sent to Chamberlain on 18 April, with the approval of the French War Committee: 'The battle being waged at present in Scandinavia is essential to the further prosecution of the war. [. . .] This is why I am deeply convinced that we must leave no stone unturned to ensure that the co-ordination and development of our efforts proceed with an increasing efficiency.'[3] This kind of verbal heroism having worked wonders on the French parliament,[4] there was no conceivable reason to refrain from exporting it . . .

The men who attended the opening session of the Supreme War Council in the afternoon of 22 April at the Quai d'Orsay were all seasoned veterans of such gatherings. On the British side were Chamberlain, Churchill, Generals Ironside and Ismay, as well as Admiral Pound;* on the French side, Reynaud, Daladier, General Gamelin, Admiral Darlan, Alexis Léger, Paul Baudouin and Colonel de Villelume. Reynaud began with a lengthy description of the general military situation, and underlined the Allies' marked inferiority to the Germans in both men and armaments; to win the war, Reynaud concluded (as usual), it was therefore necessary to attack Germany's supply lines. As an attack on the sources of petroleum 'raised difficult problems', there remained only one possible target: the Swedish iron ore mines, naturally. 'Nothing', Reynaud continued, 'must be allowed to divert the Allies from their Scandinavian

* Lord Halifax only arrived the next day.

undertaking. [. . .] Contingents in sufficient strength ought to be sent to the north of the peninsula in order to occupy the iron ore mines, or to destroy them if necessary. Strong bodies of troops also ought to be deployed around Trondheim to prevent the Germans from establishing bases on the Atlantic coast of Norway, to react to a possible German attack in the region of the Swedish lakes, and if necessary to help defend the mines by moving northwards.'[5]

Reynaud's speech had dragged on for the better part of an hour, with frequent pauses to allow for interpretation. Neville Chamberlain, who had hitherto remained impassive,[6] presently took the floor, and expressed complete agreement with his French counterpart: the Allies' main objective was indeed to deprive the Germans of Swedish iron ore, and naturally everyone was aware of the vital importance of Narvik in this connection. Chamberlain went on to explain why some troop contingents had been diverted from Narvik to Trondheim, after which he proceeded to describe the plan for a naval attack against Trondheim (Operation 'Hammer'), exactly as if it were still being contemplated. There followed a detailed explanation of the 'pincer movement' to be carried out from Namsos and Aandalsnes, together with a somewhat exaggerated account of the accomplishments of 'Sickle' Force. However, the Prime Minister could not help mentioning the difficulties, particularly the German bombings, and he had to admit that he had no precise information on the situation at Namsos.

That was beyond dispute. In fact, he was no better informed on the situation at Aandalsnes, Lillehammer or Narvik. Churchill intervened at this stage to give a more graphic description of the difficulties being encountered: no rear bases, no harbours worth mentioning, constant submarine attacks at sea and bombings on land, highly precarious lines of communication, no anti-aircraft defences, no air cover, no artillery.

None of this was sufficient to discourage Reynaud, who immediately returned to his initial preoccupations by thanking Mr Chamberlain for 'having expressed agreement with the programme he had outlined at the beginning of the session'. In addition, he wished to 'convey the congratulations of the French government to the British army and navy, especially to the soldiers who, having landed, had not hesitated to march on towards Oslo'. The expression 'to march on towards Oslo' should give an idea of the level of abstraction attained at this stage. But M. Reynaud proceeded to ask his British counterpart a series of questions: (a) Could the difficulties just mentioned give rise to a 'really dangerous situation'? (b) Could the shipments of British reinforcements for Norway be effectively interrupted? (c) Was it true that the Germans were compelled to send the greater part of their reinforcements by air? (d) Could minefields be laid in Swedish territorial waters in order to prevent their use by the Germans? (e) Could the Baltic be blocked by aerial mining? (f) Could the export of iron ore to Germany from the port of Luleå be hampered by the laying of mines in the Gulf of Bothnia? Having stated that he could answer all these questions without difficulty, Chamberlain answered none of them, except by alluding vaguely to the possibility of bottling up the port of Luleå – by what means was left unsaid.

After having postponed the discussion of such diverse issues as the eventuality of Italian aggression against Dalmatia or Greece, the German threat to the Netherlands, and 'Allied' plans for an offensive against the Soviets in the Caucasus, Reynaud, 'summing up the conclusions of the discussion that had just taken place', declared that 'for the moment, the main thing was to win the battle of Trondheim, to capture the port, and turn it into a strong base for further operations.'[7] M. Reynaud would probably have been dumbfounded had the British Prime Minister informed him that the naval attack on Trondheim had been cancelled two days earlier . . . But Chamberlain told him nothing of the sort: if he had not seen fit to impart that information to the Norwegians or to his own generals, he could hardly be expected to share it with the French!

Reynaud was quite satisfied with the outcome of the meeting, though Admiral Auphan, for one, described it as having yielded nothing but 'academic resolutions amounting to a fine exercise in non-commitment, in the best parliamentary tradition'.[8] Daladier was hardly more indulgent; on his own copy of the official minutes, he had jotted down: 'Farcical'.[9] On the British side, however, everyone returned to London in high spirits[10] – except Winston Churchill, who had to admit that he was 'much concerned at the complete failure not only of our efforts against the enemy, but of our method of conducting the war'.[11]

There was good reason for that. Three days earlier, the War Office had at long last appointed a single commander for the whole

Norwegian theatre (with the exception of Narvik). Yet the commander, General H. R. S. Massy, being unable to co-ordinate operations from Norway owing to the almost complete absence of means of communication, was to do so from London. Unfortunately, even in London, he had precious little to co-ordinate, and he was invited only once to a meeting of the Military Co-ordination Committee[12] – a committee that was not co-ordinating much anyway. As for the members of the War Cabinet, on whom rested the final decision, they remained as hesitant and ill-informed as ever; thus, on 23 April, they only mentioned that Brigadier Morgan's force had 'withdrawn from forward positions in the Lillehammer area' – a devastating understatement considering what had really happened; the next day, likewise, they failed to mention that Aandalsnes had been bombed and destroyed, but took note of the fact that 'the Norwegians and Morgan's forces were operating on the western line of the railway' – though by that time, as we know, Brigadier Morgan's forces were quite incapable of operating anywhere.

In fact, all the deliberations of the War Cabinet that day revealed a definite reluctance to face the realities of the strategic situation, and a propensity to seek refuge in abstract planning for highly improbable contingencies; thus, having noted the unpleasant fact that the eastern railway line connecting Oslo and Trondheim through the Østerdal was practically undefended and might enable the Germans from Oslo to link with those in Trondheim, they went on to draw the following rather startling conclusions: 'Our real objective was the control of the Gällivare ore fields. [. . .] Our only chance of reaching up from Narvik to Gällivare would be if Sweden was brought into the war. The surest way of compelling the Germans to infringe the neutrality of Sweden would be to block their direct line of approach to Trondheim from Oslo by holding both lines of the railway. They might then be forced to send troops through Sweden. Information has been received last night that the German expedition which had been reported as concentrating at Stettin has sailed. It is possible that this expedition will be landed in Sweden. We should then be in a position to use Trondheim as a base for subsequent operations in southern Scandinavia.'

That is to say, in Sweden . . . In other words, the situation could improve markedly if only the Germans cared to attack Sweden – and if Trondheim were taken in the mean time, which unfortunately was

155

not the case. The ministers eventually came back to earth with the following comment: 'Unless we could find some means of taking Trondheim within a short time, we could not hope to hold up German pressure from Oslo with the small forces which we could put in and maintain through undeveloped bases like Aandalsnes.' But, for anyone reading these minutes to the end, there was still a huge surprise in store: 'The original plan for a direct assault on Trondheim by the use of naval forces covering the landing of military forces had been abandoned in view of the very grave risks which would have had to be run [. . .] and because, at the time of the abandonment of the original plan, the pincer movement from Namsos and Aandalsnes had seemed to offer better hope of success. This earlier hope, however, had proved [. . .] unfounded, and it was for consideration now whether some form of naval attack on the Trondheim-fjord, combined with military landings at points where opposition was unlikely to be met, should not be undertaken.'[13]

Incredible but true: the plan for a naval attack on Trondheim, born on the morning of 9 April, shelved the same evening, reconsidered on the 14th, confirmed on the 16th, implemented in its preliminary stage on the 18th, and abandoned on the 20th, was about to be resurrected on the 24th! No need for alarm: it was to die again two days later. But by now the reader will surely understand what Mr Churchill meant when he mentioned on 24 April 'the complete failure [. . .] of our method of conducting the war'.

Winston Churchill was not alone in deploring the prevailing confusion and pusillanimity. Admiral of the Fleet Sir Roger Keyes was just as indignant, and saw no reason to hide it. It will be recalled that in mid-April, he had conceived a plan for the naval attack on Trondheim, and ever since then, he had been trying to persuade the Admiralty to adopt it. Upon being told by his former subordinates in the Naval Staff that no ships could be risked in the undertaking 'owing to the uncertainty about the Italian situation',[14] he had proposed to repeat the Zeebrugge exploit by using 'old cruisers and destroyers, minesweepers and small craft to make smoke'.[15] Besides, unlike the Chiefs of Staff and the members of the War Cabinet, Admiral Keyes had thought of consulting the Norwegian Military Attaché and the Legation Councillor, who were familiar with Trondheim and its approaches.[16] But it was all in vain; Churchill refused to see the Admiral under various pretexts, the Admiralty had him received on 23 April by an unqualified junior officer, while both Admiral Pound and General Ironside told him to leave his plan with them – and promptly shelved it.[17] By then, Admiral Keyes had learned of the cancellation of 'Hammer', and also of the German troop-landing inside Trondheimfjord that had caught 'Maurice' Force so completely by surprise. 'It infuriates me to think', Keyes wrote to Churchill, 'that the Navy should be so let down by the Admiralty and be responsible for allowing one German destroyer and one torpedo-boat [. . .] to exercise sea power within Trondheimfjord by giving mobility to a force which was thus enabled to cut off the advance guard of the Namsos troops and hold up the whole expedition.'[18]

No doubt a somewhat chaotic style of writing, but then the Admiral was clearly stuttering with rage; besides, it was perfectly true that the German landing operation south of Steinkjer had entirely paralysed General Carton de Wiart's offensive towards Trondheim.

On 24 April, Major Paul Stehlin, of the French Military Mission in Finland, arrived at Namsos. Eight days earlier, he had received a curious telegram from Air Force headquarters in Paris, ordering him to 'show up in Norway between 64th and 68th parallel' – that is, anywhere between Trondheim and Narvik! – to seek emplacements for the installation of new airfields.[19] In Namsos, Major Stehlin found his way to the headquarters of the French expeditionary force. 'General Audet', he recalled, 'was busy examining the latest orders issued by General Carton de Wiart. The idea was in fact to defend a bridgehead by deploying forces all around Namsos in the course of the next 24 hours. It appeared to me that such a plan excluded any possibility of an offensive northwards or southwards to recover the ground occupied by the Germans.'[20]

Indeed, de Wiart had ordered his two battalions, sorely tried by the battle south of Steinkjer, to take up defensive positions around Namsos, in co-operation with the 53rd Battalion of French Chasseurs Alpins. Further south, the 13th and 67th Battalions of Chasseurs Alpins, supported by a British battalion and the Norwegian ski troops under Colonel Getz, were operating in the Bangsund–Namdalseidet–Hjelle area; yet there were no clashes with the German troops dug in between Steinkjer and Sunnan, and the German air force had become much less active after 25 April. This, added to the frequent appearance of British carrier-based planes, and to the reception of much-needed supplies after 26 April, no doubt accounted for the drastic improvement in the morale of both British and French troops around Namsos at the time.

Naturally, local conditions were still far from ideal: reinforcements were to arrive, but it was not known when, in what strength, and what their orders would be. Moreover, the equipment received was very difficult to unload, because it had been rather carelessly stored in the holds of the ships, and also because the two quays at Namsos were in an appalling condition – hardly improved by constant German bombings. Besides, much of the equipment unloaded was either ill-adapted or entirely useless: firewood for the French,[21] and for the British unreadable maps of Norway half a century old, as well as three-ton lorries far too heavy for local roads.[22] Even when useful, the equipment was often incomplete: anti-aircraft guns with no predictors, and an entire Howitzer battery without a single round of ammunition.[23] When equipment was both useful and complete, however, it was often badly utilized for lack of training: thus the crew of a French anti-aircraft battery shot down their commanding officer at the very first salvo.[24] When training improved, it sometimes made matters worse: the French thus fired several times at British planes by mistake – and eventually shot one down.[25] The British also fired at their own planes, but missed them . . .*[26]

Relations between the Allies at Namsos were uneasy at best: the French and British commanders suspected each other of wanting to evacuate Namsos at the earliest opportunity – rightly in both cases – and co-ordination between them left much to be desired; thus, starting on 26 April, a French and a British officer were separately seeking an emplacement that could be used as an airfield, and neither knew of the other's mission.[27] At the level of the troops, encounters between Allies could even be rather rough, mainly because the British kept driving on the left side of the road. The French, in turn, frequently looted British supply stores, an exercise hardly conducive to improved Franco-British relations.[28]

---

* A British corporal who had opened fire with a heavy machine-gun on a Navy seaplane was thus said to have received a reprimand 'for having shot at and missed an Admiral flying low'.

Both French and British troops harboured strong suspicions of their Norwegian allies: the civilians were considered suspect,[29] and the soldiers seemed inactive, ill-trained and unreliable.[30] Yet both the British and the French expeditions depended on the civilians for a good deal of their food supplies,[31] and on the military for their means of transport. For all that, the British still could not bring themselves to trust Colonel Getz, a superb officer whose 4,000 men had ammunition for only one day of fighting. He was promised both rifles and ammunition by the British, but received nothing at all; his advice on strategic matters was likewise entirely disregarded by both French and British – with tragic consequences at times.

There was yet another obstacle to inter-allied relations at Namsos: on the British side, General Carton de Wiart spoke impeccable French, but no one under him could speak a word of it; the French naturally could not speak a word of English, and neither the English nor the French spoke Norwegian; the Norwegians in turn could not speak French, and spoke very bad English, though some could speak German, which neither the British nor the French could understand. Brigadier Phillips therefore urgently cabled London to request . . . a German dictionary.[32]

Despite such difficulties, General Audet and Colonel Getz got together on 26 April and prepared plans for an attack on Steinkjer. The British would approach the town from the west, the French from the north, and the Norwegians from the east along Lake Snaasa.[33] The attack was to be supported by French tanks and artillery, and launched simultaneously with the naval assault on Trondheim.[34] An attractive project, which worked wonders on the morale of all officers involved. But as the British had no skis, the Norwegians no ammunition and the French no tanks, as furthermore none of them had air cover and the naval attack on Trondheim had been cancelled a week earlier, the plan was doomed from the start. In fact, General Carton de Wiart, an experienced old warrior who could readily recognize the smell of defeat, had carefully withheld comment on the plan; that day, however, he took an initiative that was sufficiently eloquent: the War Office having offered him a reinforcement of a half-brigade of Chasseurs Alpins, the General declined, on the grounds that 'in case of evacuation, this would complicate matters'.[35] Less than 48 hours later, events were to prove him right.

South of Trondheim, in the meantime, General Paget's 15th Brigade, having landed two days earlier, was trying to stem the German advance in the Gudbrandsdal. Entrenched around the village of Kvam, it was blocking the road through the valley, thus allowing Norwegian troops from Lillehammer to regroup in the Romsdal and along the coast. General Paget was hoping to hold the front until the arrival of reinforcements, but he was perfectly aware of the precariousness of his position: with less than 3,000 men assisted by a few detachments of Norwegian ski troops, no vehicles, no artillery and no air cover, he was facing a German spearhead of 8,500 highly motorized troops supported by tanks, artillery and dive bombers; besides, he was being threatened on his left flank by a second German column coming up the Østerdal, and his sole supply line to Aandalsnes was a highly vulnerable and constantly bombed railway snaking across the Romsdal from Dombås to the coast, doubled by a narrow, snow-bound road dotted with car wrecks and pocked with bomb craters. At both ends, Dombås and Aandalsnes, with almost no anti-aircraft defence, were also bombed at frequent intervals by the Luftwaffe. In an effort to provide at least some air protection, London had dispatched a squadron of Gladiator planes that landed on a frozen lake north of Dombås on 24 April. Unfortunately, these biplanes were obsolete, ill-equipped to face local weather conditions and, once landed, entirely devoid of anti-aircraft protection. As a result, they were bombed on the ice the very next day, and twelve of them were burnt or sunk. The last six quickly ran out of fuel and ammunition, and completely ceased to operate after only 24 hours.[36]

Despite such adverse conditions, General Paget's men repulsed all German assaults on Kvam. Indeed, for the first time since the British landed in Norway, this was a real battle, not an execution. 'About 1 p.m.,' wrote one witness, 'German tanks came into action in support of their infantry, held up by "B" and "C" Companies in front of the village. [. . .] Corporal Stokes, of the York and Lancaster Regiment, was in command of the third gun beside the road at the back of the village. [. . .] With his first shot Stokes stopped the tank. His second burned it up and left it on the side of the road. There was a slight pause and then up from the dip waddled another tank. Stokes waited until it was alongside the first and then "killed" it with two shots in exactly the same way as the first. The road was not yet fully blocked, but the Germans were nothing if not persistent. Round the bend came an armoured car and drove rapidly towards the destroyed tanks. [Stokes] waited until the car was just between the two tanks and then neatly knocked it out with one shot. That blocked the road completely.'[37] 'Two men of "E" company', recalled another witness, 'were posted with their Bren gun behind a wall in the village at midday on the 25th. There they stayed firing their gun, while houses burned around them, shells fell almost continuously and the telephone wires above were severed one by one by bullets. Although their section commander went, there they stayed, cracking their pawky Yorkshire jokes, until late on the afternoon of the 26th a shell fell right on top of them.'[38]

In these two days of fighting, the Germans lost before Kvam more than fifty men, five tanks and three armoured cars. By the evening of 26 April, General Paget's men withdrew in good order to form a new line of defence at Kjørem, then at Otta. The Germans attacking these positions on 27 and 28 April again suffered heavy losses,[39] and their northward progression was considerably hampered. Yet General Paget could not hope to contain the enemy indefinitely without reinforcements, artillery or air support, as he had cabled the War Office immediately after arriving in the Gudbrandsdal. But the reply he received on 28 April was not at all the one he expected.

Ever since the arrival of the 148th Brigade, German planes had occasionally bombed the town of Aandalsnes, but without causing extensive destructions. After 25 April, however, things took a sudden turn for the worse; having observed the landing of the 15th Brigade and received explicit orders from the Führer himself, the Luftwaffe began bombing the town with devastating regularity. The British garrison had no defence against high-altitude bombing, and very little against dive-bombers; the few guns available had no range-finders, neither were there any projectors, trucks, sandbags . . . or even spades![40] By the evening of 26 April, explosive and incendiary bombs had destroyed the wooden jetty, flattened the port area, and pulverized the ammunition and equipment stored on the waterfront. What followed was graphically described in a report by Brigadier Hogg, commanding the port garrison: 'After seeing the extent of the damage and the obvious future prospects, I made a signal to War Office to the effect that unless the air situation could be put right, the base would be unworkable, a fact which was rapidly demonstrated. Got into touch with Adv. HQ by telephone and informed General Paget who agreed, and wished emphasis to be laid on his precarious position. He was without guns, and fighting an enemy possessed of field and medium artillery and having completely undisturbed mastery of the air. [. . .] Later on, when I had fuller reports on the bombing damage, I tried to get into touch with General Paget without success. Discussed evacuation plans.'[41]

The next morning at 5 a.m., Brigadier Hogg sent an urgent message to General Massy, the War Office, the Admiralty and the Air Ministry to recommend immediate evacuation. He was later to justify his initiative in the following terms: 'The position now was that I was out of touch with General Paget, that I felt evacuation was inevitable, and that if evacuation was delayed too long, the result would be a serious disaster involving the loss of the whole force, either by a surrender or by a shambles. I therefore decided to press for evacuation. Had I been in touch with General Paget, I should have left the decision to him obviously. As it was, it was my duty to make a decision, I accept full personal responsibility for that decision, and I am convinced that any other action would have meant disaster. I therefore recommended evacuation to the War Office.'[42] The reason why Brigadier Hogg later produced such detailed justification was perhaps that his initiative exerted considerable influence on the Allied strategic debate then being conducted in London.

The Supreme War Council meeting in Paris on 22 and 23 April having somewhat diverted the British ministers' attention from the harsh realities of the Norwegian situation, it was only on 24 April that they began to realize what had really happened at both Tretten and Steinkjer. That day, the Canadian Minister of Defence, Mr Norman Rogers, on a visit to London, noted that Prime Minister Chamberlain 'appeared to be grave and preoccupied'.[43] Winston Churchill, with whom he had lunch the next day, also seemed to him 'under some stress'. 'It was quite evident', continued Mr Rogers, 'that the invasion of Norway was very much on his mind. It was equally clear that he felt our own position was precarious. [. . .] In anticipation of the possibility of British and French forces not being able to maintain their positions in southern Norway, he expressed the importance of holding Narvik and the line of railway leading to Sweden.'[44]

The Canadian Minister of Defence found Lord Halifax, Oliver Stanley, Samuel Hoare and even King George VI to be just as pessimistic.[45] Commander Auphan, also in London at the time, found everyone at the Admiralty 'gloomy', and Admiral Pound 'quite overwhelmed'.[46] General Ironside, himself much depressed, noted in his diary: 'Back in a Flamingo to find Oliver Stanley and Dill sitting very glum in the War Office. Stanley said that he had told the PM that the situation at Namsos was desperate';[47] and Sir Alexander Cadogan, likewise: 'Halifax had met Ismay, who had given him most gloomy account of Norway – that we must get out. [. . .] We're obviously in a bad fix.'[48]

There was little doubt about that. The Military Co-ordination Committee, gathered the next day (26 April) to discuss the advisability of resurrecting the naval attack on Trondheim, came to an entirely negative conclusion, as Chamberlain announced to the War Cabinet later that morning: 'The MCC considered the position after the capture of Trondheim. Before Trondheim could be used by us as a base, 50 heavy and 80 light anti-aircraft guns would be required – and even then there would be difficulties in holding the port against heavy air attack. [. . .] To secure the maintenance of our forces in Norway would require the efforts of the greater part of the Home Fleet. [. . .] If Italy joined our enemies, we should then be unable to deal with her while, at the same time, attempting to maintain forces at Trondheim and Narvik.' In other words, even if Trondheim were taken, there would be no drastic change in the whole strategic situation, and if it were not, 'there was very little we could do in central Norway'. 'For this reason,' Mr Chamberlain continued, 'the Committee had come to the conclusion that plans should be got ready for evacuating our forces from Aandalsnes and Namsos in case of need, though we should in the meantime do everything possible to continue our resistance to the German advance.'[49]

The word was out, and it created quite a stir within the War Cabinet. Chamberlain, who as usual considered such matters first and foremost from a political point of view, was quick to add that 'we might mitigate the effects of our withdrawal if we could present to the world the picture that we had only gone into central Norway in order to gain time for the achievement of our real objective, which was the capture of Narvik'. In other words, something of a war stratagem! But the ministers present were still somewhat shaken at the prospect of an evacuation from central Norway. The Dominions Secretary remarked that 'every day we were able to hold out in central Norway would be of great advantage in our operations further north'. The Secretary of State for Air agreed, and the Chancellor of the Exchequer enquired 'whether a withdrawal from the Trondheim area would not be in sharp contrast with the conclusions recently arrived at by the Supreme War Council, placing Trondheim as the first objective for our operations'.

A good question, to which the Prime Minister answered with some justification that 'the French had always insisted on Narvik and the iron ore as the only objective worth worrying about in Scandinavia'. Chamberlain concluded the meeting by returning to the issue that concerned him above all: 'From the point of view of public opinion, it would be helpful if we could combine our withdrawal from central Norway with the announcement of the capture of Narvik.' But the Prime Minister was not entirely unaware of the harsh realities of the situation, for he added that 'it looked, however, as though it might not be possible to achieve the latter before we had to carry out the former'.[50]

The War Cabinet had indeed considered at length the possibility of evacuation from central Norway, but at no time had they explicitly decided to implement it, and most ministers clearly hoped that it could be delayed for as long as possible. The effect that such an evacuation would have on the Norwegian government, its army and its population was not even mentioned; on the other hand, the ministers greatly feared the reaction of the French authorities should an evacuation be decided upon. Well they might, for the very fact that the possibility had been mentioned that morning was to cause an immediate uproar in Paris.

At the British Embassy in Paris, Oliver Harvey noted that both Reynaud and Léger had been horrified upon hearing the news.[51] They were not alone; that afternoon at 3 p.m., the War Committee gathered at the Elysée, and General Gamelin also expressed the opinion that the British 'project' was 'deplorable'.[52] All the other members – President Lebrun, Daladier, Campinchi, Laurent-Eynac, Mandel, Darlan, Vuillemin and Georges – agreed with Paul Reynaud's proposal to send General Gamelin to London, in order to obtain British assent to the following programme: 'Decision to pursue operations in Norway; necessity of organizing the command structure; preparation of the attack on Trondheim with the co-operation of naval and air forces.'[53]

Well aware of what would happen to his government if ever the Norwegian affair ended like the Finnish one, Reynaud also sent a personal telegram to Chamberlain. This message was received in London with some consternation,[54] no doubt on account of the many heroic platitudes it contained – the following passage being typical of the whole: 'One must think big or stop making war, one must act fast or lose the war.'[55] In London that evening, General Gamelin and Ambassador Corbin conferred with the members of the War Cabinet, and Gamelin proposed the following course of action: to keep a wide bridgehead south of Trondheim, in the Aalesund–Molde–Aandalsnes–Kristiansund area, and also to occupy as many points as possible on the coast running north from Namsos in order to 'cover' the approaches to Narvik.[56] His interlo-cutors, including both Chamberlain and Churchill, seemed quite unconvinced, but readily agreed to a proposal by Ambassador Corbin to call an emergency meeting of the Supreme War Council for the very next day.[57] In the meantime, however, a new element intervened that was to have a decisive effect on the British War Cabi-net: the reception in London of the two telegrams sent by Brigadier Hogg from Aandalsnes.

It will be recalled that the two telegrams sent by the commander of Aandalsnes base in the afternoon of 26 April and in the early morning of the 27th were addressed to the War Office, the Admiralty and the Air Ministry, but also to General Massy. That was entirely proper, since the latter had been named Commander-in-Chief of all British forces in central Norway only a few days earlier. Now until the morning of 27 April, in the midst of the extraordinary confusion then prevailing, General Massy had been unable to contribute much to Allied strategy in Norway. But having read Brigadier Hogg's two alarming messages, he decided for the first time to exercise his prerogatives as Commander-in-Chief, and in the early morning of 27 April, he sent two very firm messages to the War Cabinet.

In the first one, which was in fact a long memorandum, he reminded the ministers that, according to General Ironside, he, Massy, 'was to be given a free hand regarding the date of the evacua-tion'. Yet the day before, he continued, the Military Co-ordination Committee had stated in its conclusions that 'the evacuation is to be delayed as long as possible consistent with military security, and should if practicable be postponed until after the capture of Narvik.'[58] That was of course fairly typical: the ministers and the Chiefs of Staff wanted both one thing and its contrary, and were counting on Divine Providence to make them compatible. But General Massy would have none of it, and he stressed with some logic that if he was to delay the evacuation as long as possible – and even after the capture of Narvik – then he quite clearly did not have a free hand to settle the date of the evacuation . . .[59]

The second note was just as long, but even more categorical; it stressed that 'Maurice' Force in Namsos now had a purely defensive role, and 'Sickle' Force at Aandalsnes, in permanent danger of being encircled from the east and the north, was now being very heavily bombed on its supply lines and its rear bases (evidently the influence of Brigadier Hogg's telegrams). General Massy's conclusion was unambiguous: both 'Sickle' and 'Maurice' Forces ought to be re-embarked without delay.[60] And the General ended with an extremely weighty argument in favour of a speedy decision: should evacuation of the expeditionary force be undertaken immediately, it could be completed by 1 or 2 May. If postponed, it would take more than a month.[61]

General Massy's two memoranda were delivered by hand to General Ironside just before the beginning of that morning's session of the War Cabinet. The Chief of the Imperial General Staff made extensive use of them, telling the ministers that 'the difficulties in carrying out [General Gamelin's] suggestions were enormous', and that at any rate 'the bombing of base establishments made the maintenance of the forces almost an impossibility. General Massy considered that we should evacuate our forces.'[62]

The members of the War Cabinet were no longer dealing with hypothetical situations or remote contingencies, but with a proposal to order a major evacuation without delay. Winston Churchill, for one, advocated 'leaving the troops now in Norway to put up the best fight they could, in conjunction with the Norwegians'. He went on to remind his colleagues that he had received 'the most urgent appeals from Sir Roger Keyes to carry out an operation of the "Hammer" type'.[63] But for Churchill's colleagues in the War Cabinet, all this was far too risky. Like the Prime Minister, they were all too well aware of the likely political repercussions back home of a military disaster in Norway – and General Ironside had made it clear that such a disaster was a very real possibility. The ministers, as is known, were particularly loath to take such clear-cut, constraining and irreversible decisions, and the written conclusions of the meeting remained suitably ambiguous.[64] But all the same, there was little doubt that immediate evacuation had in fact been decided. General Ironside thus wrote in his diary that he and General Massy got the War Cabinet 'to agree to evacuation at once'.[65] Likewise, General Massy cabled to General Carton de Wiart at *1.15 p.m.*, that is, immediately after the War Cabinet meeting: 'Evacuation decided in principle. Plan in your case gradual but rapid.'[66] As for Sir Alexander Cadogan, he wrote in his diary: 'Cabinet [. . .] lasted all morning. Very gloomy. We must get out, but it's an awful débâcle. But there it is, and it must be faced.'[67]

Perhaps, but there was no point in announcing this to the French with such brutal frankness. Neville Chamberlain obviously thought so too, as evidenced by his opening address to the Supreme War Council two hours later. To the reader who bears in mind that the British had just decided on the complete and immediate evacuation of Norway, the whole meeting will probably appear as a very bad comedy.

Having welcomed the French participants, the Prime Minister explained that the situation in Norway had worsened considerably since their last meeting of 22 April. The swift German advance, the weight of the air attacks, the destruction of the ports, the impossibility of landing heavy material precluded 'the type of attack operations feasible in the last war'. As a result, 'we could not [. . .] take Trondheim'. But Chamberlain hastened to reassure Reynaud that this was not tantamount to a decision to evacuate, only that evacuation would have to be carried out 'sooner or later', and that 'it could not long be delayed'. As for General Gamelin's suggestions of the day before, the Prime Minister continued, they were presently being studied by the military experts.[68]

At this stage, Chamberlain was being less than frank; naturally, the evacuation could not be 'long delayed', since the decision to evacuate forthwith had just been taken unilaterally three hours earlier! As for General Gamelin's suggestions of the day before, we know that they had been rejected by civilians and military alike . . . No doubt somewhat embarrassed at having to disguise the truth to such an extent, Chamberlain hastened to change the subject: at Narvik, he assured them, the position was far better, and a vigorous attack would soon be launched. Besides, it was probably unwise to 'limit ourselves to the consideration of one aspect of the war': there was always the danger of an attack by Italy, which would 'compel us to leave central Scandinavia'. The Prime Minister ended by wandering even further afield: another alternative to operations in central Scandinavia might well be an Allied attack on 'stocks and sources of supply in Germany' and 'navigation on the Rhine'.

Paul Reynaud thereupon took the floor. Himself a past master at parliamentary rhetoric, he had taken a connoisseur's interest in Chamberlain's efforts to push central Norway into the background. Naturally, Reynaud immediately undertook to bring it back to the fore. He did not believe, he said, in the possibility of an Italian attack, whereas there was no doubt that 'an Allied retreat from central Norway would be a moral and political disaster'. The French Premier therefore proposed to 'save face' by 'maintaining some elements of resistance around Trondheim' (along the lines exposed by General Gamelin); then, of course, he proposed to 'proceed with the capture of Narvik', and also to offer the Swedes an indemnity in exchange for the destruction of their iron ore mines.

After having gently poured cold water on the last proposal, Chamberlain made the startling statement that he agreed with the other two – including General Gamelin's strategic plan! As the latter called for the continuation of operations both south of Trondheim and north of Namsos, Paul Reynaud naturally concluded that he had succeeded in persuading his British interlocutors, and he immediately 'expressed his pleasure that an agreement had been reached on General Gamelin's proposals'.[69]

The 'misunderstanding' was to persist until the very end of the meeting. After a few more exercises of theoretical strategy on their favourite theatre of operations – the Mediterranean – the French were to return to Paris convinced that they had won the day: 'We have shown them what to do, and given them the will to do it,' Paul Reynaud claimed without undue modesty.[70] Yet only two hours after his departure, urgent orders were dispatched from London to Aandalsnes and Namsos. They could be summed up in two words: immediate evacuation.

*

Together with General Ruge and his staff, King Haakon and his ministers were still awaiting the great naval operation against Trondheim, which after all had been promised them ever since 9 April. On 21 April, Admiral Evans visited the King at Vågå, and told him that the attack would start that very day. King Haakon, who was beginning to have some doubts as to the reliability of British promises, answered that he would not pass on the news to his ministers, because 'if the attack did not take place [. . .] they would lose faith in the British'.[71] To be sure, their faith had already taken a few rude jolts: at Aandalsnes, they had seen raw, ill-equipped, undisciplined troops, without vehicles or artillery, who marched to the front with four footballs and 50,000 cigarettes.[72] Colonel Thue, commanding the 4th Norwegian Infantry Regiment stationed in the Romsdal, had added the following description in a report to his government: 'Very young lads who appeared to come from the slums of London. They had taken a very close interest in the women of Romsdal, and engaged in wholesale looting of stores and houses. [. . .] Besides, they would run like hares at the first sound of an aircraft engine.'[73]

It was hard to deny the evidence, as the Foreign Office grudgingly acknowledged shortly thereafter: 'Drunk British troops had on one occasion quarrelled and eventually fired upon some Norwegian fishermen. Again, some of the British Army officers had behaved "with the arrogance of Prussians" and the Naval Officers were in general so cautious and suspicious that they treated every Norwegian as a Fifth Columnist and refused to believe vital information when it was given them.'[74]

The repercussions on military operations had been disastrous from the very start, and all this caused consternation both at government councils and at General Ruge's headquarters. But the landing of General Paget and his regular brigade on 24 April was to bring a surge of hope among the Norwegians; Paget had visited General Ruge on 26 April to work out a common strategy, and the Norwegian Commander-in-Chief, most impressed by Paget's determination and professionalism, decided the very next day to put him in command of all Allied forces operating in the Gudbrandsdal. General Ruge regrouped his other units – some 4,000 men in all – further north to prepare them for participation in the great attack against Trondheim.[75] Officially, of course, the latter had been maintained; upon arriving at Aandalsnes, General Paget had informed

Sir Cecil Dormer of the plan's cancellation five days earlier,[76] but neither the general nor the diplomat had been authorized to share that information with the Norwegian authorities. As a result, the latters' entire strategy remained centred on the capture of Trondheim. Dormer, who visited them on 26 April, had the following to report: 'I saw the Minister of Foreign Affairs, who was joined by the PM, the Minister of Defence and the Minister of Supply. To my surprise they appeared comparatively cheerful, but that was evidently because they did not know the military situation. They produced plans of the Trondheim defences and of a landing ground which the Germans were constructing there. [. . .] They did not know that we had given up the idea of attacking Trondheim. [. . .] All the Government hopes centred on our retaking the ancient capital.'[77]

General Ruge's hopes as well; somewhat ill-at-ease at having to conceal such crucial information from his ally, General Paget commanded the defence of Kjørem the next day, with the support of General Ruge's ski detachments. A successful defence, no doubt, but little more than a desperate rear-guard action unless air support and artillery arrived without delay, as General Paget had been requesting ever since his arrival in Norway.

At dawn on 28 April, General Paget received the fateful order from the War Office: evacuation of all his forces 'as soon as possible'. He was also instructed to withhold that information from General Ruge, whom British authorities still could not bring themselves to trust. Paget was clearly startled by the order of evacuation, and most embarrassed at the idea of having to conceal it from his Norwegian allies. 'When on 28 April', he later recalled, 'I received orders from the War Office to evacuate my forces, the forward elements of which were 100 miles from the base, it was evident that I could only hope to do so with the co-operation of General Ruge, on whom I depended for transport by road and rail and for flank protection. [. . .] I decided that the right course to take was to be perfectly frank. [. . .] I therefore went to his HQ and acted accordingly.'[78]

It was an extremely painful interview that took place at Norwegian headquarters shortly after 5 a.m. General Ruge took the news with great calm, but also with some incredulity: 'So Norway is to share the fate of Czechoslovakia and Poland. But why? Why? Your troops haven't been defeated!'[79] According to General Paget, Ruge then fairly lost his temper: 'He spoke strongly of the betrayal of his country. He said that when we laid the minefield off the Norwegian coast, we must have appreciated that a German invasion would in all probability result, and yet we had taken no adequate steps to meet it. He had been promised a British division in the south, and had received only my force of five battalions and no artillery. He had kept his army in being by the assurance that strong British forces were coming to their aid, but now they would no longer have any confidence in him or the British.'[80]

A long pause ensued, then General Ruge excused himself and left the room.[81] When he returned, he had entirely regained his composure, and to the amazement of his British visitors, he declared: 'Let us return to our plans. Please tell me what help I can give you to carry out your orders.'[82] Agreement was quickly reached: General Ruge was to provide the British troops with transportation, flank protection, and evacuation of the wounded; the British, in turn, would cover the retreat of all Norwegian units left in the Romsdal.[83] Both Generals then proceeded to send telegrams to the War Office. Paget wrote that evacuation was 'unduly hazardous under present conditions', and that he could hold Dombås for a time 'if further landings were planned and if air and artillery support were provided at once'.[84] As for General Ruge, he recalled the promises made by the British since 9 April, and went on to say that a British evacuation now would 'totally wreck the confidence of the Norwegian army and people'.[85]

A lengthy process of disengagement, retreat and re-embarkation now began, under permanent pressure from the Germans and constant harassment by their Luftwaffe. Like General Massy in London, General Paget reckoned that, all going well, the evacuation could be completed by 2 May; but naturally, in view of the military situation, there was not the slightest assurance that all would go well . . . On that same 28 April, Aandalsnes, Molde and Kristiansund were bombed almost around the clock. The same evening, London undertook to implement one of the decisions taken at the Supreme War Council, and the next morning at 7 a.m. Sir Cecil Dormer – who had found refuge in a lunatic asylum near Molde – received an urgent message. 'His Majesty's government', he later wrote, 'wished me to invite King Haakon and his Government to leave Molde by a British cruiser that night, either for any other Norwegian port or for England, as His Majesty might later decide. I was to say nothing about the plans for evacuation, but steps were to be taken to see that the King did not fall into German hands.'[86]

Being an excellent diplomat, Dormer had somewhat toned down the contents of this message in his report; for the real telegram contained the following rather stern passage: 'His Majesty's Government have decided that His Majesty the King of Norway, his entourage and members of the Norwegian Government should be evacuated with last Allied troops to leave Molde area, and if necessary, this is to be done even against the King's wishes so that he may not – repeat not – fall into German hands. [. . .] His Majesty should not – repeat not – be informed of evacuation plan at present, and force should only be resorted to after first night of evacuation if King then [refuses?] to leave.'[87]

Together with French Minister de Dampierre, Dormer therefore went to see Koht and the other members of the government. It was not easy to break the news, of course, but Count de Dampierre noted that upon hearing it his interlocutors remained 'astonishingly calm', though Koht could not help exclaiming in English: 'You are killing us!'[88] Indeed, Dormer confirmed, 'Mr Koht was much upset, and for a time I feared that the Government might throw their hands in.' But Sir Cecil received help from an unexpected quarter: 'While I was with them, a Heinkel dropped a bomb near enough to make me hope that it would reconcile the Government to the idea of departure.'[89] That afternoon, the British diplomat was finally informed that the King and his government agreed to embark.

They had very little choice. At 9.30 p.m. that evening, several cars with the King, the members of the government and the ministers of France, Poland and the United Kingdom sped through Molde, heading for the port. The whole town was ablaze, and a German plane dropped an incendiary bomb that fell right behind the royal car. 'Well intended,' observed the King drily, 'but the execution seems to be lagging behind.'[90] The cars finally reached the port, where the cruiser *Glasgow* awaited them. The King and his companions, picking their way through the flames and smoke of the fiercely burning quay, between great spurts of water projected by the ship's hoses, managed to board *Glasgow* at 10.30 p.m.; they were followed by several wounded men from the base at Aalesund.* Shortly after

* And 23 tons of gold bullion.

midnight, the cruiser and her escort destroyer cast off, leaving behind them the town of Molde engulfed in a sea of flames.

Once safely out at sea, the King and his government met to decide on their destination. Leaving Norway was out of the question, but what point of the coast was to be chosen? Mosjøen? Bodø? Tromsø? 'The Government', noted Sir Cecil Dormer, 'were in favour of Mosjøen. [. . .] The King preferred Tromsø, [. . .] but was unwilling to insist; I [. . .] undertook to persuade the Government to acquiesce. I had no little difficulty, however, with Mr Koht, who insisted that by going as far north as Tromsø the Government would be cut off from the rest of Norway and would be accused by the people of running away. He was in a very nervous state of mind. I pointed out that it was no use going to a port which would be certain to be destroyed the following day, that Tromsø was as much part of Norway as anywhere south and that the Captain had to consider the safety of his charges. [. . .] But Mr Koht was past listening to me and burst from the ward room where our conversation was held, exclaiming: "You are killing us, you are killing us!" '[91]

What followed was described by Prime Minister Nygaardsvold in a report to parliament after the war: 'As there was still no consensus within the Government [. . .] it was finally decided to call a vote. The latter yielded a very slight majority in favour of Tromsø.[†] This was duly entered in the minutes of the session, together with the dissenting opinion of the minority. Once the decision had been formally adopted by a Royal Decree taken in Government Council, we proceeded to inform the Captain that the King and his government had decided to go to Tromsø . . . to which the Captain answered laconically that we could have spared ourselves all the trouble, since that was where he was going anyway. Indeed, he had received orders from his government to land us in a safe spot – Tromsø, in other words.'[92]

But even then, Prime Minister Nygaardsvold did not know the full story; for in fact, Captain Pegram, the officer commanding the cruiser *Glasgow*, had received no other instruction from His Majesty's Government than to set King Haakon and his government ashore at a place of their choosing. But while the members of the Norwegian government were still engaged in heated deliberations,

† Six votes to five.

Captain Pegram had received a visit from King Haakon. 'His Majesty', the Captain later reported to the Admiralty, 'privately told me that he wished to go to Tromsø, and that I might perhaps tell his government I was not prepared to take my ship elsewhere.'[93]

As the reader surely understands by now, King Haakon VII was definitely a force to be reckoned with.

# CHAPTER TEN

# Political Backlash

On 28 April, as Paul Reynaud awaited the speedy implementation of the 'decisions' taken the day before at the Supreme War Council, the atmosphere in Paris remained highly charged – as US Ambassador William Bullitt wrote to President Roosevelt that same day: 'Reynaud is violent on the subject of lack of brains in the British Government and the British High Command. Daladier [. . .] blames Reynaud as well as the British for not foreseeing the German riposte, and preparing adequately to meet it.' Of course, Reynaud also blamed Gamelin, who was supported by Daladier, who etc. . . . It was indeed a vicious circle, and Ambassador Bullitt added the following – hardly surprising – observation: 'Both Reynaud and Daladier expect defeat in Norway to produce most serious repercussions in France. Reynaud foresees his own fall and Daladier thinks that he as well as Reynaud will be completely discredited'.[1]

A defeat in Norway was therefore out of the question; now, evacuation would clearly be a defeat, so evacuation was entirely ruled out. At most, a small tactical retreat might be politically tolerable, but Paul Reynaud had made it perfectly clear at the Supreme War Council that he wanted the Allied expeditionary force to remain south of Trondheim and north of Namsos, in order to 'save face'. Not a man to underrate his powers of persuasion, he was now convinced that the British had accepted his strategy, and were doing their utmost to implement it.[2] That day, in fact, Paul Reynaud was even thinking that they might go one step further; for he had just received a visit from Captain de Brantes, Assistant Military Attaché in London, who was back from a quick trip to Namsos. The Captain reported that he had found there 'two good and undamaged quays', and that General Audet's morale was 'very high'. Late that night, Reynaud therefore sent for the British Ambassador to tell him the news, which in his opinion justified an even bolder strategy than that 'decided' upon at the Supreme War Council. 'Namsos', he stated, 'should be utilized for landing further troops and material.'[3]

Thus, more than 24 hours after the evacuation order had been sent to Namsos and Aandalsnes, Reynaud was still in the dark ... He was only to learn the 'news' another 16 hours later, in the afternoon of 29 April. 'I hear', Colonel de Villelume noted that evening, 'that only two hours after the Supreme War Council the day before yesterday, the British had sent out an order to evacuate not only Namsos, but also the area around Trondheim that Gamelin wanted held. [. . .] So they have openly flouted the decisions of the Supreme War Council.'[4]

'Openly' may not be quite the right word, but at any rate Reynaud immediately began mobilizing the whole apparatus of French diplomacy to try to get these orders rescinded. On 30 April, he wrote a personal letter to Chamberlain asking him to cancel the evacuation order 'in the name of friendship between our two peoples'.[5] In London, these pressures were supplemented by the timid efforts of Norwegian diplomacy. Naturally, the Norwegians knew even less than the French about British plans, and they were still expecting ... the naval attack on Trondheim! On 29 April, the Norwegian Minister in London, Eric Colban, showed Lord Halifax a message he had received from Foreign Minister Koht; the latter instructed Colban to insist that the order to withdraw British forces from the Romsdal be cancelled, since that withdrawal would cause the complete collapse of Norwegian resistance *if carried out before the liberation of Trondheim*[6] and before the situation had improved'.[7]

Pressures in the same sense were naturally being exerted on His Majesty's Government by Admiral of the Fleet Sir Roger Keyes, who was still asking – nay, demanding – to be put in charge of the naval assault against Trondheim ... the very same assault that had been jettisoned ten days earlier. On 29 April, Admiral Keyes sent Churchill his thirteenth letter in as many days, loudly deploring the 'shocking inaction of the Navy at Trondheim, for which you and your pusillanimous, self-satisfied, short-sighted naval advisers must bear responsibility'. The fourteenth letter duly arrived the next day, with both condemnations and exhortations: 'You told me that [. . .] there was no difficulty about forcing a way into Trondheimfjord. Why in Heaven's name then was it not done? It is not much use making plans, unless they are put into action in time to avert a disaster like the one at Steinkjer. [. . .] With Trondheim in our possession, we could have landed large forces, properly equipped with heavy guns, tanks, etc. and established a well defended base, and the enemy would not have been able to drive us out easily. There would then have been no question of our abandoning the Norwegians, as apparently we are about to do. [. . .] I have been busy all day seeing people, and have collected a great deal of support for my views, as to the immediate necessity for a smashing Naval blow at Trondheim – *whatever may happen later*. The French Ambassador gave me an interview this morning, agreed with me, and said he would pass my views on to Paris at once. [. . .] When am I going to be allowed to take a hand in the conduct of the Naval war?'[8]

Two days earlier – in his twelfth letter – Sir Roger had included the following unambiguous warning: 'If the scuttle is persisted in, the Government will have to go, and I shall do my damnedest to speed them.'[9] The time was not far off, and Sir Roger was to prove as good as his word . . . But in the meantime, the War Cabinet were abiding by their decision to evacuate all central Norway* – and, considering the situation on the spot, one could hardly hold it against them.

On 29 April, General Paget received a reply to his telegram of the day before, proposing to make a stand at Dombås provided he received air cover and artillery support; the reply, signed by General Massy, was short and definitive: 'Fighter support impossible. Essential you realize this and make best getaway possible.'[10] That, of course, was not as simple as it sounded: General Paget had promised to cover the retreat of Ruge's 4,000 men along the Romsdal, and to do that, he had to hold on to Dombås for at least 48 hours with his three battalions just withdrawn from Otta. After that, he would have to evacuate his men along a narrow valley, using a road dotted with craters and a railway cut in a dozen places, all that under a constant deluge of bombs and the permanent threat of attacks on his flanks and rear. Only after having escaped all these hazards would Paget's force reach the town of Aandalsnes, itself blazing fiercely and with hardly a building left intact.

* A concession was however made to General Gamelin, in agreeing to order an overland movement from Namsos to Mosjøen. But the War Office forgot to check whether such a movement was practicable before issuing the order to General Carton de Wiart.

That same day, Colonel Dudley Clarke, bearing instructions from General Ironside, once again landed at Aandalsnes in the midst of a fierce morning air raid. Having found his way to British base headquarters, he attended a conference between Brigadier Hogg, Lieutenant-Colonel Lewis* and Brigadier Morgan. 'It was apparent,' he reported, 'that there were difficulties in communication between Base Sub-Area and Advanced Force HQ, and Brig. Hogg seemed unaware of Gen. Paget's plans. He seemed to think that Gen. Paget's force might be unable to reach the base, and even feared a breakthrough by the enemy that day. He was therefore making his own evacuation plans independently. The following resulted from the Conference: (a) Embarkation from Molde was impractical, as most of the trawlers had been sunk and none of the ferry boats would face the crossing under air attack. There was therefore no means of getting troops to Molde. (b) In view of Brigadier Hogg's fear of a possible break-through as well as highly probable severing of the lines of communication, a message was sent to the War Office urging for embarkation to begin that night.'[11]

In the meantime, defensive positions against land attack on the town were to be set up and manned without delay – a daunting task: the last munitions depot had just blown up, the petroleum reserve was still smouldering,[12] and the road to Dombås, badly broken up, flooded, machine-gunned and littered with stranded vehicles, was almost unusable. But the good fortune that had so completely deserted the expeditionary force in its offensive operations began to smile persistently on its efforts at disengagement and re-embarkation. Between 29 April and 1 May, weather conditions gradually worsened, making German air attacks increasingly difficult;† moreover, despite the thousands of bombs rained on them every day, none of the cruisers and destroyers participating in the evacuation were sunk. Best of all, General Paget's 15th Brigade, supported by Norwegian ski troops and four artillery pieces sent up by General Ruge, managed to hold on to Dombås until the evening of 30 April.[13] At that stage, there was a genuine fraternity of arms between British and Norwegian troops; the latter, having made their way to the coast

* Chief of 'Primrose' detachment at Aalesund.
† These difficulties were no doubt much increased by British bombings of Fornebu, Stavanger and Aalborg airports on 29 April.

behind the defensive screen of the 15th Brigade, proceeded to assist General Paget's retreat with all available means.

For the next 48 hours, the gradual retreat towards Aandalsnes of 1,800 British and 300 Norwegian soldiers, by train, ski and on foot, represented a startling military exploit that threatened several times to turn into a complete catastrophe. But eventually, the force reached Aandalsnes in the evening of 1 May, and at 2 a.m. the next day, the last destroyer carried away the rearguard of what had been 'Sickle' Force.* The campaign in the Gudbrandsdal was over; it was a defeat, but not a disaster. In London, Neville Chamberlain was so relieved that he lost no time in informing the Commons of the successful evacuation.[14] That was a horrendous mistake, of course: further north, at Namsos, another re-embarkation was proceeding, on which the Germans, now alerted, would not fail to concentrate all their efforts.

At Namsos, General Carton de Wiart received the order of evacuation in the evening of 27 April, and communicated it to General Audet the following morning. Both commanders greeted the news with relief,[15] and the very few officers who deplored it[16] quickly realized that there was no alternative: that same day, heavy German bombing on the port of Namsos destroyed the greater part of the material they had received two days earlier. Between 28 April and 2 May, the British and French troops that had advanced towards Steinkjer during the last three days were gradually pulled back towards Namsos. The British fell back from Fjellbotn to Namdalseid, and the French from Lake Gilten to Berge and Klingen. Everywhere, rearguard detachments were left behind to conceal the retreat from the Germans . . . but also, alas, from the Norwegians.

General Carton de Wiart, for one, had taken quite seriously the War Office instructions not to inform the Norwegians of the evacuation. As a result, the Norwegian troops under Colonel Getz, deployed around Lake Snaasa in accordance with the attack plan agreed upon on 26 April, continued their advance towards Steinkjer, without suspecting that the Allied troops on their flank were being gradually thinned out, until they vanished entirely on the

---

* Since its landing on 24 April, 15th Brigade had lost 850 soldiers and 30 officers.

evening of 2 May. Colonel Getz was thus left alone in close proximity to the enemy, entirely unprotected and with a gaping right flank. He had indeed noticed a few puzzling movements by his allies, but they had told him that these were in connection with the naval attack on Agdenes fortress near Trondheim[17] – a successful deception no doubt, if deceiving one's ally can be rated a success in war.

As the British and French forces had almost entirely pulled back towards Namsos, the French commander received yet another order; as Major Stehlin later recalled: 'General Gamelin, who was conducting imaginary operations on a map back in Paris, had sent directly to General Audet an order to move part of our forces northwards, towards Mosjøen, with the apparent design of supporting operations at Narvik.'[18] That, of course, was a transparent effort to mitigate the political effects of the retreat, which the British War Cabinet had endorsed two days earlier in order to please the French. General Carton de Wiart therefore received an identical order, not without considerable surprise: 'I knew the road to be covered with deep snow and impassable for infantry, and I could see no point in the move. [. . .] I wired the War Office to that effect.'[19] General Audet and Major Stehlin entirely agreed, and let it be known in Paris as well.[20]

On 30 April, for the first time in a week, German forward detachments began to probe Allied positions near Namsos, while air attacks on the town intensified dramatically; that day, in Namsos harbour, the anti-aircraft sloop *Bittern* received a direct hit and sank. The port's anti-aircraft defences were woefully inadequate, as was the protection afforded on 1 May by a few fighters from the aircraft carrier *Ark Royal*.[21] The town of Namsos had been literally razed to the ground; amid the smouldering ruins, however, a second telegram arrived from General Gamelin, insisting on the movement to Mosjøen which both British and French officers considered utterly useless and impracticable.*[22] On top of it all, the British officers learned in the afternoon of 2 May that their Prime Minister had publicly announced the evacuation of Aandalsnes . . .[23]

In the end, despite innumerable difficulties, a flotilla of French and British ships arrived at Namsos on the evening of 2 May, and

---

* To please the General, a detachment was eventually sent to Mosjøen by sea.

performed the remarkable feat of embarking 4,200 men at night in less than four hours. The fleet then managed to slip away without being attacked inside the fjord. On 3 May, on the open sea, the Luftwaffe did strike a heavy blow, but too late to compromise the success of the evacuation.*

A few hours later, at 10.30 p.m. on the evening of 2 May, Colonel Getz – who was still expecting the naval assault on Trondheim[24] – received two messages signed by Generals Audet and Carton de Wiart. The two officers informed him that they were leaving, and they begged his forgiveness. Colonel Getz, a loyal and courageous officer, found himself abandoned with his troops north-east of Steinkjer, with the enemy deeply infiltrated on his right flank and rear. Nevertheless, he managed to extricate himself and make his way back to Namsos; in the ruins of the town, his soldiers found the smoking carcasses of a dozen trucks, several shattered anti-aircraft guns, a few crates of food and 300 rifles without ammunition. 'We are leaving a quantity of material here,' General Carton de Wiart had written to him, 'which I hope you can come and take, and know it will be of value to you and your gallant force.'[25]

On the evening of 3 May, Colonel Getz and his men, surrounded and short of ammunition, agreed to surrender. That same day, General Hvinden-Haug signed the capitulation of all Norwegian forces south of Trondheim.[26] Two days earlier, General Ruge, after considerable hesitation, had finally left Molde aboard a British destroyer to join the King and the government at Tromsø.[27] In central Norway, the combat thus ended for lack of combatants.

Ever since 9 April, the press, the BBC and the official communiqués had been presenting the slightest initiative by British forces in Norway as a magnificent feat of arms that could not fail to hasten the victorious outcome of the campaign.[28] Each naval operation, each landing of troops, every arrival of senior officers in Norway was the subject of lengthy discussion on the radio or in the press, with excellent effects on the morale of the population – and disastrous consequences for the security of operations. But as victories became scarce and setbacks began accumulating, the members of His Majesty's Government grew increasingly worried by the political

---

* The destroyers *Bison* and *Afridi* were sunk, and more than 250 men lost.

consequences of a sudden disillusionment of public opinion. On 22 April, already, Oliver Stanley was telling his colleagues that 'reports which had appeared in the press [. . .] gave the impression that the Allies were sweeping victoriously forward after successful landings in considerable strength at a number of places in Norway. Unless the press could be persuaded to alter their tone, the public might suffer a severe shock if things went badly in Namsos.'[29] Four days later, Chamberlain was warning his ministers that 'to admit failure in Norway would be a serious blow to the Government's prestige'.[30] That such loss of prestige might adversely affect the existence of Mr Chamberlain's government was clearly implied. In fact, it will be recalled that at exactly that time, General Carton de Wiart had been asked to refrain from evacuating his troops and to remain at Namsos 'for political reasons'.

After 26 April, however, the issue of evacuation had to be faced squarely, and Chamberlain warned his colleagues that 'a severe reaction' of public opinion might be expected.[31] From then on, the fear of imminent censure by public opinion, press and opposition clearly dominated the debates of the War Cabinet. On 29 April, Chamberlain for once mentioned the plight of the Norwegians, only to comment that 'it was obviously undesirable, on political grounds, that they should manoeuvre us into the position of appearing to desert them.' The next day, it was likewise mentioned at the War Cabinet that the Ministry of Information was 'steadily preparing' public opinion for the possibility of a defeat. Chamberlain told his colleagues with obvious relief that he 'had seen the leaders of the opposition, and they had made no criticism of the Government's action'.[32]

That was probably out of courtesy; but the rumblings of public discontent were already clearly perceptible, and on 29 April, a deputation from the Watching Committee of Peers and Members of Parliament, led by Lord Salisbury, formally protested to Lord Halifax about the 'want of initiative shown by the Government' in its war policy.[33] The next day, Harold Nicolson, an MP and member of the Committee, wrote in his diary: 'The general impression is that we may lose the war.'[34]

It was indeed. Details of the setbacks suffered in Norway during the last ten days were becoming known throughout the country, and rumours were rife concerning the woeful inadequacies in the organization and equipment of the expeditionary force.[35] Moreover, on 30 April, the news of the evacuation that had barely begun at Namsos and Aandalsnes was already known 'to scores of people'. Worse still, it appeared that the indiscretion had come 'from a person in authority'![36] This could only aggravate the general dissatisfaction, and that same day Conservative MP Sir Henry Channon noted that 'in the House, there is more talk of a cabal against poor Neville. "They" are saying that it is 1915 over again.'[37] The next day, Harold Nicolson found a similar mood in the House of Lords; on 2 May, Channon, an old friend of the Prime Minister, was 'beginning reluctantly to realize that Neville's days are, after all, numbered'.[39] On 3 May, General Ironside also heard that 'there is a first-class row commencing in the House.' and that 'there is a strong movement to get rid of the PM.'[41]

The Government were of course fully aware of the 'mounting tide of opinion against them'.[42] At War Cabinet meetings in the first days of May, more and more time was spent shoring up the Government's defences against the gathering storm in Parliament. Naturally, the capture of Narvik could still save the day, and ever since the end of April, discreet pressure in that sense had been exerted on Lord Cork and his staff.[43] Unfortunately, the German defenders of Narvik, displaying little interest in the political survival of Mr Chamberlain's government, obstinately refused to surrender. Besides, British officers on the spot were unanimous in their opinion that an immediate attack was out of the question.[44]

Something else obviously had to be found. On 1 May, the Prime Minister, in an effort to disarm his critics, announced some changes in the organization of defence; Winston Churchill, who already chaired the meetings of the Military Co-ordination Committee in the absence of the Prime Minister, would now also be responsible 'on behalf of the Committee' for giving 'guidance and direction to the Chiefs of Staff Committee'.[45] But most government critics dismissed the arrangement as purely cosmetic; for one thing, it was clear that the 'guidance and direction' given to the Chiefs of Staff Committee were to be those of the Military Co-ordination Committee and of the War Cabinet, with Churchill merely acting as their spokesman. Moreover, everyone knew that Chamberlain tended to put Churchill forward every time he was accused of conducting the war with insufficient vigour.[46] The next day, Chamberlain, grasping yet another opportunity, proudly announced the success of the Aandalsnes evacuation – a dangerous blunder that did nothing to appease the MPs, to say nothing of the military. The rest of his speech did not go down well either, as Harold Nicolson – a firm supporter of the Prime Minister – could not help remarking that day: 'I find that there is grave suspicion of the Prime Minister. His speech about the Norwegian expedition has created disquiet. The House knows very well that it was a major defeat. But the PM said that "the balance of advantage rested with us" and that "Germany has not attained her objective". They know that this is simply not true. If Chamberlain believed it himself, then he was stupid. If he did not believe it, then he was trying to deceive. In either case he loses confidence.'[47] The press was even less indulgent, with the *Manchester Guardian* seeing in the Prime Minister's 'capacity for self-delusion' nothing less than a national peril.[48]

In his speech of 4 May, Chamberlain had promised a parliamentary debate on Norway for 7 May. In the meantime, of course, new arguments would have to be found for the defence of the Government – all the more so as the soldiers, sailors and airmen were coming back from Norway, and had many a tale to tell their families . . . and their MPs. Mr Chamberlain was not the last to rehearse his own defence, as his personal archive bears witness; it contains among others the following unsigned 'Note on Intelligence', dated 6 May: 'If necessary it could be said that we had believed that it would be possible to forestall the Germans in the Norwegian ports, but their treacherous action in advance of hostilities prevented this.'[49] That was a reference to the largely mythical 'Trojan horse' story of an all-powerful German Fifth Column in Norway before the invasion – a favourite theme of the British press since 9 April; the argument of Quisling's treason was also to be used as justification.[50] After all, faced with an enemy using such dishonest means, could one really wonder that a British government composed of such decent men had been so thoroughly taken by surprise? The argument was actually used in the course of several 'exploratory' talks with members of the Opposition after 4 May, and found to be perfectly serviceable. Whether it would prove sufficient was of course a different matter.

In the midst of this highly charged atmosphere stepped Norwegian Foreign Minister Halvdan Koht and Defence Minister Ljungberg. They had been asked by their government to try to learn something of British strategic intentions in Norway – a mission that seemed far from useless, since their government had only learned the day before – 4 May – that the naval attack on Trondheim had been cancelled![51] But both Koht and Ljungberg quickly found out that, in London, strategy was being largely eclipsed by politics. The Norwegian Foreign Minister, who had a brief talk with Mr Chamberlain in the afternoon of 6 May, found him uncommunicative, ill-at-ease and very defensive.[52] 'When I pointed out', Koht later recalled, 'that there had been a certain lack of communication between the Norwegian and Allied High Commands, he immediately interjected: "That was not our fault!" I merely replied that I had no wish to complain, and that I was aware that it took two to co-operate.'[53] Koht came back from the interview somewhat perplexed, but a glance at the calendar would have been enough to understand Mr Chamberlain's nervousness: the great debate in the Commons on the Norwegian Affair – and on Chamberlain's whole war policy – was to begin the next day.

The parliamentary session of 7 May opened in an atmosphere of great uncertainty: the Government would of course have to justify their actions, inactions, procrastination and unpreparedness, without revealing anything that could be of use to the enemy. In addition, they knew that they would have to face much more than their usual parliamentary opposition: many members of the Conservative Party were also expected to denounce the Government's policy, though their exact number remained unknown. Finally, as if all that were not enough, the Government had been receiving for the last eight days increasingly detailed and urgent warnings of an imminent German attack in Belgium and the Netherlands.

The Opposition were naturally preparing to pronounce a merciless indictment of the Prime Minister's whole war policy. Yet everyone in the Liberal and Labour Parties knew that the Conservatives held a solid majority in the Commons; there was therefore no question of replacing the Government with a Labour administration. The best they could hope for was the resignation of the Prime Minister, which would pave the way for the formation of a coalition Cabinet. But the new Prime Minister could only be a member of the very administration they were about to denounce: Lord Halifax, or perhaps Winston Churchill . . .[54] Much tact was thus called for in the indictment of the Government – especially since no one could foresee the reaction of the Conservative majority. But for the next two days, transcending political cleavages and personal sympathies, the hideous spectre of imminent defeat was to haunt every conscience, dominate every debate, and create an atmosphere at once exceptionally strained and intensely emotional.

As soon as Chamberlain entered the House, he was greeted with shouts of 'Who missed the bus?' - an irreverent allusion to his unfortunate words of 4 April. The Prime Minister, who seemed both tired and embarrassed, began his speech with a tribute to the troops, who 'carried out their task with magnificent gallantry'; after which, in a somewhat halting voice, he undertook to make more palatable the decidedly bleak events of the last three weeks:

'I hope that we shall not exaggerate the extent or the importance of the check we have received. The withdrawal from Southern Norway is not comparable to the withdrawal from Gallipoli. [. . .] There were no large forces involved. Not much more than a single division. [. . .] The German strike was made easy by treachery from inside Norway and had been prepared long beforehand by the concealment of troops and materials in apparently innocent-looking ships [. . .] The campaign is not yet finished . . .'[55]

*Interruptions:* 'Hitler missed the bus!'

'While I think the implications of the Norwegian campaign have been seriously exaggerated . . .'

*Interruptions:* 'Who missed the bus?'

'. . . and while I retain my complete confidence in an ultimate victory, I do not think that the people of this country yet realize the extent or the imminence of the threat which is impending against us . . .'

*An Honourable Member:* 'We said that five years ago!'

'For my part I try to steer a middle course . . .'

*Interruptions*

'Neither raising undue expectations . . .'

*Interruptions:* 'Hitler missed the bus!'

'. . . A great many times, some Honourable Members have repeated the phrase "Hitler missed the bus". . .'

*Interruption:* 'You said it!'[56]

Chamberlain struggled on, ending with an appeal to close ranks that fell on stony ground. 'The very crowded House', wrote Sir Henry Channon, 'was restive and bored, and the Egyptian Ambassador even slept. The Prime Minister sat down at last.'[57] Lloyd George and Herbert Morrison asked a few questions, after which Clement Attlee took the floor; the Labour Party leader had little gift for oratory, yet no one could miss the pertinence of his arguments – except perhaps the Egyptian Ambassador:

> The evacuation was a wonderful feat of arms, but after all, it is a retirement. It does represent a setback. [. . .] High hopes were raised. [. . .] We are paying the penalty now, because after great expectations, there is necessarily disappointment. It is no good trying to minimise the event. [. . .] We were informed on 19th March that we had a force of 100,000 men ready to go to Finland. [. . .] What I cannot understand is the rapid disposal of all these troops. [. . .] I have heard stories of some boys being sent to Norway, quite young and having very little training. [. . .] I want to know whether the right kind of troops were sent. [. . .] I ask whether at any time, there was not delay and discussion where action was necessary? [. . .] I am not in the least satisfied [. . .] that the present War Cabinet is an efficient instrument for conducting the war. [. . .] Norway comes at the culmination of many other discontents [. . .] In a life and death struggle, we cannot afford to leave our destinies in the hands of failures or men who need a rest.[58]

This merciless indictment was closely followed by that of the Liberal leader, Sir Archibald Sinclair: 'In the field of propaganda [. . .] economically, above all diplomatically, and to a lesser extent militarily we have suffered a grave reverse.'[59] Brushing aside the argument of the Norwegian army's shortcomings,[60] Sinclair went on to enumerate some of the most glaring deficiencies in the armament, supplying and overall command of the British troops. The scandal of the loading and unloading of ships, the lack of air cover, the pitiful state of the very few anti-aircraft guns available at Namsos and Aandalsnes, the complete absence of skis and snowshoes, the troops' lack of training[61] – all were reviewed until Sinclair concluded that 'this breakdown in organization occurred because there had been no foresight in the political direction of the war.'[62]

187

When the Liberal leader sat down, the applause was not limited to Opposition benches; but curiously enough, Sinclair's eloquence was not the sort that could turn the tide of opinion and carry the House – neither was Attlee's, of course. Several Tory Members then rose to defend the Government, but they appeared inexperienced, unconvinced, and thus utterly unconvincing. However, the Honourable Members were soon jolted out of their torpor by the appearance of Sir Roger Keyes, dressed in full uniform of Admiral of the Fleet with six rows of medals. This imposing appearance, added to the profound conviction of the hero of Zeebrugge – and his most unparliamentary language – cast a spell on the House. The story he had to tell may sound familiar to us, but most Members of the House were hearing it for the first time, and the effect was devastating. 'The capture of Trondheim', assured Sir Roger, 'was essential, imperative and vital. Ever since April 15th, I have been urging the Admiralty to take more vigorous naval action.'[63] Admiral Keyes – a long-time Conservative – went on to detail his fruitless attempts to obtain command of the naval attack on Trondheim, the repeated rebuffs he had met with, the real causes of the disaster at Steinkjer, the hesitations of the War Cabinet, and ultimately the abandonment of any offensive project. 'A shocking story of ineptitude,' he roared. 'The Gallipoli tragedy has been followed step by step.'[64]

A great many MPs were to remark on the impression produced by that intervention. 'The House', noted Harold Nicolson, 'listens in breathless silence. It is by far the most dramatic speech I have ever heard, and when Keyes sits down, there is thunderous applause.'[65] For Harold Macmillan, likewise, 'Whether the decision not to force our way in Trondheimfjord was right or wrong, this speech revealed what Members already suspected – an alarming absence of fixity of purpose and of co-operation within the Services'.[66]

Admiral Keyes's diatribe had clearly shaken the House; but then, Harold Macmillan himself had created quite a stir in that same assembly after the Finnish Affair, without seriously affecting the Prime Minister's position. Yet another attack, coming on top of the breach opened by Admiral Keyes, was to seal the fate of the Government; this time again, it came from a Conservative Member: Leopold Amery.

A former cabinet minister, a friend and colleague of both Austin and Neville Chamberlain, Leo Amery had held a Birmingham seat for over 25 years, and commanded great respect in the House. As a Privy Councillor, he had the right to be heard on the first day, but the exact moment remained at the Speaker's discretion. 'This time,' Amery recalled, 'I knew that what I had to say mattered and, what was more, I was desperately anxious that it should have its intended effect. So I followed impatiently the alternation between speakers who declared that all was well with the best of governments which had just won a successful campaign and those who dwelt on the military disaster which was the natural climax of years of incompetence.'[67]

But time passed, the Honourable Members gradually drifted out for dinner, and by the time Amery's name was called, there were only about a dozen members left. 'I nearly decided to leave the reasoned criticism of the Government to another day and speak for a few minutes at most. But Clem Davies, who had come up behind me after I had risen, murmured in my ear that I must at all costs state the whole case against the Government, and went off to collect an audience from the Smoking Room and Library. By the time I had made a few comments on the preceding speeches I had at any rate the makings of a House. So I proceeded at once to the direct attack.'[68]

That was hardly an overstatement; for more than an hour, only a few feet away from the government benches, Amery delivered a devastating indictment of Chamberlain's whole war policy: 'The Prime Minister gave us a reasoned, argumentative case for our failure. It is always possible to do that after every failure. [. . .] Wars are won, not by explanation after the event, but by foresight, by clear decision and by swift action. I confess that I did not feel that there was one sentence in the Prime Minister's speech this afternoon which suggested that the Government either foresaw what Germany meant to do, or came to a clear decision when it knew what Germany had done, or acted swiftly or consistently throughout the whole of this lamentable affair. [. . .] I am not going to discuss the reasons for the actual evacuation. They may well have been conclusive in the actual circumstances. But the circumstances should never have arisen, and it is the story of these events – of the decisions, of the absence of decisions, of the change of decisions which brought about these circumstances [. . .] which call for our enquiry.'[69]

Whereupon Amery fired a long salvo of questions at the government benches. Why were the warnings from Stockholm and Copen-hagen at the beginning of April not taken seriously? Why were such inadequate forces sent to Norway, without proper equipment and without transport? Why and by whom was the 'Hammer' blow at Trondheim countermanded? 'What we have lost', Amery went on, 'is one of those opportunities which do not recur in war. If we could have captured and held Trondheim, and if we could have rallied the Norwegian forces, then we might well have imposed a strain on Ger-many which might have made Norway to Hitler what Spain once was to Napoleon.'

'By then', Amery later recalled, 'I had got a keenly attentive House. What was more important, the murmurs of approval and the open applause were coming more and more from the Conservative benches which were filling round me.'[70] Obviously encouraged, Amery continued: 'We cannot go on as we are. There must be a change. First and foremost, it must be a change in the system and structure of our governmental machine. This is war, not peace. [. . .] Just as our peace-time system is unsuitable for war conditions, so does it tend to breed peace-time statesmen who are not too well fitted for the conduct of war. Facility in debate, ability to state a case, caution in advancing an unpopular view, compromise and procras-tination are the natural qualities [. . .] of a political leader in times of peace. They are fatal qualities in war.[71] [. . .] Somehow or other we must get into the Government men who can match our enemies in fighting spirit, in daring, in resolution and in thirst for victory.'

At this point, Amery quoted a passage from Cromwell's statement to John Hampden: 'You must get men of spirit that are likely to go as far as they will go, or you will be beaten still. It may not be easy to find these men. They can be found only by trial and by ruthlessly dis-carding all who fail and have their failings discovered.'[72] But this had reminded Amery of even more powerful words by Cromwell, which he hesitated to quote until he 'felt himself swept forward' by the mood of the House:[73] 'I have quoted certain words of Oliver Cromwell, I will quote certain other words. [. . .] This is what Crom-well said to the Long Parliament when he thought it was no longer fit to conduct the affairs of the nation: "You have sat too long here for any good you have been doing. Depart, I say, and let us have done with you. In the name of God, go!" '[74]

The effect produced on the House was tremendous: 'A terrific attack,' wrote Harold Nicolson;[75] 'terrible words', according to Winston Churchill;[76] and for Harold Macmillan: 'By the speech he was to make on this day, he effectively destroyed the Chamberlain Government. This is no exaggeration.'[77] Probably not, but it is clearly an anticipation; the debate went on until late that evening, and was resumed the next day. Sharp, merciless attacks were launched on the Government from Tory, Labour and Liberal benches. On the morning of 8 May, Herbert Morrison, in the name of the Labour Opposition, asked for a vote of confidence to be held at the end of the day's debate.[78] At these words, Neville Chamberlain immediately rose to speak: 'I say to my friends in the House – and I have friends in the House ...: I accept the challenge. I welcome it indeed. At least we shall see who is with us and who is against us, and I call on my friends to support us in the lobby tonight.'[79]

A most unfortunate statement, which caused consternation even on government benches; the Prime Minister appeared to be treating as a simple party matter – and even a matter of loyalty to his person – what had evidently become a life-and-death issue for the whole nation. Chamberlain's *faux pas* was promptly exploited by the Opposition, beginning with the old Liberal leader Lloyd George, who was to produce his last major speech in the House on that occasion: 'He said: "I have got my friends". It is not a question of who are the Prime Minister's friends. It is a far bigger issue. The Prime Minister must remember that he has met this formidable foe of ours in peace and in war. He has always been worsted. [. . .] He has appealed for sacrifice. The nation is prepared for every sacrifice so long as it has leadership, so long as the Government show clearly what they are aiming at and so long as the nation is confident that those who are leading it are doing their best. I say solemnly that the Prime Minister should give an example of sacrifice, because there is nothing which can contribute more to victory in this war than that he should sacrifice the seals of office.'[80]

One after the other, Sir Stafford Cripps, Duff Cooper, Commander Bower and A. V. Alexander rose to stress the incongruity of Mr Chamberlain's last words.[81] Many young Conservatives in uniform recited the endless list of insufficiencies and blunders pervading the Norwegian expedition, and, like Duff Cooper himself, made it clear that they would vote against the Government that evening.[82] For all that, the Prime Minister's political opponents were now distinctly uneasy: they naturally wanted to see Chamberlain go, but Churchill alone seemed able to see England through the mortal perils that were now threatening; there was therefore no question of sacrificing him in the process as well. Yet here was Churchill sitting on the government bench, in full solidarity with his colleagues, and scheduled to close the debate that evening as spokesman for an utterly discredited administration. 'We were determined to bring down the Government,' wrote Harold Macmillan, 'and as every hour passed, we seemed more likely to achieve our purpose. But how could Churchill be disentangled from the ruins? If the chief issue of the first day had been the overthrow of the Government, the chief anxiety of the second was the rescue of Churchill.'[83]

Actually, many of the speakers had already been preparing that rescue since the day before; concentrating their attacks on the Prime Minister and the Government's defence policy since 1935 – a perilous exercise for the Labour Members – they repeatedly drew a sharp distinction between Churchill and his government colleagues. Thus, on 7 May, Admiral Keyes, in the midst of a devastating indictment of the Admiralty, made the following startling mention of its First Lord: 'I am longing to see proper mention made of his great abilities. I cannot believe it will be done under the existing system.' Likewise, Herbert Morrison elicited from the Prime Minister an admission that Churchill's new powers of direction over the Chiefs of Staff were too recent to give him any special responsibility in the Norwegian fiasco.[84]

The next day, the same phenomenon recurred with amazing regularity; Commander Bower reminded the House of Churchill's past attacks against the Chamberlain government; A. V. Alexander, after a ringing denunciation of both the War Office and the Air Ministry, had nothing but praise for the First Lord of the Admiralty.[85] Duff Cooper was even more explicit: 'Tonight, we shall no doubt listen to an eloquent and powerful speech by the First Lord. [. . .] He will be defending with his eloquence those who long refused to listen to his counsel, who treated his warnings with contempt. He will, no doubt, be as successful as he has always been, and those who so often trembled before his sword will be only too glad to shrink behind his buckler.'[86]

Lloyd George followed their example, and pronounced a few memorable words in the process: 'Everybody knows that whatever

Admiral of the Fleet Sir Roger
Keyes: 'If the scuttle is persisted in,
the Government will have to go,
and I shall do my damnedest to
speed them.'

Naval commander at Narvik Lord
Cork and Orrery: 'Short man, great
sailor, resolutely offensive spirit.'

General Bethouart: 'Graduate of
St Cyr military school, an expert on
mountain warfare by training . . .
and a diplomat by necessity.'

General Dietl: 'Führer's companion
from the "heroic times" of Munich,
and brilliant defensive strategist.'

Norwegian Commander-in-Chief
General Otto Ruge: 'An erect, spare
figure with keen, blue eyes. A
kindly, friendly man with something of the appearance of a Master
of Foxhounds.'

was done was done half-heartedly, ineffectively, without drive and unintelligently. [. . .] Is anyone here satisfied with the steps we took to train our army? Nobody is satisfied. The whole world knows that. And here we are in the worst strategic position in which this country has ever been placed. [. . .] I do not think that the First Lord was entirely responsible for all the things that happened there.'

> Winston Churchill: 'I take complete responsibility for everything that has been done by the Admiralty, and I take my share of the burden.'
> Lloyd George: 'The Right Honourable Gentleman must not allow himself to be converted into an air-raid shelter to keep the splinters from hitting his colleagues.'[87]

From all sides of the House, the Honourable Members themselves were thus doing their very best to shield Churchill from the broadsides aimed at the government. As a result, when Churchill finally rose to speak that evening, he found himself in the delicate situation of having to defend his former opponents who were now his government colleagues, against opponents of the Government who happened to be his partisans – and probably his future colleagues as well. The First Lord of the Admiralty therefore sought to avoid controversy by dwelling on the considerable difficulties of the Norwegian campaign, and appealing for unity in the prosecution of the war: 'Let pre-war feuds die; let personal quarrels be forgotten; let us keep our hatreds for the common enemy.'[88]

The vote that followed was clearly of decisive importance: 'It was the whole future of Britain and the Empire which was at stake,' wrote Harold Macmillan.[89] Though apparently the Government won, the result was in reality a stinging defeat for Chamberlain: 281 had voted for the Government, 200 against – and that included 33 Tories, while 60 more had abstained.[90] Never since his assumption of power in 1937 had the Prime Minister found himself with such a tenuous majority. 'There was no doubt', wrote Churchill, 'that in effect, though not in form, both the Debate and the Division were a violent manifestation of want of confidence in Mr Chamberlain and his Administration. After the Debate was over he asked me to go to his room, and I saw at once that he took the most serious view of the sentiment of the House towards himself. He felt that he could not go on. There ought to be a National Government. One Party alone could not carry the burden. Someone must form a Government in which all Parties would serve, or we could not get through.' With his usual pugnacity, Churchill would not admit defeat, and sought to persuade the Prime Minister to carry on. 'But Chamberlain was neither convinced nor comforted, and I left him about midnight with the feeling that he would persist in his resolve to sacrifice himself if there was no other way, rather than attempt to carry the war further with a one-party Government.'[91]

Actually, Chamberlain was hesitating, and he changed his mind several times. During the whole morning of 9 May, rumours were rife in the corridors of the House, in the clubs and at party headquarters. Would Chamberlain step down? Who would succeed him? It was being whispered that the Labour Party preferred Halifax*[92] . . . So did Chamberlain, of course. One thing at least seemed certain: a coalition government had to be formed. Chamberlain had just consulted Clement Attlee and Arthur Greenwood, to find out whether they would agree to join a government of which he remained Prime Minister. They had replied that they would submit the question to their Party Congress assembled in Bournemouth, but had also added that in their opinion, the answer would almost certainly be negative.[93]

That afternoon, Chamberlain invited both Churchill and Halifax to Downing Street. 'We took our seats at the table opposite Mr Chamberlain,' Churchill recalled. 'He told us that he was satisfied that it was beyond his power to form a National Government. The response he had received from the Labour leaders left him in no doubt of this. The question therefore was whom he should advise the King to send for after his own resignation had been accepted. His demeanour was cool, unruffled, and seemingly quite detached from the personal aspect of the affair. He looked at us both across the table.'[94]

Actually, it was clear that Chamberlain would have preferred to see Halifax succeed him. He admitted as much in a letter to his sister two days later,[95] and for the moment he went so far as to say that

---

* That was correct, but they could see no one other than Churchill to 'win the war', and appeared to view him rather in the role of a Minister of Defence.

Halifax 'was the man mentioned as the most acceptable'.[96] But Churchill had been duly prepared for this interview by Anthony Eden and by an old friend of the Prime Minister, Sir Kingsley Wood; the latter had indeed warned Churchill that Chamberlain 'would want Halifax to succeed him and would want Churchill to agree'. Kingsley Wood's advice: 'Don't agree, and don't say anything.'[97]

Winston Churchill followed that advice to the letter: 'Usually, I talk a great deal, but on this occasion I was silent. [. . .] A very long pause ensued. [. . .] Then at length Halifax spoke. He said that he felt that his position as a Peer, out of the House of Commons, would make it very difficult for him to discharge the duties of a Prime Minister in a war like this. He would be held responsible for everything, but would not have the power to guide the Assembly upon whose confidence the life of every government depended. He spoke for some minutes in this sense, and by the time he had finished it was clear that the duty would fall upon me – had in fact fallen upon me.'[98]

That was not yet certain, for on the following morning the news exploded like a bombshell: Hitler had attacked Belgium and the Netherlands. Upon hearing this, Neville Chamberlain changed his mind once again, and decided to remain at his post.[99] Kingsley Wood stepped in once again to persuade the Prime Minister that this fresh crisis made the formation of a government of national unity all the more necessary. Chamberlain eventually relented, and that evening at 6 p.m., Winston Churchill was invited to Buckingham Palace, where the King asked him to form the new Government. On his way back from the Palace, he confided to his bodyguard, Inspector Thompson: 'I hope that it is not too late. I am very much afraid that it is. We can only do our best.'[100]

# CHAPTER ELEVEN

# Checkmate

On 10 May, Halvdan Koht had received solemn assurances from Lord Halifax that the German offensive in the West would not affect Britain's resolve to pursue operations in northern Norway.[1] For once, this was nothing but the truth: the new British Prime Minister firmly intended to bring the siege of Narvik to a victorious conclusion, and then use the town as a springboard for further operations southwards – and probably eastwards as well.

At Narvik, the situation had not evolved appreciably since 24 April. But this time, the Allies had reason to be optimistic, for they had at Narvik everything they had lacked at Namsos and Aandalsnes: overwhelming numerical superiority, with a total force amounting to 30,000 men,* opposed to General Dietl's 4,000 soldiers and sailors dug in, in and around Narvik; an adequate anti-aircraft defence, with 48 heavy guns and 60 light ones;[2] an increasingly efficient air support, pitted against German planes that found themselves at the extreme limit of their operational capacity; the landing in early May of the long-awaited tanks and landing craft; the thaw, which made progress on land somewhat easier; and of course General Béthouart, whose arrival at long last put an end to the paralysis affecting the British High Command at Harstad.

General Antoine Marie Béthouart, a graduate of the French Military Academy at Saint-Cyr, had always displayed a keen interest in mountain warfare. A military adviser in Finland during the First World War, then a Military Attaché in Yugoslavia, he had achieved his life's ambition upon being given command of the 5th Half-Brigade of Chasseurs Alpins stationed at Bellay. Appointed in January 1940 to command the abortive Petsamo expedition, he had finally

---

* In addition to the British forces, there were now four battalions of Chasseurs Alpins, four Polish battalions and two battalions of the Foreign Legion.

landed at Namsos in April, under the command of General Audet. As is known, there was precious little to be done there, and even before his troops had been evacuated, Béthouart was ordered to leave for Harstad, where he duly landed on the morning of 28 April.

At his very first meeting with the two British commanders, General Béthouart realized the complete incompatibility of their strategic conceptions. Lord Cork, relying on the power of the fleet, wanted to stage a landing as close as possible to the town of Narvik; but General Mackesy, still haunted by the prospect of an 'Arctic Gallipoli', prepared an enveloping – and necessarily quite slow – movement from Salangen in the north, Bogen in the west and Ballangen in the south. For General Béthouart, this was hardly an attractive strategy: it would compel his mountain troops to cover some fifty miles of rugged mountain terrain in the melting snow before reaching the outer defence perimeter of Narvik. Besides, owing to the somewhat haphazard conditions of embarkation in France, his men had no mountain shoes, no boots, and no snow goggles.

Yet General Béthouart, having reconnoitred the sea approaches to Narvik with Lord Cork, was not in favour of an immediate landing at Narvik either. He deemed it preferable to start with the occupation of the Øyord Peninsula, which could then be used as a springboard for the final assault on Narvik. The attack against the main objectives of the peninsula, Bjerkvik, Meby and Øjord, would of course have to be made both by land and by sea, but General Mackesy was very reluctant to contemplate a naval assault. Luckily, the Norwegian ski troops of General Fleischer's 6th Division succeeded in chasing the Germans out of Gratangen, thus shortening the land approach to Øyord Peninsula by more than 35 miles.

By 4 May, General Mackesy still would not hear of a naval assault on Bjerkvik; but his resistance was considerably weakened when Lord Cork, with the backing of both the Government and the Admiralty, proceeded to demand an immediate landing at Narvik itself! To Mackesy, of course, a landing at Bjerkvik and the Øyord Peninsula no doubt appeared far safer. After 48 hours of negotiations and wires to and from London, the matter was finally resolved: Lord Cork was allowed to defer the direct attack on Narvik, and to put General Béthouart in charge of a combined assault on Bjerkvik.

'General Fleischer', Béthouart recalled, 'was furious at the

British, with whom he had had no liaison for the past three weeks.'[3] But General Béthouart, for one, fully realized the value of General Fleischer's co-operation for the success of his plans, and agreement on a common strategy was quickly reached: operating from Gratangen and Foldvik, the Norwegian ski troops on the left flank and the French Chasseurs Alpins on the right would converge on the northern approaches to Bjerkvik. General Bohucz-Szysko's Polish brigade, with its rear base at Bogen, would attack Bjerkvik from the west. Finally, the naval landing would be carried out by the 13th Half-Brigade of the Foreign Legion, with massive support from British naval artillery. By launching all these attacks simultaneously, it was hoped to catch the German defenders by surprise and wipe them out with the least possible delay. There was another interesting feature about the action: it was to be the first attack effectively carried out by the Allies since the beginning of the campaign.

On 12 May, shortly before midnight, a formidable armada approached the little port of Bjerkvik: three destroyers, four armoured landing craft containing 120 men each, then the ironclad *Resolution* and the two cruisers *Effingham* and *Vindictive*, escorted by five other destroyers. The sun shone almost as in broad daylight, and General Béthouart, aboard *Effingham*, prepared to direct the landing operations: 'I was standing on the command bridge with Lord Cork, who introduced the gunnery officer, placed him at my disposal, and added: "You will command the fire." [. . .] A study of aerial photographs and observations made during our reconnaissance of 8 May had allowed us to determine the main objectives to hit in order to cover the landing, and then assist the troops on shore. The ground was white with snow. Nothing moved. The Germans had probably taken cover in the houses along the beach. I had received assurances from General Fleischer that the civilian population had been evacuated. The tanks were lowered on the landing craft with cranes, but the operation was slow and difficult. I told the gunnery officer to prepare to concentrate his fire on the closest objectives, the most dangerous for the landing. I followed the progress of the landing craft; I felt that the time had come and, my heart beating a bit faster, I shouted the fateful words: "Fire!" The scorching blast of the heavy pieces firing at our feet lashed our faces and tore the cigarettes from our mouths. There was a deafening roar. Several houses caught fire immediately, then the church blew up and burned; it had been used as a munitions depot. Another house containing a supply of flares was hit by a shell, triggering a terrific firework display. It all built up into a huge furnace that splashed with red the snow of the surrounding mountains.'4

From the command bridge of the second cruiser, Captain of the Foreign Legion Pierre-Olivier Lapie also witnessed the shelling: 'An extraordinary sight that smacked of scene-shifting and film-staging: "Give me 30 yards of shelling, please!" Some houses were burning. An ammunition dump exploded. Flames were shooting up. [. . .] After an hour of shelling, there was a sudden silence, and the sea near the beach appeared dotted with small black craft, loaded with men. The first battalion was heading for shore to spearhead the attack on Bjerkvik.'5 But the German mountain troops of the Windisch Group were solidly entrenched, and from three sides, they raked the beach with murderous machine-gun fire. 'Following my recommendations,' wrote General Béthouart, 'the officer commanding the first echelon did not insist, and proceeded to seek a less exposed landing place. The whole group veered left, found a creek sheltered behind a promontory, and rushed to land. Two heavy machine-guns were in their way, but the Germans manning them had fled. The second echelon followed, and soon I could see the whole line of Foreign Legionnaires deploying on the snow for a flank attack on Bjerkvik, supported by tanks.'6

Among these men was Corporal of the Foreign Legion Charles Favrel. 'Then the assault began,' he recalled, 'and a frightful butchery ensued, in the course of which we slaughtered more civilians than Germans. Machine-guns riddled the doors and windows with their cross-fire, then the infantrymen rushed forward hurling grenades, and entered the houses left untouched by the conflagration. [. . .] With rifle in hand, I was to scour a dreadful calvary strewn with mangled corpses, cradles overturned on dead babies, and the wounded moaning in pools of blood.'7 General Fleischer's information was thus incorrect: the civilian population of Bjerkvik had not been evacuated . . . But the assault went on, punctuated by the distant echo of cannon fire to the north: the Chasseurs Alpins and the Norwegians from Gratangen were attacking the enemy rear. The Austrian Gebirgsjäger hung on to every street corner; they sprayed the streets with murderous machine-gun and small-arms fire, and mined the ground before moving on to a new line of defence. It took the Legionnaires two more hours to overwhelm the last defenders and secure their hold on Bjerkvik; after which, just like at Namsos, the town was systematically plundered – though without British participation this time . . .[8]

In the meantime, other operations were proceeding further east: the 2nd Battalion of the Foreign Legion, supported by two tanks, landed at Meby and stumbled on strong resistance, which was finally smothered by heavy fire from *Effingham*'s batteries. The Legionnaires then marched on to the military camp at Elvegaardsmoen, which they reached around 7.30 a.m. and captured after three hours of fierce hand-to-hand fighting. Huge stores of armaments and supplies were found in the barracks and bunkers: 100 heavy machine-guns, tons of ammunition, a complete field hospital with 60 German wounded, and even General Dietl's correspondence, fresh from the previous day's air drop.[9] After that, the enemy still had to be cleared from the high ground around the camp, and the Legionnaires, though exhausted by a night of heavy fighting, resumed their forward movement. 'Beyond the camp,' wrote General Béthouart, 'the battalion came up against a rocky eminence known as Hill 220. Three German machine-gun nests opened fire on the Legionnaires. A tank destroyed two of them, but the third kept shooting. At that, three Legionnaires undertook to scale the steep slope. They were Spaniards. They had almost reached the top, when the Germans saw them, lowered the muzzle of their machine-gun and killed two of them. But the lone survivor [. . .] leapt to the top and hurled the machine-gun and its crew into the abyss.'[10]

But for General Béthouart, the main objective still lay ahead: the southern extremity of Øyord Peninsula, which could serve both as an artillery position and a springboard for the attack on Narvik. As soon as Bjerkvik had been secured, Béthouart sent the Foreign Legion's motorcycle platoon speeding down the coastal road to the village of Øyord. Its flanks were covered by the Poles just arrived from Bogen, and by two destroyers closely hugging the shore. This time, however, there was no battle: the Germans, frightened by the shelling of Bjerkvik, had withdrawn to the mountains. 'Thus,' recalled General Béthouart, 'we had captured without firing a single shot the objective that interested me most.'[11]

Undoubtedly a brilliant victory – the very first – which was to prove of crucial importance in the storming of Narvik. For the moment, however, the situation in the whole theatre of operations remained most preoccupying: for one thing, of course, the evacuation of central Norway could not fail to influence the strategic situation further north. Almost as soon as the Allies had left Namsos, German mountain troops under General Feuerstein mounted a daring overland offensive towards Mosjøen. Both the British and the French had found the road impassable, but that did not deter a well-equipped army that could move in broad daylight without fear of air attack. A few detachments from the 14th Norwegian Infantry Regiment had thrown up roadblocks along the way, and the British sent five 'Independent Companies' of 300 men each under Colonel Colin McVean Gubbins to carry out guerrilla operations in the region. That force, code-named 'Scissor' – one more tool – was to meet with very limited success, and was even bypassed by a bold German amphibious operation quite comparable to that of Steinkjer. On 10 May, indeed, the Germans landed two companies of infantry at Hemnesberget, between Mosjøen and Mo, thus compelling the British and the Norwegians to beat a hasty retreat towards the north.[12]

After that, Mosjøen fell within 24 hours, and Mo was directly threatened. It therefore became imperative to divert troops from the Narvik theatre, in an effort to stem the swift northward progress of the German mountain troops. Two battalions of the British 24th Brigade bound for Bodø therefore boarded the Polish ship *Chrobry*, but the latter was sunk by German bombers before reaching Bodø, and the troops had to be brought back to Harstad, having lost all their equipment in the shipwreck. Three days later, one of the battalions, entirely re-armed and re-equipped, boarded the cruiser *Effingham* . . . which unfortunately ran aground twelve miles off Bodø. The battalion was therefore once again returned to Harstad, having once again lost all its equipment. Only then did the British commander decide to listen to the Norwegians and put the troops on board fishing vessels.

Thus, the Allies no longer had unlimited time to take Narvik: even if the road from Mo to Bodø was all but impassable, and communications from Bodø to Narvik could not allow the quick passage of strong German units, the fact remained that General Dietl would soon receive overland reinforcements from the south – in addition to the ones he was receiving by air drops and through Sweden.*

For Churchill, the success at Bjerkvik was conclusive proof of the incompetence of General Mackesy, who had strongly advised against the operation . . . *Vae Victis!* Only one day after the occupation of Bjerkvik, Mackesy was unceremoniously replaced by General Auchinleck, who had landed at Harstad three days earlier. After that, relations between Allied commanders on the spot improved markedly. On the other hand, co-ordination between London and Paris remained unsatisfactory, mostly because General Gamelin continued to run a highly theoretical war from his office at Vincennes, while both Reynaud and Daladier, for political reasons, insisted on sending to Norway an increasing number of French troops – who remained stuck in the gigantic bottleneck around the Clyde.[13]

In the Narvik theatre, there was no lack of material difficulties as well: many of the Polish 'mountain' troops had never even seen a mountain; the French Chasseurs Alpins were critically short of skis and snow-shoes; the 3,500 Norwegians operating north and northeast of Narvik had only insignificant reserves of ammunition, while both the British and French had as many casualties from frostbite as from enemy action.[14] Here again, the arrival of new supplies often posed new problems before it solved the old ones – as Béthouart wrote on 15 May to General Gamelin: 'I am experiencing considerable difficulties [. . .] because I have no information on the exact cargo of each ship, and because that cargo has not been loaded in a rational way.'[15]

As British, French, Norwegian and Polish troops were converging on Narvik from the Ankenes Peninsula to the Kuberg mountains, understanding between allies on the battlefield was not much better than at Namsos or Aandalsnes. At the root of that incomprehension lay – as usual – a linguistic problem: the French could not understand the British, the British could understand neither the Poles nor the French, and neither French, Poles nor British could understand

---

* Between 19 and 22 April, a train with 24 wagons had crossed Sweden and reached Narvik with both food and medical equipment. On the 25th, another train with 5 wagons had also brought 300 'health service personnel'.

the Norwegians. Immediately after landing at Harstad, General Béthouart had cabled to Paris: 'The lack of interpreters for both English and Norwegian is causing us great difficulties. I am urgently requesting interpreters, including officers. I only have one interpreter, and he speaks Russian.'[16] Indeed, that was unlikely to be much help . . . but even a whole month later, though the interpreters had arrived at last, the problem was no nearer a solution, because these interpreters could speak excellent Finnish, but not a word of Norwegian. At Supreme Headquarters in Paris, no one appeared to know the difference.[17]

Actually, this was not the only obstacle to co-operation with the Norwegians; geography was another, since for security reasons the King, the Government and the Commander-in-Chief were quartered very far from the theatre of operations – and even from each other. During the temporary absence of Sir Cecil Dormer, the British Chargé d'Affaires thus wrote to the Foreign Office on 12 May: 'We followed the acting Minister of Foreign Affairs (Lie, formerly Minister of Supply), to a place about 100 kilometres from Tromsø. Actually, it is a village (Kvesmenes) at the head of the Lyngen-fjord. [. . .] Kvesmenes is almost completely cut off from everything else – including most other members of the Government – the roads being snow- and water-logged. To get here we (Admiral Boyes and myself) took about 48 hours in small and smelly boats which were periodically bombed and machine-gunned by German planes. Other members of the Government are in other almost inaccessible valleys, the King and the Crown Prince in a third. I can get to His Majesty when required, but it takes the whole day, and the car has to be periodically dug out of ditches and snow-drifts. It was not a practical possibility to live nearer to him, and he is anyhow desperately anxious to keep hidden (he lives in a tiny farm well off the road). Lie is a great stand-by – by far the best member of the Government, and in particular far better than Koht [. . .] but the whole show is desperately crocky and amateurish. As for our own show, the less I say about it in a censorable letter, the better.'[18]

Upon returning from England, Dormer himself painted a strikingly similar picture: 'We arrived in Tromsø on the 19th May, where the general atmosphere seemed the reverse of satisfactory. There were a few stray junior officials in the town, but the Government were scattered over a wide area in the country round. [. . .] The

King and General Ruge [. . .] though living near one another, were completely isolated from anyone else. [. . .] The Prime Minister, who was suffering from nervous strain, was living in seclusion.'[19]

Actually, as Sir Cecil cautiously indicated, this was not only a problem of physical isolation or lack of communication (for the telephone was not working either). There were also within the Government quite a few personal quarrels and antipathies, a marked incompatibility of temper between Koht and his main collaborators within the makeshift 'Foreign Ministry', and last but not least, Prime Minister Nygaardsvold's 'nervous strain', which had as much to do with the shock of 9 April as with his inability to cope with the latest developments. After 18 May, the problem of geographic isolation, at least, was settled by a decision to gather the whole Government at Tromsø.[20] Whether that would suffice to make the Government's decision-making process more efficient naturally remained to be seen.

At that time, there was precisely an issue that demanded the Government's prompt attention: the 'Mowinckel Plan', which had been submitted to Messrs Mowinckel and Hambro by Swedish Foreign Minister Günther. It envisaged nothing less than the cessation of hostilities in northern Norway, followed by the creation of a Demilitarized Zone around Narvik; the Franco-British forces would evacuate northern Norway, while Swedish troops occupied Narvik to guarantee that the agreements were respected. Northern Norway would thus become an 'Unoccupied Zone' – with all the drawbacks inherent in such status: the Germans could naturally denounce the agreement overnight, invade the whole area and capture the Government. The plan gave rise to heated debates within the Government, with tempers flaring at times. Prime Minister Nygaardsvold was as usual somewhat vacillating, but Halvdan Koht, Trygve Lie and especially King Haakon vehemently opposed the idea as tantamount to a betrayal of the Allied cause.[21] At long last, to the intense relief of the Allies, the Norwegians decided to shelve the plan.

It must be admitted that the behaviour of these self-same Allies had caused some perplexity among the Norwegians. Whereas a certain fraternity of arms now prevailed among Norwegian and Allied troops closing in on Narvik, relations at a higher level remained somewhat strained. This was no doubt due to the unfortunate precedents of Namsos and Aandalsnes, but there was also something else, which General Ruge himself later acknowledged in these terms: 'We were not informed of the instructions of our British counterparts. We had the impression that the Allies were not frank enough with us.'[22] As usual with General Ruge, this was an understatement: actually, the Norwegians were told as little as possible, and in fact largely neglected. On 15 May, General Ruge thus sent the following cable to the Foreign Office: 'In a very short time, we shall be short of Norwegian ammunition both for infantry arms and for guns. [. . .] We must receive British and French arms and ammunition. [. . .] If not, the moment will come very soon when all Norwegian units must be taken out of the front until re-armed.'[23] General Ruge was to receive nothing at all.

The Norwegian authorities were also at a loss to interpret certain British initiatives on the spot, most notably the precipitate evacuation of Mo and the amazing weakness of the anti-aircraft defences at Bodø, which was soon to cause yet another disaster. The Norwegians never ceased to wonder at the seemingly limitless nonchalance displayed by their British allies, and in this, admittedly, they were not alone. 'At the harbour,' wrote French Lieutenant Dewavrin, 'I never failed to meet British dockworkers disguised as soldiers, taking the umpteenth cup of tea of the day's umpteenth tea-break, as a tank or a truck dangled forlornly in the air, precariously suspended from a crane cable.'[24] It would, however, be fair to add that the good people of Harstad were not above supplying the British soldiers with a particularly potent brew that had a devastating effect on quite a number of His Majesty's subjects . . .

Returning to the (hopefully) more sober atmosphere of the High Command, General Ruge had made yet another interesting and highly disquieting observation: 'We gradually acquired the impression that the Allies hesitated to involve themselves too deeply in new undertakings.'[25] Unfortunately, that impression was entirely correct. On 13 May, to be sure, the new British Minister of War, Anthony Eden, was still assuring Norwegian Minister Colban that 'the Allied action in Norway would be pursued with the utmost energy'.[26] But only a few days later, the Allies began in earnest to reconsider the opportunity cost of their engagement in northern Norway. The reason for that was perfectly obvious: for the Franco-British armies on the western front, the campaign was already taking a definite turn for the worse.

The greater part of the British army, commanded by Lord Gort, had advanced into Belgium with the First French Army Group to meet the German invasion. By 12 May, the Allied armies had reached their assigned positions along the Dyle and the Meuse in the north; they were confronting twenty-two German divisions, including three armoured ones. But the surprise came further south: on 14 May, seven Panzer divisions, having crossed the Ardennes and the Meuse, crashed through French positions at Sedan and Dinant. Supported by dive bombers, followed by motorized infantry, they wreaked havoc in the lines of the French Second and Ninth Armies, which fell back in confusion. On the northern front, the French, Belgian and British divisions, already hard-pressed and badly battered, were now in danger of being cut off from their supply lines by the unexpected breakthrough at Sedan. At 6 o'clock on the morning of 15 May, Paul Reynaud received a frantic phone call from Daladier: 'Our army is dissolving. [. . .] The battle is lost.'[27] An hour and a half later, in London, Churchill was awakened with the news that Reynaud was on the phone: 'We are defeated; we have lost the battle,' the French Premier told him in substance. Churchill was sceptical, but agreed to 'come over and talk'.[28]

In the north, the Dutch had capitulated, while in the centre, west of Dinant, the French Ninth Army had all but disintegrated. Churchill, however, relying on his First World War experience, persisted in considering all this as a temporary setback: 'It was ridiculous to think that France would be conquered by 120 tanks.'[29] At 3 p.m. on 16 May, Churchill flew to Paris for an urgent meeting of the Supreme War Council; he was accompanied by Generals Dill and Ismay.

Landing at Le Bourget, Churchill and Ismay were immediately struck by the atmosphere of depression that seemed to reign everywhere. Ismay was even told that the Germans could be in Paris 'in a few days at most'.[30] When the party arrived at the Quai d'Orsay, bonfires were already burning in the gardens; they were being fed with great heaps of archives. Reynaud, Baudouin, Daladier and General Gamelin were all there, and Churchill noted that 'utter dejection was written on every face'.[31] Naturally, Churchill immediately undertook to cheer his interlocutors with colourful reminders – in no less colourful French – of past difficulties overcome together.

However, he was himself dumbfounded to hear General Gamelin say that the French army was unable to counter-attack, having no strategic reserve. 'I admit this was one of the greatest surprises I have had in my life,'[32] Churchill later recalled. Gamelin and Reynaud repeatedly asked for more fighter squadrons to cover their troops, and Churchill, in spite of serious misgivings, promised and obtained from the War Cabinet the dispatch of ten more squadrons.[33]

Churchill's efforts had not been in vain; the next day, 17 May, Reynaud felt sufficiently emboldened to make a move he had been contemplating for some time: he would remove Daladier from his post and take personal charge of the Ministry of War. He would also appoint Georges Mandel as Minister of the Interior, Marshal Pétain as Vice-President of the Council, and at long last replace Gamelin by appointing General Weygand Commander-in-Chief. To be sure, Weygand was 73, and no one regarded him as a military genius; but he had been Marshal Foch's Chief of Staff during the First World War, and this would no doubt encourage the dispirited French troops. Besides, there was no one else; General Weygand was therefore called back from Syria. In the mean time, the French government had abruptly ceased to insist that the British send an ever-increasing number of French troops to Norway. On the contrary, they were now clamouring for the speediest possible return of the Chasseurs Alpins still stranded around the Clyde.

Back in London on 17 May, Churchill told the War Cabinet of the extreme gravity of the situation in France, and he was quite naturally led to evoke the dispersion of resources due to the pursuit of operations in Norway: 'We should consider whether Narvik was eating up what we needed for our own defence, particularly in destroyers, anti-aircraft guns and fighters.'[34]

Here matters rested for the time being, the capture of Bjerkvik having given rise to fresh hopes. Churchill, ever optimistic, had even stated that 'it seemed likely that Narvik would be captured at any moment'.[35] But during the next few days, the situation in France was to worsen considerably. At Rethel, Charleroi, St Quentin, the German tanks swept everything before them, and the Allied units were in full retreat. On the Somme, the German columns, instead of heading south, had turned westwards towards the sea, and were threatening Amiens and Abbeville. The French and British armies were all but trapped in the north by the German advance, and still the Allied counter-offensive failed to materialize. On 19 May, General Gamelin had ordered the northern armies to force their way southwards and attack the Panzer divisions on the Somme. But the order was cancelled by General Weygand, who replaced him the next day. On the 21st, Weygand himself gave orders for a north-south attack on the German columns, but by then the Allied front was dissolving in chaos; many French units did not receive the order, others could not carry it out, and Lord Gort was already thinking of a possible withdrawal towards Dunkirk.

Faced with such grave perils, the War Cabinet seemed uncertain as to what policy they should follow in northern Norway. As for Churchill, he told his ministers on 20 May that he was disappointed with the progress of operations at Narvik, 'which were causing a heavy drain on our resources in equipment and shipping'. He added that in his view, the operations were not being pressed hard enough, and the War Cabinet should perhaps consider the dispatch of a direct order to Lord Cork to take Narvik by assault.[36] Naturally, this was easier said than done: the Germans at Narvik had received reinforcements by air, they clung solidly to their positions south and north-east of the town, and the beaches were still covered with about three feet of mud and melting snow. Yet the pressure of events in France was steadily mounting, and even Churchill had stated at the War Cabinet of 20 May that 'the Chiefs-of-Staff should now consider carefully whether we were likely to get a dividend out of our occupation of Narvik, even after we had succeeded in capturing it. It was clear that the troops, ships and equipment occupied in the operation were urgently needed elsewhere.'[37]

Churchill was of course highly reluctant to abandon the siege. On 22 May, he was still stressing the considerable political value of the capture of Narvik;[38] but that same day, he had to admit that an imminent invasion of the British Isles had now become a distinct possibility.[39] Actually, the Prime Minster was receiving confused and contradictory news of the fighting; he could only offer advice to Reynaud and Weygand, and instruct Lord Gort to follow the directives he received from the French. But Lord Gort was receiving no instructions from the French, and Weygand was taking no advice from the British. In fact, there was a glaring lack of liaison between the French and the British, and Churchill was forever thundering at

Royal Navy Vessels entering Narvik fjord, April 13, 1940: 'England expects every man to do his duty.'

British naval artillery pounding the port of Bjerkvik, in preparation for the Anglo-French landing of May 13, 1940: An extraordinary sight that smacked of scene-shifting and film-staging: "Give me 30 yards of shelling, please!"'

German troops storming a hamlet near Lillehammer.

'the liaison that did not liaise'. He returned to Paris on 22 May for another meeting of the Supreme War Council; there he expressed agreement with General Weygand's plan to re-establish communications between the northern and southern armies, but voiced some concern at the lack of leadership in the north.[40] The commander there, General Billotte, had been killed, and General Blanchard had replaced him, but there was still no satisfactory liaison between Lord Gort and General Blanchard.

In London, on 23 May, the War Cabinet had before them a report from the Chiefs of Staff; their conclusions were unambiguous: they recommended the capture of Narvik, to be followed by the complete evacuation of Norway.[41] Their main argument was that in view of the situation in France, it was impossible to supply Lord Cork with sufficient troops and material to allow him to hold northern Norway indefinitely. All this was logical, but disastrous, as Winston Churchill was quick to point out, adding that he 'deprecated asking troops to incur heavy losses in assaulting a town which it was proposed to evacuate immediately afterwards'. The Chief of the Air Staff did stress that 'the Chiefs of Staff fully appreciated the political advantages of being able to say that we had captured Narvik', but the Prime Minister immediately answered that 'these advantages had been considerably minimized by the situation on the Western Front'.

Still, an evacuation was something terribly difficult to swallow, and the First Lord of the Admiralty, A. V. Alexander, expressed the hope that 'no decision would be taken at that meeting to abandon Norway. [. . .] There were grave political considerations which needed full consideration.' Churchill replied that 'he did not ask for an immediate decision. Plans for evacuating Norway should, however, be worked out at once. [. . .] He had no doubt that this country would shortly be subjected to a very heavy attack. The guns, destroyers, aircraft carriers, shipping and troops at present devoted to the Norwegian project were urgently needed for our own defence.' The Foreign Secretary and the Lord Privy Seal agreed, but they also stressed the importance of capturing Narvik. Churchill pointed out that, at any rate, 'it would be some weeks before withdrawal could be effected'; he expressed the familiar hope that in the interval 'we should take every advantage of our position in northern Norway to mine the approaches to Luleå to the maximum possible extent' –

and brought up yet another idea that is unfortunately more familiar still: 'We should on no account mention withdrawal to the Norwegians until it had actually begun. We should then offer the King of Norway and his entourage asylum in this country.'[42]

After all that, one must naturally expect a repetition of the painful scenes that had marred the evacuation of Namsos and Aandalsnes. For there was no mistaking the evidence: whatever the precautions in vocabulary, the principle of an evacuation had already been decided by Winston Churchill, and tacitly accepted by his colleagues; in fact, Lord Cork received the very next day, 24 May, instructions from the Defence Committee* to 'evacuate Narvik as soon as possible'[43] – an order that was only endorsed the following day by the War Cabinet. Naturally, in order to evacuate Narvik, it was preferable to occupy it beforehand. This Lord Cork had a free hand to accomplish, provided of course things went very fast, for it was now the fate of Great Britain that hung in the balance, and it would be decided very far from northern Norway.

The decision-making process was now evidently much faster and more efficient than under Chamberlain – though the decisions arrived at were not necessarily more rational. Thus, we already know that Lord Cork was not authorized to inform the Norwegian authorities of the evacuation order. But there was more: he was not authorized to inform the French either! For the Admiral, it was already somewhat unsettling to carry out an attack on Narvik while having in his pocket an order to evacuate the whole country . . . But to hide it from his allies on top of that seemed so utterly senseless that Lord Cork decided to disregard the instruction – at least as far as the French were concerned. On 27 May, he sent the following telegram to the Chiefs of Staff: 'In view of active operations being carried out by French forces in close contact with Norwegians, I have felt bound to communicate decision to General Béthouart, which I did yesterday 26th May. General Béthouart represented to General Auchinleck, who entirely agrees, that there may be extreme difficulty in withdrawing British and French troops now fighting side by side with Norwegians in contact with enemy without betraying them.'[44]

It was indeed to prove most difficult. But for now, the final assault

* The successor of the Military Co-ordination Committee.

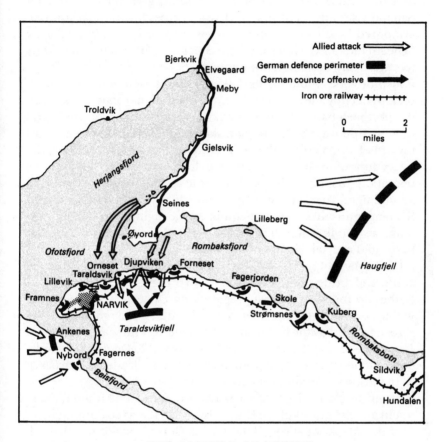

THE CAPTURE OF NARVIK
28 MAY 1940

on Narvik was about to be launched. On the night of 27–8 April, the attack was to come from three different directions: in the north-east, the 13th Half-Brigade of the Foreign Legion and a Norwegian battalion, setting out from Øyord, would cross the Rombaksfjord in armoured landing craft and land on Orneset beach, immediately beneath the railway line; a second echelon would then land slightly westward, at Taraldsvik. Simultaneously, south-west of Narvik, the Polish brigade would attack Ankenes and, crossing the Beisfjord, seek to occupy the southern sector of Narvik harbour. Finally, on the northern bank of the Rombaksfjord, a battalion of Chasseurs Alpins, supported by Norwegian ski troops, would attack eastward towards Hundalen, on the enemy's rear. Just like at Bjerkvik, the heavy guns of the Royal Navy were to lend massive assistance to the operation. Just like at Bjerkvik, too, the assault was to be launched at midnight, and this was no coincidence: as Trondheim and Stavanger airports were not equipped for night take-offs, the Germans at Narvik would thus be deprived of air support during the first – and crucial – hours of the attack.

On 27 May at 11.45 p.m., the whole armada was in place. From the command bridge of the cruiser *Cairo*, Lord Cork and General Béthouart followed the last preparations. Once again, the General was to command the fire, then direct the attack on land. Behind the screen formed by the heavy ships, five landing craft carrying the 1st Battalion of the Foreign Legion skirted the Øyord Peninsula, crossed the mouth of the Rombaksfjord, then headed for Orneset. At that, General Béthouart gave the signal to open fire.

Along the shore, the Austrian soldiers of the 139th Mountain Regiment and the sailors of the Haussels Group saw a red flare shoot up over the attack squadron. 'After that,' a German sailor recalled, 'all the cannons spewed out a devastating fire. Hundreds of shells crashed without interruption on the railway, exploded with a thunderous roar in front of tunnel entrances, rained down with a terrific whine on the cliffs on Framnes, detonated among the houses of Vassvik, as huge boulders came hurtling down the slopes of Fagernesfjell with an earth-shaking roar. In the town as in the harbour, at Fagernes and on the shores of Ankenes, wooden houses burned like torches. Each detonation [. . .] sent thousands of iron and rock fragments whistling in all directions. [. . .] The whole coastline from Orneset to Taraldsvik was blotted out by a thick cloud of powder and dust, which was constantly pierced by the flashes of new explosions.'[45]

Behind that avalanche of fire, the 1st Battalion of the Foreign Legion landed at 0.15 a.m. without encountering serious opposition. Immediately behind the beach, the fifty Germans of Naval Artillery Company Nöller who had survived the shelling left their shelters and almost immediately stumbled on the attacking Legionnaires; ferocious hand-to-hand combat ensued, compelling the Germans to give up their positions and re-group along the railway line, high above the beach. From their new positions, they dominated the assailants, who now had to scale the cliffs of Orneset under heavy machine-gun fire. Moreover, German artillery had opened fire on the wharfs of Øjord just as the 2nd Battalion of the Foreign Legion was about to embark; severe losses ensued, embarkation was delayed, and the lack of reinforcements considerably weakened the Orneset bridgehead.

But the Legionnaires of the 1st Battalion doggedly fought on. Braving murderous machine-gun and mortar fire, they stormed the cliff and reached the railway line. An artillery piece firing from a tunnel along the railway line hampered their progress, but they hauled a mountain cannon up the slope with their bare hands and destroyed the enemy piece. Soon, a Norwegian battalion landed from fishing boats on Orneset beach; with the Foreign Legion, they undertook to storm Hill 457, where the Germans were now entrenched high above the beach and the railway. The assailants met with very strong resistance and immediately suffered severe casualties. By 4 a.m., the 2nd Battalion of the Foreign Legion had not yet landed, while south of Narvik, the Poles approaching Ankenes were caught under heavy artillery fire.

For the Allies, things were soon to deteriorate even further; at 4.30 a.m., Messerschmidt bombers appeared above Narvik, and immediately targeted the Allied fleet. 'The whole artillery of *Cairo*', General Béthouart recalled, 'fired in vain at the assailants, who dropped a hail of bombs. [. . .] Everyone ducked instinctively. Two bombs exploded on the ship, one on the fo'c'sle in front of us, the other between the two funnels. Splinters rained upon us. We got up. The Admiral, wearing a helmet, bent over the railing and exclaimed "Oh!" [. . .] All the crew of the cannons had been mown down: 20, 30 mangled corpses, and blood spattered everywhere. Replacement crews emerged from the hatchways, pushed the corpses aside and resumed the fire. Behind us, a heavy machine-gun had been hit, and its ammunition was burning. Watney asked a sailor for life belts. "Won't do you any good, sir. We're about to blow up." '[46]

*Cairo* did not blow up; but the whole squadron was compelled to retreat under a hail of bombs, thus leaving the Allied troops without artillery support. The Germans immediately grasped the opportunity to launch a counter-offensive on the slopes of Hill 457; 'Then came the counter-attack,' a French Legionnaire noted, 'two German companies rushed down on us. A Legionnaire leapt forward, but was almost immediately cut down, his legs torn off by a burst of machine-gun fire.'[47] 'Some of our men had almost reached the top of the first slope,' wrote another French officer, 'when down below, along the railway line and the pass leading to Orneset, the Germans were driving a wedge in our flanks and setting up their heavy machine-guns. Soon, they would cut off our companies fighting on the slope from the landing beach of Orneset.'[48] Corporal Favrel belonged to one of these companies: 'The intensity of the shooting half a mile behind us', he wrote, 'seemed to indicate that a very strong attack was being brought to bear mainly on the Norwegian unit that had just taken over from us. We were cut off from the battalion, which must also have been cut off from the rest of the brigade, since the fighting now raged half-way up the slope, and the Norwegians fell back on the eastern side of Orneset beach, which the cross-fire of mountain cannons, mortars and machine-guns was fast rendering untenable. That fire also swept the fjord, blocking the arrival of landing craft loaded with reinforcements, supplies and ammunition.'[49]

Indeed, in a landing craft less than 150 yards from the beach, Major Paris, General Béthouart's Chief of Staff, had just been killed outright by a bullet in the forehead. 'The shore was raked with bullets,' observed a Legionnaire; 'in the middle of the fjord, a ship carrying ammunition was hit by a shell. She crackled like phosphorus, sputtered a long time, then, all at once, blew up and sank. The situation had become terribly alarming. The bridgehead was about to be pushed back into the sea.'[50] At Ankenes too, the Germans had taken advantage of the withdrawal of the Allied naval support to launch a devastating counter-offensive, and the left flank of the Polish battalion was falling back with heavy losses.

Shortly after 6 a.m., however, British Hurricanes appeared over Narvik, and the 2nd Battalion of the Foreign Legion finally landed at Taraldsvik. On the heights of Orneset, the German counter-attack began to weaken, and the hard-pressed Legionnaires of the 1st Battalion were quick to react. 'On the slopes,' recalled an eyewitness, 'in the midst of all the disorder, confusion and wavering, a cry suddenly rang out: *"A moi! La Légion!"* Despite a mortal head wound, Captain de Guittaud rallied his company and launched it against the enemy; the wounded rose; a lieutenant, pistol in hand, led the way for his section; 20 Legionnaires out of 35 were killed. The Company lost 60 men. [. . .] Legionnaires and Norwegians, side by side, now held fast, and the Norwegians [. . .] progressively overtaking the men of the Foreign Legion, inched their way to the top.'[51]

By 7 a.m., the Allies were slowly gaining the upper hand; on Hill 457, littered with corpses and bomb craters, the Germans were being increasingly isolated in their defensive positions; the 2nd Battalion of the Foreign Legion and a Norwegian detachment, following the railway line, were now meeting weaker resistance in their progress towards Narvik. South-west of the town, a company of the 2nd Polish Battalion reached Nybord, a strategic point from where it could hold Ankenes under constant artillery fire. Meanwhile, in the north-west, the French Chasseurs Alpins and the Norwegian ski troops were slowly but methodically driving the Germans back in the Haugfjell and along the Rombaksfjord.

In Narvik, at Major Haussel's headquarters, the situation was now considered untenable: communications with General Dietl's HQ further east had been cut, there were no more reserves, and the axis of the enemy progress clearly indicated that they were attempting an enveloping movement. With only 150 mountain troops and 250 sailors, the Major could not hope to stave off a direct assault on the town for very long. As for a counter-attack, it was now entirely out of the question. However, the road running eastward along the Beisfjord remained open for a possible escape . . . At 6.50 a.m., Major Haussels ordered his troops to evacuate the town, taking with them all light weapons and as much ammunition as possible.[52] Many isolated groups failed to receive the order, and they continued to resist until late in the afternoon, both at Fagernes and atop Hill 457.

Around 5 p.m., however, advance elements of the Norwegian battalion entered the eastern suburbs of Narvik, and learned that the Germans had evacuated the town. The Foreign Legion made a circular movement west of the town, and covered the harbour area. A few hours later, General Béthouart himself entered Narvik, greeted by an enthusiastic population. The very next day, the Norwegians, the Poles, the French and the motorized section of the Foreign Legion were to initiate operations to push back the remnants of General Dietl's troops towards the Swedish border.[53]

This was obviously a magnificent victory, though it must have seemed derisory to the victors themselves; for back in France, the battle for the north was by now virtually lost. The German armoured divisions, converging from south, west and north, inexorably closed in on the Allied armies re-grouped in a large bridgehead around Dunkirk. On 28 May, the Belgian army capitulated. The day before, the War Office had informed Lord Gort that his task was to 'evacuate the maximum force possible', and the British were beginning to fight their way towards the sea. General Blanchard's troops, having received no such orders, were slow in following, and five French divisions were trapped around Lille. By 30 May, the badly battered British divisions had all succeeded in reaching the defensive perimeter around Dunkirk, and half the 1st French Army had joined them. A gigantic naval effort was under way to evacuate the troops from Dunkirk. Churchill himself was back in Paris on 31 May for yet another meeting of the Supreme War Council; at this very grave juncture, when the Allied armies were struggling for survival in the north, he wanted to avoid any misunderstanding between the British and the French: the evacuation, he insisted, should proceed *'bras dessus, bras dessous'*![54] Never before had France and Britain found themselves in such mortal peril.

At Narvik, however, the French and the British had another reason to be bitter: the town that had been conquered at such expense in blood and toil was to be evacuated almost immediately; in fact, the first preparations to that effect had begun even before the assault. But by 1 June even the operations being pursued east of the town were halted, and the re-embarkation of the 26,000-man expeditionary corps began in earnest; and yet at that date, neither the Norwegian government nor General Ruge had been informed of what was afoot.

The question of when to inform the Norwegians of the complete evacuation of northern Norway had been debated several times at the War Cabinet since 24 May, without any decision being taken. Finally, on 27 May, it was decided that 'the question should be brought before the War Cabinet again in two or three days'.[55] On 29 May, Lord Halifax raised the question anew, but the Prime Minister answered that 'he was in favour of waiting a few days before taking a decision'.[56] Even at this late hour, no one in London seemed to trust the Norwegians . . . and everyone feared their reaction upon hearing the news of the evacuation; indeed, an immediate Norwegian capitulation would make re-embarkation far more perilous than it already was. Yet the experience of the Aandalsnes evacuation ought to have given the British a much higher opinion of General Ruge's loyalty to his allies.

At Tromsø, the Norwegian authorities, though still unaware of the impending evacuation, had not been spared a few very rude shocks. On 27 May, the Luftwaffe had bombed and entirely destroyed the town of Bodø, without encountering significant opposition from the British planes and anti-aircraft guns. Two days later, at Tromsø, the good news of the capture of Narvik had been entirely eclipsed by surprising and most disquieting information: the British were said to be preparing the evacuation of the whole area around Bodø, thus effectively opening the road to Narvik for the Germans. Sir Cecil Dormer, who conferred the next day with the members of the Norwegian government, reported the following to Lord Halifax: '[Mr Koht] and the Prime Minister were visibly suffering under some great strain when I was received by them this morning, and I soon learned that this was caused by the news that the British troops were on the point of evacuating the whole Bodø area. [. . .] Mr Koht [. . .] stated that the decision had apparently been reached without consulting General Fleischer, the Norwegian commander, that it was contrary to the explicit assurances which had been given to him in London, and, moreover, that it would bring the Germans considerably nearer to Tromsø, where the Government were hoping that they would be able to establish themselves firmly.'[33]

At this point, Storting President Carl Hambro intervened in the conversation and embarked on a violent attack on Great Britain, concluding with the statement that 'the Norwegians felt that they could no longer trust the British'.[58] He added that there did not appear to be any co-operation between the Royal Navy and the

British army. Sir Cecil Dormer answered somewhat heatedly that Mr Hambro was in no position to pass judgment on matters such as these and that, on the contrary, co-operation was excellent – to which Mr Hambro retorted that 'if that were true, then it was even worse'.[59]

'Mr Koht', Sir Cecil pursued, 'spoke more calmly, but said that it was of the utmost importance that there should be a conference of the Allied and Norwegian commanders to discuss the whole position and to learn our future plans. He also told me that General Fleischer wished to go on fighting at Bodø even if we withdrew, but needed some British reinforcements, and he dwelt at some length on the importance of holding that area. Mr Nygaardsvold, who from the start had looked the picture of misery, with averted head resting on his hands, then interposed his one and only remark, saying that to-morrow there was to be a State Council, the next day would be too late, so that the conference must take place this very afternoon; otherwise he would have to go to the King and they would stop fighting (or some such remark). His exact words were not very audible, but I paid no attention to them, as he showed every sign of extreme nervous strain.'[60] Naturally, Sir Cecil readily agreed to a conference between the commanders. That, after all, was no great commitment; and in the meantime the Norwegians still knew nothing about the decision to evacuate the whole country – even if they had already picked up a few tell-tale signs.[61]

At Narvik, the Allied commanders were increasingly reluctant to keep the Norwegians in the dark; General Auchinleck, who had taken over from Mackesy, wrote to General Ironside on 30 May: 'The worst of it all is the need for lying to all and sundry in order to preserve secrecy. Situation vis-à-vis the Norwegians is particularly difficult, and one feels a most despicable creature in pretending that we are going on fighting when we are going to quit at once.'[62] This could not go on for long; whereas on 31 May the War Cabinet once again postponed the decision whether or not to inform the Norwegians,[63] Lord Cork decided that same day to take matters into his own hands: 'General Auchinleck and myself were invited to Tromsø to discuss future operations. The position was obviously impossible. It was decided that the information must be imparted.'[64] The next morning, indeed, Sir Cecil Dormer was brought to Harstad in a flying boat, and informed by Lord Cork of the decision to evacuate;

Sir Cecil undertook to inform the Norwegian government immediately.

At Tromsø, that same morning, the Norwegian government had gathered in the presence of King Haakon, and the minutes of the meeting showed that the Norwegians strongly suspected what was afoot: 'We all agreed that if the Allies were to evacuate their troops entirely – and there are indications that this is a distinct possibility – our situation would become practically desperate. Indeed, apart from the fact that we lack anti-aircraft guns and planes, we have almost entirely run out of ammunition. More than a month has now passed since Great Britain promised to send us rifles and ammunition.'[65]

Having reached Tromsø by late afternoon, Sir Cecil first visited Defence Minister Ljungberg, with whom he was on particularly good terms, and broke the news with a wealth of oratorical precautions: 'I said, speaking personally and in strict secrecy, that the Allies would, I thought, decide to evacuate and if so, His Majesty's Government would be prepared to bring away at the same time the King and the Government.'[66] The connoisseur is bound to admire Sir Cecil's choice of hypothetical and conditional formulations to convey a decision that had after all been reached nine days earlier – and was already being implemented . . . At any rate, Ljungberg could easily read between the lines, and he immediately asked whether the Allies could leave his army enough weapons and supplies to continue the struggle alone. Sir Cecil answered in the negative: 'Everything must be taken away'.[67] However, he hastened to add, 'This consideration [. . .] seemed to indicate the desirability of reviewing the question of adopting the so-called Mowinckel Plan, according to which the Germans would undertake not to attack northern Norway if the Allied forces evacuated it and the Swedes occupied Narvik.'[68] Ljungberg assented, and so did Koht, who had just joined the conference.

Thus the Mowinckel Plan, rejected two weeks earlier in both London and Tromsø, was now being grasped as a last chance of salvation by both Britain and Norway. The day before, the Swedish Ambassador in London had discussed the plan with Lord Halifax, who found it 'most curious', but added nonchalantly that 'as these were curious times we lived in' he would again put the proposal before the Cabinet.[69] The Swedish diplomat had few illusions, but to his utter amazement, the War Cabinet approved the Mowinckel Plan the very next day.[70]

Actually, this was not as surprising as it seemed. On the one hand, of course, the plan, if accepted by the Germans, would allow the Norwegian authorities to keep part of their territory, and the British to save face at a time when they were pulling back to their islands in all haste. But His Majesty's ministers considered the situation soberly, and they saw little chance of Hitler proving so magnanimous. Yet they were also perfectly aware of the usefulness of negotiating on the Mowinckel Plan during the whole period of evacuation; for the British authorities were above all preoccupied with the possible reactions of the Norwegians upon learning of the evacuation: their immediate surrender, for instance, would be catastrophic for the Allies, not only because it would endanger the evacuation, but also because it would leave the Norwegian government at the mercy of the Germans; and that government, in spite of its apparent weakness, controlled an asset that was of vital importance to the Allied war effort – more than a thousand merchant ships and their crews.[71] Thus, even if the Mowinckel Plan proved a failure – the most likely outcome – it would at least allow the Allies to gain much needed time: to evacuate their troops, of course, but also to persuade the Norwegian authorities to join them.

Actually, the members of the Norwegian government were not naïve either – though this fact was far more recent. Naturally, Mr Koht would leave no stone unturned to ensure the success of the Mowinckel Plan; but by 1 June, most of his colleagues had already understood that the plan was doomed, and that evacuation was the only practical alternative. On 3 June, while Koht discussed the Mowinckel Plan with his Swedish counterpart in Luleå, General Ruge was summoned to Tromsø. 'The decision had been taken,' he recalled. 'The King, the Government and the President of the Storting were to leave for England in order to continue the struggle. I expressed complete agreement.'[72]

During the next few days, while Polish troops and Foreign Legionnaires continued to operate in the Sildvik area and along the railway line to push the Germans back to the Swedish border, other units and most of the heavy equipment were being discreetly pulled back towards Harstad and embarked. But at Tromsø, in the mean time, several prominent Norwegians were beginning to have second thoughts about their decision to leave Norway. Prince Olav was one of them, and as early as 3 June, he had informed the Government that he proposed to remain in Norway in order to share the fate of his compatriots. 'I was well aware', he was to explain 23 years later, 'that defeat and evacuation [. . .] would have an extremely depressing effect on the Norwegian people, and I thought I would be able to persuade them that it was necessary to pursue the struggle.'[73]

A noble resolve, but the Norwegian cabinet unanimously opposed it.[74] Two days later, it was General Ruge's turn to inform the Government that he was unwilling to leave the country. He considered that, having already abandoned his troops once in central Norway, he could not do so again without completely losing the respect of his men. In spite of pressing rejoinders by the Government, General Ruge remained adamant: he would capitulate with his troops once the King, the Government and their followers had left Norway and were well out of reach of the enemy.

But there was yet a third man who could not bring himself to leave his people: King Haakon himself. On 5 June, only two days before the date set by the British for the end of the evacuation, Sir Cecil Dormer received an unexpected message: 'About 10 p.m.,' he wrote, 'I had a visit from Mr Johan Anker, of yachting fame, a personal friend of King Haakon, who brought me a letter from HM, written in pencil and marked private, to the effect that on further reflection, he felt it his duty to remain behind in Norway.'[75] Dormer immediately relayed the news to London, where it caused understandable consternation; a note was immediately drafted by the Foreign Office to dissuade the King from such a dangerous course.[76]

It was to prove superfluous, for at dawn the next day, long before the arrival of that note, Dormer was already travelling on the muddy and crater-pocked road leading to the King's retreat. 'I nearly got ditched,' he recalled, 'the melting snow making the roads almost impassable. But all went well and to my great relief, I found that the King had not come to any final decision. I pointed out that by staying in Norway after the Allied forces had evacuated it, His Majesty would become a virtual prisoner, unable to help his people in any way or even be in touch with them. The Germans would issue orders purporting to be made with his approval: in short he would be playing into their hands. By coming to England, accompanied by his

Government, he would on the other hand be a free agent, and Norway could carry on her struggle alongside the Allies. HM's hesitations were soon dispelled and after a short conversation he agreed to abide by the arrangements already made, after which we turned to lighter topics. He told me that he had not informed his government of his letter to me and that there was no need for them to know of it. The conversation took place in HM's tiny bedroom, so as to be out of earshot of others. The Crown Prince and Lieut. Eric Smith, whom I had brought with me, were also present. Before taking my leave, I told HM that the hour of departure was fixed for the following night. The Crown Prince accompanied us to the gate where, to my consternation, he suggested that, though the King was right in going to England, he ought to stay behind. I argued that that would be almost as bad as for the King to stay, for the Germans would be certain to play off one against the other and bring about a situation resulting in the King's deposition. He accepted this view and I was then able to hasten back to Tromsø to telegraph that all was well. On my arrival I found a telegram from the FO [. . .] instructing me to take the action which I had already taken. It was now the turn of some members of the Norwegian Government, including the Prime Minister, to vacillate. [. . .] It was clear that they were hoping against hope that the Germans would accept the Mowinckel plan, which would have enabled them to stay on in Norway, but as two, then three days went by without an answer from Stockholm this hope had to be abandoned. Nevertheless I was afraid that something might happen to cause them to change their minds at the last moment. The new hitch arose when the Prime Minister announced that he would not leave unless his wife arrived in time to come with him.'[77]

Norway – and Great Britain – obviously owed a great debt of gratitude to Sir Cecil Dormer. Until the evening of 6 June, the Norwegian ministers continued to vacillate, and at the very last moment some of them even requested a postponement of the evacuation. But Dormer refused to budge: the evacuation was to be completed the very next day, and the last ship to leave would be the cruiser *Devonshire*; she was at the Norwegian government's disposal, but would sail in any event at eight o'clock in the evening.[78]

The next day, at 2 p.m., there was a last Council of Ministers at the seat of the Tromsø bishopric.[79] Towards the end of the session, the

Prime Minister submitted to his colleagues a proposal that 'the King, the Crown Prince and the Government depart for an allied country, and that this decision be announced by proclamation to the Norwegian people'. The proposal, then the text of the proclamation to the people, were quickly accepted, after which the King made a short speech: 'Having duly weighed the situation, I have come to the firm conclusion that in the present situation, my government and myself have no other alternative than to leave the country, in order to pursue from abroad our work for the benefit of Norway.'[80] The King was so overpowered by emotion that he was unable to continue.[81] Actually, he was not quite sure that his decision had been the right one; a short while later, he talked with Bishop Hansen, who recalled their conversation in the following terms:

'What did you think when you learned of this?' the King asked me with tears in his eyes.

'It's terrible,' I replied, 'but I understand that there is nothing else to do, since the Allies are leaving.'

'It's so good to hear you say that. I am so afraid of the Norwegian people's judgment.'[82]

At 70, King Haakon was about to leave his country, without knowing whether he would ever see it again. Would he even reach England safely? And, if he did, what could he do there? Many of his ministers were tormented by the very same thoughts. Would their departure cut them off completely from the Norwegian people? The latter had already passed a severe judgment on the extraordinary carelessness of their defence policy. Would they not also condemn their exile?

Shortly after 6 p.m., in Tromsø harbour, the last British soldiers, Norwegian volunteers from the army, navy and air force, members of the Diplomatic Corps, the staff of the ministries and the ministers themselves all boarded *Devonshire*. The King, Prince Olav and their aides-de-camp finally arrived, to the intense relief of Dormer and of the captain of the cruiser. 'From where we stood at the railing,' recalled Trygve Lie, 'we could see the King and the Crown Prince climbing the ship's ladder. The King seemed extremely depressed. It was certainly one of the most painful hours of his life.'[83] At eight o'clock sharp on the evening of 7 June 1940, *Devonshire* hoisted anchor and disappeared in the heavy mist, heading north-north-west.

That same evening, further south, the two Polish battalions and the Legionnaires who were still pursuing operations near the Swedish border had silently pulled back towards Narvik; to camouflage their withdrawal, the Poles had even left dummies in front of their former positions. In the port of Narvik, while heavy material, vehicles and ammunition were being either destroyed or sunk, the rear guards of the last two battalions embarked around 10 p.m. Demolition experts of the Foreign Legion blew up a large portion of the railway line above the town, as well as their own anti-aircraft guns. The pack mules of the expeditionary force had been turned loose, and were wandering through the deserted streets. Finally, at midnight, General Béthouart and his staff boarded the last destroyer, which hastened to join the rest of the convoy at the mouth of the fjord. German planes were nowhere in sight. For the victors of Narvik, it was to be a successful retreat.

Two days earlier, General Auchinleck had received a telegram from the War Office ordering him 'not to hand over any rifles or ammunition to Norwegians'.[84] But in the early hours of 8 June, as the last British naval units had reached the high seas, a new message was handed to Lord Cork, ordering him to leave the Norwegians 3,000 rifles with corresponding ammunition.[85] To the very last, confusion had reigned supreme.

On 9 June, the soldiers of the Norwegian 6th Division were disbanded under the supervision of General Ruge. The next day, an armistice was declared in northern Norway.[86] The Norwegian campaign was at an end. A few days later, the French campaign would also end . . . and the Battle of Britain would soon begin in earnest. It was not the end; it was not even the beginning of the end; but it was already the end of the beginning.

# LOOKING BACK

In June 1940, in Paris as in London, no one thought of taking a closer look at the results of the Norwegian campaign; the very existence of France and Britain was threatened, and the news of the capture of Narvik, like that of the complete evacuation of the country, was quickly submerged in the great maelstrom of the French disaster. But 'when the clamour of the gun dies away, the clamour of the history writer begins'.[1] What, then, were the concrete results of that two-month campaign, and what influence did it exert on the subsequent events of the Second World War?

Losses on both sides during the campaign were roughly comparable. During land operations, the British had lost 1,869 men, either dead, missing or severely wounded; the French and the Poles had lost 530, and the Norwegians 1,335. To this must be added about 250 men (mostly British) who died or were lost at sea. The Germans, for their part, had lost a total of 5,296 men, either dead or missing.[2] As for material losses, 242 German planes had been destroyed – one third of them transport planes – and only 112 RAF planes; in view of the considerable numerical superiority of the German air force, this represented a relatively equal loss in numbers. There was likewise a relative parity in naval losses; in the course of the campaign, the British had lost three cruisers, seven destroyers, one aircraft carrier and four submarines;[3] the Germans, three cruisers, ten destroyers, six submarines, with four cruisers and six destroyers heavily damaged. But if such losses were relatively insignificant for the Royal Navy, they effectively crippled the far weaker Kriegsmarine, which lost in Norway the greater part of its surface strength for the rest of the war.

For Germany, of course, the most important strategic result was no doubt the acquisition of naval and air bases east and north-east of the British Isles and in the area of the North Cape; it now had an additional springboard for attacks on Britain, an ideal starting-point for raids on the enemy's maritime communications, and of course a guarantee against any British attempt to impose a naval blockade of Germany. Yet the drawbacks were just as obvious: on the one hand, the unique strategic vantage-point that was Norway could only be very partially exploited by the Germans, owing to the huge naval losses they had incurred in conquering it.[4] Besides, the British had discreetly carried out a 'preventive' landing in Iceland by mid-May, thus offsetting part of the German strategic gains. Economically, of course, victory in Norway was highly profitable for the Germans; once they had repaired Narvik harbour, they could receive an uninterrupted supply of both Swedish and Norwegian iron ore: 600,000 tons in 1941, 1.8 million tons in 1943.[5]

Naturally, the victory in Norway greatly enhanced Germany's prestige among neutral countries such as Sweden – and potential belligerents such as Italy. But of course the victories in France had an even greater impact from that point of view. For the Germans, however, the campaign was also to have another, highly unexpected consequence: until the very end of the war, Hitler remained firmly convinced that Winston Churchill would attack him in Norway; as a result, he had the whole country turned into a fortress, defended by formidable coastal batteries, half a million men and the greater part of the German navy. This veritable obsession led him to commit a number of strategic blunders in other theatres – especially the Mediterranean. Thus is ultimate defeat sometimes already inscribed in the most brilliant victories . . .

It is not easy to discern the advantages that accrued to Great Britain from that unfortunate campaign. It is customary to state that the destruction of the German fleet in Norway prevented Hitler from launching a large-scale naval attack on the British convoys during the re-embarkation at Dunkirk. Actually, it is highly doubtful whether the Führer would have done such a thing, even with all the necessary means at his disposal: 'On land,' he used to say, 'I am a hero; at sea, a coward.'[6] It is no less traditional to point out that the Norwegian campaign led to the complete re-organization of the British decision-making process, including the creation of a Defence Ministry. But that re-organization was due far less to the pressure of events in Norway than to the intervention of Winston Churchill, who was already contemplating it at the beginning of the war – and even some time before that. Finally, it is also customary to write that the lessons of the Norwegian campaign proved invaluable to the Allies, since they led to a substantial improvement in the planning and execution of combined operations later in the war. That argument is no more convincing than the two others, for it could easily be demonstrated that at Dakar, in Crete and at Dieppe, the same mistakes were repeated – plus a few others that were more disquieting still. In fact, there is no reason to stop at the Second World War: some mistakes of the very same type were faithfully repeated during the Falklands War of 1982!

What could perhaps be considered a positive element, however, is that the Norwegian campaign effectively discouraged the British military from launching further operations under similar conditions of dramatic aerial inferiority. During the next four years, Churchill was to use all possible means – and a few impossible ones as well – to get his generals to plan and carry out large-scale landing operations in Norway. There is little doubt that the British military's victorious resistance to such strong pressures was firmly grounded in the disastrous memories left by the Norwegian fiasco of 1940.

All things considered, the only substantial – and even decisive – advantage that Great Britain was to draw from that ill-fated undertaking was the replacement of Neville Chamberlain by Winston Churchill. Indeed, nothing other than the dismal story of setbacks suffered in Norway could have led to the resignation of Chamberlain before 10 May 1940; but after that date, there was not the slightest chance that the Members of Parliament would have risked opening a political crisis in the midst of the Battle of France – and no one can possibly say what would have happened if Neville Chamberlain had remained Prime Minister of Great Britain in the summer of 1940.

# NOTES

## INTRODUCTION

1 AEB, 11075/ Oslo 35/40, J. U. de Schooten to Spaak, no. 84–59, 27/1/38.
2 *Ibid.*, J. U. de Schooten to Pierlot no. 1118, 2/8/39.
3 *Morgenbladet*, 24/1/39.
4 YNGVAR HAUGE, *Kongen av Norge*, Aschehoug, Oslo, 1960, p. 62.
5 *Ibid.*, p. 65.

## CHAPTER I

1 E. SPEARS, *Assignment to Catastrophe*, Heinemann, London, 1954, vol. I, p. 27.
2 FO 371/23657, Note from Industr. Intell. Cttee to CID, London, 30/8/ 39.
3 *Ibid.*
4 W. S. CHURCHILL, *The Second World War*, vol. I, Cassell, London, 1948, p. 420.
5 ADM 205/2, First Sea Lord Records, 18/9/39.
6 W. S. CHURCHILL, *The Second World War*, vol. I, *op. cit.*, pp. 421–2.
7 W. S. CHURCHILL, *The Second World War*, vol. I, *op. cit.*, p. 423.
8 *Ibid.*, p. 424.
9 T. FELSTEAD, *Intelligence*, Hutchinson, London, 1941, p. 62.
10 FO 371/23659, Intelligence Department of Ministry of Economic Warfare, 27/11/39.
11 FO 371/23659, War Cabinet meeting, 30/11/39.
12 F. KERSAUDY, *Stratèges et Norvège*, Hachette, Paris, 1977, pp. 25–6.
13 *Ibid.*
14 K. FEILING, *Neville Chamberlain*, London, 1946, pp. 428–9; and M. COWLING, *The Impact of Hitler*, CUP, London, 1975, p. 356.
15 J. MORDAL, *La campagne de Norvège*, Self, Paris, 1949, p. 37.
16 W. N. MEDLICOTT, *The Economic Blockade*, vol. I, HMSO and Longman, London, 1957, pp. 36–7.
17 See J. B. DUROSELLE, *L'Abîme*, Imprimerie Nationale, Paris, 1982, pp. 72–7, 117–20; E. BONNEFOUS, *Histoire politique de la Troisième République*, vol. VII, PUF, Paris, 1967, p. 137.
18 H. MICHEL, *La drôle de guerre*, Hachette, Paris, 1971, p. 241.
19 On this question, see F. KERSAUDY, *La Norvège et les Grandes Puissances*,

pp. 214–16, 315–17; R. GIRAULT, 'Les relations franco-soviétiques après septembre 1939' in *Français et Britanniques dans la drôle de guerre*, CNRS, Paris 1979, pp. 263–91.

20 P. AUPHAN, *La marine française dans la Deuxième Guerre mondiale*, France-Empire, Paris, 1967, p. 79.

21 W. S. CHURCHILL, *The Second World War*, vol. I, *op. cit.*, pp. 429–30.

22 *The Times*, 6/12/39.

23 ADM. 205/2, First Sea Lord Records, Note by DNI to First Sea Lord, 5/12/39.

24 W. S. CHURCHILL, *The Second World War*, vol. I, *op. cit.*, p. 430.

25 FO 371/23660, War Cabinet Conclusions 111 (39), 11/12/39.

26 *Ibid.*, War Cabinet Conclusions 116 (39), 15/12/39.

27 R. MACLEOD, *The Ironside Diaries, 1937–1940*, London, Constable, 1962, p. 185.

28 FO 371/23667, War Cabinet Conclusions 118 (3 c), 18/12/39.

29 FO 371/23667, War Cabinet Conclusions no. 120 (39 ), 20/12/39.

30 *Ibid.*

31 FO 371/24820, MCC meeting, 20/12/39.

32 J. R. M. BUTLER, *Grand Strategy*, vol. II, September 1939–June 1941, London, HMSO, 1957, p. 101.

33 *Ibid.*

34 D. DILKS, *Cadogan Diaries*, p. 239.

35 ADM 116/4471, *Admiral Drax to First Lord*, 28/12/39.

36 FO 371/24820, W. Churchill to Prime Minister, 29/12/39.

37 *Ibid.*, War Cabinet meeting, WM 40, 2/1/40.

38 MACLEOD, *Ironside Diaries, op. cit.*, p. 191.

39 DILKS, *Cadogan Diaries, op. cit.*, p. 243.

40 *Förspelet til det tyska angreppet på Danmark och Norge den 9 avril 1940*, KGL Utrikesdepartementet, Stockholm, 1947, pp. 22–3.

41 FO 419/34, Tel. from King Haakon VII, 8/1/40.

42 W. S. CHURCHILL, *The Second World War*, vol. I, *op. cit.*, p. 444.

43 *Ibid.*

44 See: R. OMANG, *Altmarksaken*, Gyldendal, Oslo, 1953.

45 FO 415/34, Sir C. Dormer to Viscount Halifax no. 50, 19/2/40, Oslo.

46 AE, X. Rapport du ministre Dampierre au Quai d'Orsay, 28/3/40, Oslo.

47 W. S. CHURCHILL, *The Second World War*, vol. I, *op. cit.*, p. 445.

48 WO 106/1858, Cabinet Papers, Norwegian Operations, COSC, 16/1/40.

49 WO 106/204 B, Scandinavia, Stratford.

50 WO 106/1858, COSC 16/1/40, *op. cit.*; WO 193/772 'Memo by CIGS'.

51 F. KERSAUDY, *Stratèges et Norvège 1940*, Hachette, Paris, 1977, pp. 123–4.

52 H. ISMAY, 'Le Comité des chefs d'état-major pendant la guerre', *L'Armée, la Nation*, Bruxelles, 6e année, no. 3, mars 1951, p. 28.

53 MACLEOD, *Ironside Diaries, op. cit.*, p. 210.

54 G. ROSSI-LANDI in *Français et Britanniques dans la drôle de guerre, op. cit.*, pp. 48–51.

55 F. KERSAUDY, *Stratèges et Norvège, op. cit.*, pp. 125-6.
56 WO 106/1858, Cabinet Papers, Norwegian operations. Lord Halifax to Lord Chatfield, 23/1/40; ADM 1165458, NID, 24/1/40.
57 SHAT, Hautes Instances, 61 P. 4 - CQG, Cabinet de la Défense Nationale, Conseil Suprême, 5/2/40.
58 SHAT, Hautes Instances, Conseil suprême, *op. cit.*
59 *Ibid.*
60 ACC, Letter from Vice-Admiral Odend'hal to Captain Auphan,13/2/40, London.
61 J. MINART, *P.C. Vincennes*, T. I. Berger-Levrault, Paris, 1945, p. 187.
62 MINART, *P.C. Vincennes, op. cit.*, p. 186.
63 J. KENNEDY, *The Business of War*, W. Morrow, New York, 1958, p. 46.
64 WO 193/772, General Massy to General Sir Guy Williams, 6/2/40.
65 FO 371/24818, Lord Halifax to Marquess of Lothian, 20/2/40, London.
66 *Ibid.*, War Cabinet meeting, 23/2/40.
67 *Ibid.*, War Cabinet meeting, 29/2/40.
68 UD 2/35 G. Sov. Finl VII, 15/2/40, Helsinki.
69 *Ibid.*
70 L. WOODWARD, *British Foreign Policy in the Second World War*, vol. II, HMSO, London, 1957, p. 88; V. TANNER, *Finlands Väg*, Holger-Schildts, Stockholm, 1950, p. 248.
71 *Ibid.*
72 C. G. E. MANNERHEIM, *Mémoires*, Hachette, Paris, 1952, p. 287.
73 *Ibid.*, p. 288.
74 K. A. MERETSKOV, *Na službe narodu*, Izd. Pol. Lit., Moscow, 1968, p. 189.
75 L. WOODWARD, *British Foreign Policy*, vol. II, *op. cit.*, p. 92.
76 G. ROSSI-LANDI in *Français et Britanniques, op. cit.*, pp. 48-51.
77 M. GAMELIN, *Servir*, T. III, Plon, Paris, 1946, p. 204.
78 J. MORDAL, *La campagne de Norvège, op. cit.*, p. 103.
79 J. HARVEY, *The Diplomatic Diaries of Oliver Harvey, 1937-1940*, Collins, London, 1970, p. 338.
80 L. WOODWARD, *British Foreign Policy, op. cit.*, pp. 92-3.
81 *Ibid.*
82 *Ibid.* Also: *Innstilling*, Bilag, Bd. I, p. 221.
83 C. G. E. MANNERHEIM, *Mémoires, op. cit.*, p. 292.
84 D. DILKS, *Cadogan Diaries, op. cit.*, p. 261.
85 R. MACLEOD, *Ironside Diaries, op. cit.*, p. 226.
86 WO 193/772, War Cabinet Meeting, 11/3/40.
87 R. MACLEOD, *Ironside Diaries, op. cit.*, p. 226.
88 J. KENNEDY, *The Business of War, op. cit.*, p. 47.
89 WO 106/1893, General Mackesy to DMO & P, 8/3/1940, London.
90 *Ibid.*
91 J. KENNEDY, *The Business of War, op. cit.*, p. 48.
92 *Ibid.*
93 R. MACLEOD, *Ironside Diaries, op. cit.*, p. 227.

94 J. KENNEDY, *The Business of War, op. cit.*, p. 49.
95 *Ibid.*, p. 49.
96 *Ibid.*, p. 50.
97 R. MACLEOD, *Ironside Diaries, op. cit.*, p. 228.
98 J. KENNEDY, *The Business of War, op. cit.*, p. 50.
99 CAB 65/12 War Cabinet Meeting, 12/3/40 Confidential Annexe, minute 2.
100 J. KENNEDY, *The Business of War, op. cit.*, p. 50.
101 CAB 65/12 War Cabinet Meeting, 14/3/40, Confidential Annexe, minute 4.
102 M. GILBERT, *Winston S. Churchill,* vol. VI, Heinemann, London, 1983, p. 190.

## CHAPTER II

1 DGFP, séries D, Doc. no. 19, Hossbach minutes, 5/11/37.
2 H. RAUSCHNING, *Hitler m'a dit,* Ed. France, Paris, 1939, p. 171.
3 F. KERSAUDY, *Stratèges et Norvège, op. cit.*, pp. 42–52.
4 *Ibid.*, pp. 72 and 108.
5 V. QUISLING, *Russland og vi,* Mallingske, Oslo, 1930.
6 *Morgenbladet,* 11/3/50.
7 MGFA, Nachlass Boehm, n 172/14, H. W. Scheidt to Admiral Boehm, 31/1/55.
8 STRAFFESAK MOT V. A. L. J. QUISLING, Eidsivating Lagstols Landssvikavdeling, Oslo, 1946, p. 346.
9 WALTER HUBATSCH, *Quellen zur neuesten Geschichte,* Stuttgart, 1953/1, p. 62.
10 MGFA, Nachlass Boehm, N 172/14, *op. cit.*
11 FRANZ HALDER, *Kriegstagebuch,* T. III, Kohlhammer, Stuttgart, 1962, p. 13.
12 MGFA, KTB - SKL, Teil C 8 - 1017/1 OBDM - Führer, 26/1/40, p. 210.
13 EARL F. ZIEMKE, *The German Northern Theater of Operations,* DAP, Washington, DC 1959, p. 12.
14 IFZG ZS 979 Vernehmung Adm. Krancke 15/6/48.
15 E. F. ZIEMKE, *The German Northern Theater, op. cit.*, p. 15.
16 IFZG, ZS 979, *op. cit.*
17 TMI, Tome XV, Déposition de l'amiral Raeder, 17/5/46, p. 251.
18 HEINZ G. SERAPHIM, *Das Politische Tagebuch Alfred Rosenbergs,* Musterschmidt, Göttingen, 1956, p. 102.
19 IFZG, ZS 979, *op. cit.*
20 TMI, Tome XXVIII, PS 1809, Tagebuch Jodl, p. 406.
21 BERETNING TIL FOLKETINGET, Bilag Bd. XII, Copenhagen 1951, pp. 283–5.
22 BERETNING, *op. cit.*, Bilag Bd. XII, p. 283.

23 *Ibid.*, p. 284.
24 NHM, F.O.II 09 Div., BKS 24, Bericht und Vernehmung des General-obersten von Falkenhorst, 30/9/45, p. 6.
25 *Ibid.*, p. 12.
26 E. F. ZIEMKE, *The German Northern Theater, op. cit.*, p. 17.
27 TMI, T. XXVIII, PS 1809, *op. cit.*, p. 409, 29/2/40; and BERETNING, *op. cit.*, p. 285.
28 K. VON TIPPELSKIRCH, *Geschichte des Zweiten Weltkrieges*, Athaenäum, Bonn, 1956, p. 55.
29 TMI, T. XVIII, PS 1809, *op. cit.*, p. 409, 3/3/40.
30 MGFA, KTB-SKL, Teil a, 1000/7, p. 98, 13/3/40.
31 BERETNING, *op. cit.*, T. XII, p. 38, Doc 24, 6/3/40; and p. 68, Doc. 38, 13/3/40.
32 *Ibid.*, Bilag, p. 17, doc. no. 14.
33 DGFP, vol. 9, p. 67. Doc. no. 41, 2/4/40.
34 BERETNING, *op. cit.*, t. XII, p. 287.
35 MGFA, KTB-SKL, Teil B, 1005/2, 1/4/1940.

## CHAPTER III

1 D. DILKS, *Cadogan Diaries, op. cit.*, pp. 262-3; R. MACLEOD, *Ironside Diaries, op. cit.*, p. 228.
2 Parliamentary Debates, H. of C., vol. 358, 1939-40, col. 1922.
3 *Ibid.*, col. 1900, 2214.
4 *Ibid.*, col. 1850, 1874, 1912.
5 HAROLD MACMILLAN, *The Blast of War*, Macmillan, London, 1977, p. 59.
6 CAB 83/5, MCC Memorandum no. 61/1940, 8/3/40.
7 CAB 65/12, War. Cab. 71, Confidential Annexe no. 6, 18/3/40.
8 On the origins of this project, see W. S. CHURCHILL, *The Second World War*, vol. I, *op. cit.*, pp. 399-401.
9 WO 193/772, War Cabinet Meeting, 19/3/40.
10 FO 371/24821, Cabinet Conclusions 73 (40), 20/3/40.
11 J. B. DUROSELLE, *L'Abîme, op. cit.*, pp. 99-101.
12 FO 371/24821, Note by Sir A. Cadogan, N 3504, 19/3/40.
13 W. S. CHURCHILL, *The Second World War*, vol. I, *op. cit.*, p. 455.
14 R. MACLEOD, *Ironside Diaries, op. cit.*, p. 234.
15 PAUL DE VILLELUME, *Journal d'une défaite*, Fayard, Paris, 1976, p. 249.
16 Commission d'Enquête Parlementaire, T. II, Paris, 1952, p. 351, Communication de M. Paul Reynaud au gouvernement britannique, 25/3/40.
17 R. MACLEOD, *Ironside Diaries, op. cit.*, pp. 234-5.
18 D. DILKS, *Cadogan Diaries, op. cit.*, p. 265.
19 R. MACLEOD, *Ironside Diaries, op. cit.*, p. 237.

20 D. DILKS, *Cadogan Diaries, op. cit.*, p. 265.
21 J. R. M. BUTLER, *Grand Strategy*, vol. II, *op. cit.*, p. 121.
22 SHAT, Hautes Instances, 61 p. 4, GQG, Cabinet de la Défense Nationale, Conseil Suprême du 28/3/40.
23 BUTLER, *Grand Strategy*, vol. II, *op. cit.*, p. 121.
24 SHAT, Hautes Instances, Conseil Suprême, *op. cit.*
25 *Weissbuch* no. 6, p. 255, doc. no. 30; J. MORDAL, *La campagne de Norvège, op. cit.*, Annexe IV, p. 430.
26 See F. KERSAUDY, *La Norvège et les Grandes Puissances, op. cit.*, pp. 599–604.
27 WO 106/1969, Note by DMO & P., 30/3/40.
28 *Ibid.* Note for DCIGS, 2/4/1940.
29 *Ibid.* Memo by CIGS for COSC, 3/4/1940.
30 WO 193/773 WO for meeting of COSC, 4/4/1940.
31 D. DILKS, *Cadogan Diaries, op. cit.*, p. 266.
32 W. S. CHURCHILL, *The Second World War*, vol. I, *op. cit.*, pp. 460–1.
33 *Time*, 3 April 1940.
34 LLEWELYN WOODWARD, *British Foreign Policy in the Second World War*, HMSO, London, 1970, vol. I, p. 116.
35 ADM 199/2202, War Diary, Home Command, 7/4/40.
36 *Aftenposten*, 2 April 1940.
37 *Daily Telegraph*, 4 April 1940.
38 *Innstilling, op. cit.*, Bilag Bd II, pp. 143–4, 148, 152, 156, 161.
39 DEUTSCH-NORWEGISCHER VERLAG, *Zwischen Storting und Downing Street*, Oslo, 1942, p. 28. Also: T. LIE, *Leve eller dø, op. cit.*, p. 101.
40 MVBZ, Archief van het Nederlandse Gezandschapt te Londen, C-8/ Doos 28 no. 58, V. H. de With tot Van Kleffens, 16/8/43.
41 *The Times*, 1 April 1940.
42 *The Times*, 3 April 1940.
43 *Innstilling*, Bilag Bd II, p. 165.
44 AE, X. Note diplomatique remise par le ministre de France Dampierre au ministre des Affaires étrangères de Norvège, 5/4/40.
45 FÖRSPELET, *op. cit.*, p. 379.
46 I. MAISKI, *Vospominanja Sovjetskovo Posla*, Nauka, Moskva, 1965, p. 55.
47 AE, X. Note remise au ministre des Affaires étrangères de Norvège par le ministre de France, 8/4/40.
48 C. HAMBRO, *Historiske Dokumenter, op. cit.*, p. 99.
49 AE, X. Note du ministre des Affaires étrangères de Norvège au ministre de France, 8/4/40.
50 C. HAMBRO, *Historiske Dokumenter, op. cit.*, p. 102.
51 MGFA, KTB-SKL, Teil B, 1005/2, p. 211.
52 *Innstilling, op. cit.*, p. 97.
53 *Innstilling, op. cit.*, p. 98.
54 LEIF C. ROLSTAD, *April 1940, en Krigsdagbok*, Gyldendal, Oslo, 1980, p. 21.

## CHAPTER IV

1 RA, Koht ARKIV, Trumål, 5/11/45, pp. 2-3.
2 T. LIE, *Leve eller dø, op. cit.*, p. 16. This is confirmed by H. KOHT in *Norway Neutral, op. cit.*, p. 75.
3 T. LIE, *Leve eller dø, op. cit.*, p. 16.
4 FO 371/24829. Tel. from Sir C. Dormer, received 3.25 a.m., 9/4/40.
5 Interview of Sir C. Dormer, *op. cit.*
6 T. LIE, *Leve eller dø, op. cit.*, p. 17.
7 *Ibid.*, also RA, Koht arkiv, Trumål, 29/5/63.
8 L. C. ROLSTAD, *9 April, op. cit.*, p. 21.
9 T. LIE, *Leve eller dø, op. cit.*, p. 17.
10 L. C. ROLSTAD, *9 April, op. cit.*, p. 21.
11 H. KOHT, *Norway Neutral, op. cit.*, pp. 65-6.
12 UD U27 6/26, 9 April 1940, Notat av. J. Bull.
13 W. HUBATSCH, *Weserübung, op. cit.*, pp. 86-7, and O. K. GRIMNES, *Oscarsborg festning*, FKA, Oslo, 1972, pp. 6-8.
14 H. KOHT, *Norway Neutral, op. cit.*, pp. 203-9.
15 H. KOHT, *Norway Neutral, op. cit.*, pp. 74-5.
16 H. KOHT, *Norway Neutral, op. cit.*, p. 75.
17 *Ibid.*, also: T. LIE: *Leve eller dø, op. cit.*, p. 23.
18 H. KOHT, *Norway Neutral, op. cit.*, p. 76.
19 T. LIE, *Leve eller dø, op. cit.*, p. 23.
20 FO 371/24834 Report by Sir Cecil Dormer, 20/4/40.
21 *Innstilling*, Bilag Bd II, *op. cit.*, p. 255.
22 *Innstilling*, Bilag Bd II, *op. cit.*, p. 209.
23 *Ibid.*, p. 214. (According to declarations by General Laake himself . . .)
24 NHM, FO II O9 Div., Vernehmung Falkenhorst *op. cit.*, pp. 12-13.
25 C. J. HAMBRO, *7 Juni, 9 April, 7 Juni*, Gyldendal, Oslo, 1956, pp. 131-2.
26 T. LIE, *Leve eller dø, op. cit.*, p. 114.
27 H. KOHT, *Norway Neutral, op. cit.*, p. 81.
28 C. J. HAMBRO, *7 Juni, op. cit.*, pp. 114 and 115.
29 T. LIE, *Leve eller dø, op. cit.*, p. 116.
30 *Ibid.*, p. 118.
31 T. LIE, *Leve eller dø, op. cit.*, p. 117.
32 T. LIE, *Leve eller dø, op. cit.*, p. 119.
33 FO 371/24834 Report by Sir C. Dormer, *op. cit.*
34 FO 371/24829 FO to Sir C. Dormer, 12.55, 9/4/40.
35 C. J. HAMBRO, *7 Juni, op. cit.*, pp. 134-7.
36 C. J. HAMBRO, *7 Juni, op. cit.*, p. 147.
37 C. J. HAMBRO, *7 Juni, op. cit.*, p. 152.
38 MGFA N 172/14, Nachlass Boehm, H. W. Scheidt an Adm. Boehm, 16/1/55, p. 9.

39 ERICH PRUCK: 'Abwehraussenstelle Norwegen' in *Marine Rundschau*, 1956, no. 4, pp. 114–15.
40 MGFA N 172/14 Nachlass Boehm, *op. cit.*, pp. 9–10.
41 H. G. SERAPHIM, *Das politische Tagebuch Rosenbergs*, Musterschmidt, Göttingen, 1956, p. 104: 9/4/40.
42 NRK 51 987/1 (original recording of the speech).
43 C. J. HAMBRO, *7 Juni, op. cit.*, p. 154.
44 C. J. HAMBRO, *7 Juni, op. cit.*, p. 156.
45 *Ibid.*, pp. 164–5.
46 NRK 2643, 10/3/55, General Helset om Midtskogen.

## CHAPTER V

1 H. ISMAY, *Memoirs, op. cit.*, pp. 118–19.
2 On the whole question, see CCA, Redw 1/2, Diary of Adm R. E. Edwards; W. S. CHURCHILL, *The Second World War*, vol. I, *op. cit.*, p. 467.
3 T. K. DERRY, *The Campaign, op. cit.*, p. 64.
4 CAB 65/6, WC 85 (40) 9/4/40, 8.30 a.m.
5 *Ibid.*, WC 86 (40) 2/4/40, 12H.
6 *Ibid.*
7 CAB 65/6, WC 86 (40), *op. cit.*
8 ADM 116/4471. 'Summary of events', 9 April.
9 PAUL BAUDOUIN, *Neuf mois au gouvernement*, la Table Ronde, Paris, 1948, p. 21.
10 *Ibid.*, p. 22.
11 *Ibid.*, pp. 22–3.
12 PAUL REYNAUD, *Envers et contre tous*, Flammarion, Paris, 1963, p. 323.
13 PAUL DE VILLELUME, *Journal d'une défaite*, Fayard, Paris, 1976, p. 263.
14 FNSP, Archives Daladier, 3 DA 5 Dr 5, Conseil Suprême interallié, 9/4/40, pp. 3–12.
15 *Ibid.*
16 *Ibid.*
17 CAB 83/3, MCC no. 17, 9/4/40, 9.30 p.m.
18 W. S. CHURCHILL, *The Second World War*, vol. I, *op. cit.*, p. 474.
19 FO 371/24834. Report by Sir Cecil Dormer, *op. cit.*, p. 5.
20 FO 371/24829 Naval attaché, Stockholm, to DNI, 10/4/40, 8.07 a.m.
21 AEB, 11064, GB. Baron Cartier de Marchienne à M. Spaak, no. 4708-1583, 10/4/40.
22 WO 106/1812. DMO for GIGS, Narvik appreciation, 10/4/40, 3 p.m.
23 CCAC, DMCL (Maclachlan MSS). '*Source Todd*', 9/4/40.
24 WO 106/1812, Narvik appreciation, *op. cit.*
25 *Ibid.*
26 CAB 65/12, WM 87 (40) 10/4/40.

27 CAB 65/6, WC 87 (40) 10/4/40.
28 W. S. CHURCHILL, *The Second World War*, vol. I, *op. cit.*, p. 474.
29 WO 106/1812 DCIGS. Operations to capture Narvik, 11/4/40.
30 *London Gazette*, Supplement, 8/7/1947, Lord Cork's Despatch.
31 Quoted in W. S. CHURCHILL, *The Second World War*, vol. I, *op. cit.*, p. 482.
32 WO 106/1812, Operations to capture Narvik, *op. cit.*
33 W. S. CHURCHILL, *The Second World War*, vol. I, *op. cit.*, p. 482.
34 L. E. H. MAUND, *Assault from the Sea*, Methuen, London, 1949, p. 24.
35 P. DE VILLELUME, *Journal d'une défaite*, *op cit.*, p. 271.
36 ADM 205/4. Scand. 'Notes of informal meeting', 11/4/40, 9.35 a.m.
37 CAB 65/6, WC 88 (40) 11/4/40, 11.30 a.m.
38 L. WOODWARD, *British Foreign Policy*, vol I, *op. cit.*, pp. 120–1.
39 FÖRSPELET, *op. cit.*, p. 381, Uppteckning av Gen. Thörnell.
40 FO 371/24834. Mr Mallet, Stockholm, to FO no. 236, 13/4/40.
41 FO 371/24835 'De la part de M. Coulondre', Stockholm 13/4/40.
42 *Ibid.*, Mr Mallet to FO no. 208 DIPP, 13/4/40.
43 *Ibid.*, Note for the Cabinet no. N4643, 11/4/40.
44 FO 971/24830, Tel. by Sir C. Dormer, transm. by Mr Mallet, Stockholm, no. 205, 12/4/40.
45 CAB 83/3, MCC no. 19, 11/4/40.
46 *Ibid.*
47 CAB 65/12, WM 89 (40) 12/4/40.
48 T. K. DERRY, *The Campaign in Norway*, *op. cit.*, p. 66.
49 FO 371/2/830 FO to Mallet, Stockholm, 11/4/40, 5.45 p.m. See also *Daily Mail*, 11/4/40 and *Yorkshire Post*, 11 and 12/4/40.
50 CAB 65/12, WM 90 (40) 12/4/40.
51 CAB 65/12, WM 91 (40) 13/4/40.
52 *Ibid.*
53 CAB 65/12, WM (40) 13/4/40.
54 WO 106/1859, Battle Summary no. 17, p. 23.
55 CAB 83/3, MCC no. 22, 13/4/40, 10.30 p.m.
56 R. MACLEOD, *Ironside Diaries*, *op. cit.*, pp. 257–8.
57 *Ibid.*, p. 258.
58 CAB 65/12, WM 92 (40) 14/4/40.
59 CAB 65/12, WM 92 (40) 14/4/40.
60 L. E. H. MAUND, *Assault from the Sea*, *op. cit.*, p. 26.
61 L. E. H. MAUND, *Assault from the Sea*, *op. cit.*, p. 27.
62 CAB 65/12, WM 92 (40), 14/4/40.
63 T. K. DERRY, *The Campaign*, *op. cit.*, p. 66.

## CHAPTER VI

1 L. C. ROLSTAD, *April 1940, op. cit.*, p. 27.
2 ROBERT DE DAMPIERRE, *L'équipée d'une légation de France*, Plon, Paris, 1945, p. 41.
3 FO 371/24832. Report by Mr Rowland Kenney, 7/5/40.
4 JOHAN NYGAARDSVOLD, *Beretning om den Norske Regjeringens virksomhet fra 9 April 1940 til 25 Juni 1945*, Stortinget, Oslo, 1947, p. 6.
5 T. LIE, *Leve eller dø, op. cit.*, p. 134.
6 J. NYGAARDSVOLD, *Beretning, op. cit.*, p. 7.
7 W. HUBATSCH, *Weserübung, op. cit.*, p. 466, Anhand L.4.
8 *Ibid.*, pp. 466–7.
9 UD, U 27. 6/26, Notat av møtet mellom Kongen og min. Bräuer, 10/4/40.
10 UD, U 27. 7/6, Notat 10/4/40.
11 *Innstilling*, Bilag Bd II, p. 275.
12 T. LIE, *Leve eller dø, op. cit.*, p. 136.
13 *Innstilling*, Bilag Bd II, p. 275.
14 *Ibid.*, pp. 275–6.
15 *Ibid.*, p. 276.
16 *Ibid.*
17 UD, U 27.6/26 Notat av telefonsamtale, 10/4/40. See also: K. KOHT, *Norway Neutral, op. cit.*, p. 87.
18 NRK, 2641/1, *C. J. Hambro taler*, 4/5/55.
19 T. LIE, *Leve eller dø, op. cit.*, p. 135.
20 L. C. ROLSTAD, *April 1940, op. cit.*, p. 32.
21 *Ibid.*, p. 38.
22 OTTO RUGE, *Krigens dagbok*, Halvorsen og Larsen, Oslo, 1946, p. 260.
23 O. U. MUNTHE-KAAS, *The Campaign in Norway*, International Symposium of Historians, Helsinki, 1978, p. 11.
24 O. RUGE, *Krigens dagbok, op. cit.*, p. 357.
25 See for example: L. C. ROLSTAD, *April 1940, op. cit.*, pp. 38–9 and NRK, 52087–8 (Klausul), O. Solumsmoen: Dagbok fra Aprildagene; 21/9/71.
26 O. RUGE, *Krigens dagbok, op. cit.*, pp. 350, 351.
27 N. og K. GLEDITSCH, *Glimt fra Kampårene*, Dreyers, Oslo, 1954, p. 27.
28 O. RUGE, *Krigens dagbok, op. cit.*, p. 352.
29 NRK, 50395/1, 18/2/65. Krigen i Norge.
30 L. C. ROLSTAD, *April 1940, op. cit.*, p. 50. (According to the notes of Margaret Reid, secretary to Captain Foley.)
31 FO 371/24834. Tel. received from Norway, 14/4/40. (Special distribution and WC.)
32 L. C. ROLSTAD, *April 1940, op. cit.*, pp. 57–8.
33 FO 371/24834. Tel. 13/4/40, *op. cit.*, 5 p.m.
34 T. K. DERRY, *The Campaign, op. cit.*, p. 67.

35 NA, St. Dpt, 740.0011, EW 39/3208. G.2 Report no. 1 by Capt. R. M. Losey, 19/4/40, Stockholm.
36 L. C. ROLSTAD, *April 1940, op. cit.*, p. 53.
37 FO 371/24834. Message from Norwegian C.-in-C. to HM's government, 14/4/40, 3.45 p.m., N 4359.
38 Quoted in ODD LINDBÄCK-LARSEN, *Krigen i Norge 1940*, Gyldendal, Oslo, 1965, p. 67.
39 NRHQ, 8th Bat., the Sherwood Foresters, 'Campaign in Norway', by E. G. C. Beckwith, Hon. Colonel, 1958, p. 2.
40 NRHQ, 'Campaign', *op. cit.*, p. 3.
41 DUDLEY CLARKE, *Seven Assignments*, Jonathan Cape, London, 1948, pp. 88, 92.
42 *Ibid.*, p. 90. Also: NRHQ, 'Campaign', *op. cit.*, p. 3 and T. K. DERRY, *The Campaign, op. cit.*, p. 99.
43 D. CLARKE, *Seven Assignments, op. cit.*, p. 95.
44 T. K. DERRY, *The Campaign, op. cit.*, p. 99.
45 N. og K. GLEDITSCH, *Glimt, op. cit.*, p. 38.
46 NRHQ, 'Campaign', *op. cit.*, p. 3.
47 *Ibid.*, and T. K. DERRY, *The Campaign, op. cit.*, p. 99; WO 106/1859, Battle Summary no. 17, p. 47. Tel-AT/2217/17.
48 NRK 50031/2, 18/1/65, *Felttoget i Sør Norge*, av. Gen. Major R. Roscher Nilsen.
49 D. CLARKE, *Seven Assignments, op. cit.*, pp. 109–12.
50 NRK 50031/2, *Felttoget, op. cit.*
51 O. LINDBÄCK-LARSEN, *Krigen i Norge, op. cit.*, p. 79; J. L. MOULTON, *The Norwegian Campaign, op. cit.*, p. 178; T. K. DERRY, *The Campaign in Norway, op. cit.*, pp. 105–7.
52 On the whole operation, see NRHQ, 'Campaign', *op. cit.*, and O. LINDBÄCK-LARSEN, *Krigen i Norge, op. cit.*, pp. 79–84; J. L. MOULTON, *The Norwegian Campaign, op. cit.*, pp. 176–89; T. K. DERRY, *The Campaign in Norway, op. cit.*, pp. 105–12.
53 See for example T. LIE: *Leve eller dø, op. cit.*, p. 185.
54 N. og K. GLEDITSCH, *Glimt fra Kampårene, op. cit.*, p. 185.
55 H. KOHT, *Norway Neutral, op. cit.*, p. 199.

## CHAPTER VII

1 WO 106/1859, Battle summary no. 17, p. 62.
2 ADM 199/485 Tel. 2341/14. To Adm. of the Fleet Lord Cork.
3 ADM 199/485 Report by Adm. of the Fleet Lord Cork and Orrery, p. 3.
4 FO 371/56332 Lord Cork on campaign in Norway, 1946, p. 4.
5 X, Joint Services, Staff College lecture, 18th lecture, Script 10, Narvik, opening phase, p. 5.

6 WO 106/1905, notes on supply situation at Narvik (no date), p. 3.
7 *Ibid.*
8 X, Staff college lecture, *op. cit.*
9 WO 106/1898. For WO from Mackesy, 0943/19, as well as WO 106/1905, notes on supply situation, *op. cit.*, pp. 1-2; and ADM 199/485 Report by Lord Cork, *op. cit.*, p. 1.
10 WO 106/1859, Battle Summary no. 17, *op. cit.*, p. 63.
11 ADM 199/485, tel. 1201/16 in: Report by Lord Cork, *op. cit.*, p. 2.
12 W. S. CHURCHILL, *The Second World War*, vol. I, *op. cit.*, p. 486.
13 WO 106/1898. 'Rupert plans for attack.' HQ Avon force to WO no. 2105/17, 17/4/40.
14 ADM 199/485. Report by Lord Cork, *op. cit.*, p. 3.
15 *Ibid.*
16 *Ibid.*, p. 4.
17 *Ibid.*, p. 5.
18 *Ibid.*, p. 6, Naval message from Flag Officer, Narvik, to Admiralty, 1635/18, 18/4/40.
19 WO 106/1859, Battle Summary no. 17, *op. cit.*, p. 64.
20 X. Staff College lecture, Script 10, *op. cit.*, pp. 7-8.
21 WO 106/1859, Battle Summary no. 17, *op. cit.*, p. 64.
22 T. K. DERRY, *The Campaign, op. cit.*, p. 154.
23 WO 106/1859, Battle Summary no. 17, *op. cit.*, p. 65.
24 CCAC, Rosk 4/76, WSC to Sir C. Forbes, Secret and Personal, 17/4/40.
25 T. K. DERRY, *The Campaign, op. cit.*, p. 84.
26 A. CARTON DE WIART, *Happy Odyssey*, Jonathan Cape, London, 1950, p. 168.
27 A. CARTON DE WIART, *Happy Odyssey, op. cit.*, p.169.
28 T. K. DERRY, *The Campaign, op. cit.*, p. 87.
29 J. MORDAL, *La campagne, op. cit.*, p. 291.
30 SHAT, 4723 CEFS, Campagne de Norvège, général Audet à 3e Bureau no. 86/35, rapport sur l'expédition de Namsos, 12/5/40, pp. 3-4.
31 *Ibid.*, p. 8.
32 J. MORDAL, *La campagne, op. cit.*, pp. 291-2. Also: SHAT 4721, CEFS, Carton 3, rapport de l'adjudant Perrin, pp. 6-8.
33 O. B. GETZ, *Fra Krigen i Nord Trøndelag, 1940*, Aschehoug, Oslo, 1940, p. 55.
34 WO 106/1938, 'Maurice'. Conversation of Capt. Lindsay and Second Lt. Scott-Haston with DDMI (1), MI 2(B), 10/5/40.
35 O. B. GETZ, *Fra Krigen, op. cit.*, pp. 77-81; T. K. DERRY, *The Campaign, op. cit.*, pp. 91-6.
36 A. CARTON DE WIART, *Happy Odyssey, op. cit.*, p. 171.
37 A. CARTON DE WIART, *Happy Odyssey, op. cit.*, p. 171.
38 CCAC, ROSK 4/76 WSC to Sir C. Forbes, Secret and Personal, 17/4/40.
39 R. BUTLER, *Grand Strategy, op. cit.*, p. 135.

40 WO 106/1859, Battle Summary no. 17, p. 31, Tel. AT 0142/14, 14/4/40.
41 *Ibid.*, AT 1157/14, 14/4/40.
42 WO 106/1859, Battle Summary no. 17, *op. cit.*, p. 32.
43 On this curious episode, see BRIAN COSGRAVE, *Churchill at War*, Collins, London, 1974, pp. 164-5.
44 CAB 65/12, WM 95 (40), 17/4/40, p. 2.
45 CAB 65/12, WM 95 (40), *op. cit.*
46 *Ibid.*, p. 4; as well as W. S. CHURCHILL, *The Second World War*, vol. I, *op. cit.*, p. 493.
47 FNSP, 3 DA 7-DR 5, Avril 1940. P. Reynaud à N. Chamberlain, 18/4/40.
48 *Ibid.*, 3 DA 6-DR 5. Sdrb, Comité de guerre du 16 avril.
49 CAB 65/12, WM 96 (40), 18/4/40, p. 2.
50 W. S. CHURCHILL, *The Second World War*, vol. I, *op. cit.*, p. 492.
51 *Ibid.*, p. 493.
52 Interview with Lord Mountbatten, 4 June 1979.
53 CAB 80/105, COS paper 297 (s) (40) Operation 'Hammer', 19/4/40.
54 CAB 79/85, COS 87 (40), 19/4/40.
55 CCAC, Keyes MSS, 13/28 'Norwegian crisis, April 1940', Diary.
56 W. S. CHURCHILL, *The Second World War*, vol. I, *op. cit.*, p. 496.
57 CCAC, Keyes MSS 13/28, Diary, *op. cit.*
58 W. S. CHURCHILL, *The Second World War*, vol. I, *op. cit.*, p. 496.
59 CAB 65/12, WM (98) 40, 20/4/40, p. 1.
60 *Ibid.*, pp. 2-3.
61 CAB 65/12, WM (98) 40, *op. cit.*, p. 5.
62 CAB 65/12, WM 99 (40), 21/4/40, p. 1; WM 100 (40), 22/4/40, p. 1; 23/4/40, pp. 1-2.
63 *Ibid.*, WM 100 (40), 22/4/40, p. 1.
64 CAB 65/12, WM 101 (40), 23/4/40, p. 3.
65 CAB 65/12, WM 101 (40), 23/4/40, p. 2.
66 *Ibid.*, WM 99 (40), 21/4/40, p. 7.
67 NRK, 50031/2, 18/1/65, Gen. Major R. Roscher-Nielsen, *op. cit.*
68 *Ibid.*
69 CAB 65/12, WM 96 (40) 18/4/40.
70 W. S. CHURCHILL, *The Second World War*, vol. I, *op. cit.*, p. 508.
71 WO 106/1905. Report by Maj.-Gen. A. Carton de Wiart, p. 3.
72 A. CARTON DE WIART, *Happy Odyssey*, *op. cit.*, p. 171.
73 IWM, Sir C. Nicholson papers, DS. MISC/7, pp. 5-6.
74 IWM, Sir C. Nicholson papers, *op. cit.*, p. 9.
75 J. L. MOULTON, *The Norwegian Campaign*, *op. cit.*, p. 193.

## CHAPTER VIII

1 See in particular: G. L. DIETL, *General Dietl*, Münchner Buchverlag, Munich, 1951, pp. 118-42.

2 Tagebuch Jodl in W. HUBATSCH, *Weserübung, op. cit.*, p. 373.

3 General von Brauchitsch.

4 Tagebuch Halder in W. HUBATSCH, *Weserübung, op. cit.*, p. 374.

5 BERNHARD VON LOSSBERG, *Im Wehrmachtführungsstab*, Nölke, Hamburg, 1949, p. 70.

6 WALTER WARLIMONT, *Im Hauptquartier der Deutschen Wehrmacht*, Bernard und Graefe, Frankfurt, 1962, p. 96.

7 Tagebuch Halder in W. HUBATSCH, *Weserübung, op. cit.*, p. 374.

8 Tagebuch Jodl in W. HUBATSCH, *Weserübung, op. cit.*, p. 376.

9 *Ibid.*

10 Author's note.

11 B. VON LOSSBERG, *Im Wehrmachtführungsstab, op. cit.*, p. 67.

12 *Ibid.*, pp. 67–8.

13 Tagebuch Jodl in W. HUBATSCH, *Weserübung, op. cit.*, p. 376.

14 NHM, FO II og div, Bks 24, Vernehmung des G. O. von Falkenhorst, *op. cit.*, pp. 14–15.

15 See: HELMUT GREINER, *Die Oberste Wehrmachtführung, 1939–1943*, Limes Verlag, Wiesbaden, 1951, p. 88.

16 VICTOR MOGENS, *Tyskerne, Quisling og vi andre*, Utenriksforlaget, Oslo, 1945, p. 110.

17 DGFP, vol. 6, April 1940, pp. 136–9, Doc. no. 95, The Minister in Norway to the Foreign Ministry no. 2800, 11/4/40.

18 *Innstilling*, bd I, *op. cit.*, p. 156.

19 *Ibid.*, pp. 154–5.

20 *Ibid.*, pp. 159–60.

21 *Innstilling*, bd I, *op. cit.*, pp. 148–9.

22 *Ibid.*, pp. 162–3.

23 *Innstilling*, bd I, *op. cit.*, pp. 168.

24 Tagebuch Jodl in W. HUBATSCH, *Weserübung, op. cit.*, p. 376.

25 AA, Partei Dienststellen Norwegen, 4/3, E 087690, Konferenz Hitler–Quisling, 16/8/40.

26 Tagebuch Jodl in W. HUBATSCH, *Weserübung, op. cit.*, p. 376.

27 B. VON LOSSBERG, *Im Wehrmachtführungsstab, op. cit.*, p. 70. (See also: CAB 65/12, WM 100 (40) 22/4/40.)

28 J. L. MOULTON, *The Norwegian Campaign, op. cit.*, p. 203.

29 Tagebuch Jodl in W. HUBATSCH, *Weserübung, op. cit.*, p. 378.

30 *Ibid.*, p. 379.

31 *Ibid.*, p. 380.

## CHAPTER IX

1 W. S. CHURCHILL, *The Second World War*, vol. I, *op. cit.*, p. 503.

2 Journel officiel, 12/4/40, p. 669.

3 FNSP, E DA 7 DR 5, avril 1940, P. Reynaud à N. Chamberlain, 18/4/40.
4 See in particular P. DE VILLELUME, *Journal d'une défaite, op cit.*, pp. 281-3.
5 *Ibid.*, p. 287.
6 P. DE VILLELUME, *Journal d'une défaite, op cit.*, p. 288.
7 FNSP. Conseil Suprême, *op. cit.*; F. BEDARIDA, *La Stratégie secrète, op. cit.*, p. 435.
8 AMIRAL AUPHAN, 'A propos de l'expédition de Norvège', *Ecrits de Paris*, 1948, no. 47, p. 46.
9 F. BEDARIDA, *La Stratégie secrète, op. cit.*, p. 475.
10 See CAB 65/12, WM (40) 102, 24/4/40; R. MACLEOD, *Ironside Diaries, op. cit.*, p. 279.
11 W. S. CHURCHILL, *The Second World War*, vol. I, *op. cit.*, p. 505.
12 J. R. M. BUTLER, *Grand Strategy, op. cit.*, p. 137.
13 CAB 65/12, WM 102 (40) 24/4/40.
14 CCAC, Keyes MSS, 13/28, Notes on the Norwegian campaign, 4/12/41.
15 *Ibid.*, Keyes to Churchill, 17/4/40.
16 *Ibid.*, Diary, Norwegian crisis.
17 ADM 205/6 FSL records CIGS to Adm. Keyes 24/4/40.
18 CCAC, Keyes MSS 13/12, Keyes to WC 29/4/40.
19 PAUL STEHLIN, *Témoignage pour l'histoire*, Laffont, Paris, 1964, p. 239.
20 *Ibid.*, p. 245.
21 R. DU PAVILLON, *Les dessous de l'expédition de Norvège*, Arthaud, Paris, 1976.
22 WO 106/1905. 'Report by Gen. Carton de Wiart', *op. cit.*, p. 8 and annexe, p. 241.
23 *Ibid.*, p. 3.
24 P. STEHLIN, *Témoignage, op. cit.*, pp. 248-9.
25 R. DU PAVILLON, *Les dessous, op. cit.*, pp. 277 and 279.
26 D. J. L. FITZGERALD, *History of the Irish Guards*, Gale & Polden, Aldershot, 1949, p. 32.
27 WO 106/1905, 'Report by Gen. Carton de Wiart', *op. cit.*, p. 3; P. STEHLIN, *Témoignage, op. cit.*, pp. 246-7.
28 R. DU PAVILLON, *Les dessous, op. cit.*, p. 259.
29 WO 106/1905, 'Report by Gen. Carton de Wiart', *op. cit.*, Annex, p. 8; and R. DU PAVILLON, *Les dessous, op. cit.*, p. 223.
30 WO 106/1856, Gén. C. de Wiart to CIGS, Spillum, 25/4/40.
31 R. DU PAVILLON, *Les dessous, op. cit.*, p. 201.
32 WO 106/1856, Brig. Phillips to WO, 25/4/40. Priority.
33 The plan is described in detail in O. B. GETZ, *Fra Krigen, op. cit.*, pp. 100-3.
34 *Ibid.*
35 R. DU PAVILLON, *Les dessous, op. cit.*, p. 233; A. CARTON DE WIART, *Happy Odyssey, op. cit.*, pp. 171-2.
36 For the disastrous episode of Lake Lesjaskog, see in particular V.

MacClure, 'Gladiators in Norway', *Blackwood's Magazine*, vol. 249, Feb–Mar 1941, pp. 104–9.

37 W. Hingston, *Never Give Up, a History of the K.O.Y.L.I.*, vol. 5, Lund-Humphries, London, 1950, p. 97.

38 W. Hingston, *Never Give Up, op. cit.*, p. 96.

39 WO 106/1904, Report of operation – Sickle force in Norway, by Gen. Paget. See also: T. K. Derry, *The Campaign, op. cit.*, pp. 119–28.

40 WO 106/1905. Report on events observed at Aandalsnes, by Capt. Maxwell-Hislop, RN, 6/5/40, p. 4.

41 *Ibid.*, Sickle force. Report on certain aspects by Brigadier Hogg, 4/5/40, p. 3.

42 *Ibid.*

43 APC, MG 26 J4, N. M. Rogers. Visit to UK. Diary 1940, p. 32.

44 *Ibid.*, p. 39.

45 *Ibid.*, pp. 19, 32 and 43.

46 A. Auphan, 'A propos de l'expédition', *op. cit.*, p. 47.

47 R. MacLeod, *Ironside Diaries, op. cit.*, p. 279.

48 D. Dilks, *Cadogan Diaries, op. cit.*, p. 273.

49 CAB 65/12, WM 104 (41) 26/4/40.

50 *Ibid.*

51 O. Harvey, *Diplomatic Diary, op. cit.*, p. 352.

52 FNSP, 3 DA 6 – DR 3 – Sdrb, Comité de Guerre, 26/4/40.

53 *Ibid.*

54 FO 800/312, Lord Halifax to Ambassador Campbell, 30/4/40.

55 *Les documents secrets, op. cit.*, pp. 296–7.

56 M. Gamelin, *Servir, op. cit.*, T. III, pp. 366–7.

57 CAB 21/1378, Bridges to Cadogan, 26/4/40.

58 WO 106/1827, Memo., by C. in C., NWEF, 27/4/40.

59 *Ibid.*

60 WO 198/9, 'Sickle Force', C. in C., NWEF, 27/4/40.

61 *Ibid.*

62 CAB 65/12, WM 105 (40) 27/4/40.

63 *Ibid.*

64 *Ibid.*

65 R. MacLeod, *Ironside Diaries, op. cit.*, p. 287.

66 WO 106/1895, Massy to C. de W., 27/4/40, 13.15 p.m.

67 D. Dilks, *Cadogan Diaries, op. cit.*, p. 273.

68 FNSP, 3 DA 5 – DR 5 – Sdrb, Conseil suprême du 27 avril 1940; and CAB 99/3, SWC no. 9, 27/4/40.

69 *Ibid.*

70 FNSP, 3 DA 6 – DR 3 – Sdrb, Comité de Guerre.

71 T. Lie, *Leve eller dø, op. cit.*, p. 189.

72 FO 371/24834, Memorandum on situation at Aandalsnes, 3/5/40.

73 T. Lie, *Leve eller dø, op. cit.*, p. 189.

74  FO 371/24833, Note by J. M. Addis. N 5801, 14/6/40.
75  O. Ruge, *Krigens dagbok, op. cit.*, pp. 383–4.
76  FO 371/24834, Report by Sir C. Dormer, 4/5/40.
77  *Ibid.*
78  WO 106/1904, Report by Gen. Paget, *op. cit.*
79  NRK, 50031/2, Felttoget i Sør Norge, av Gen. Major R. Roscher - Nielsen, 18/1/65.
80  WO 06/1904, Report by Gen. Paget, *op. cit.*
81  NRK, 50031/2, Felttoget, *op. cit.*
82  D. Clarke, *Seven Assignments, op. cit.*, p. 160.
83  WO 106/1904, Report by Gen. Paget, *op. cit.*
84  WO 106/1897, To CIGS from Paget, 28/4/40.
85  T. K. Derry, *The Campaign, op. cit.*, p. 132.
86  FO 371/24834, C. Dormer to the Viscount Halifax, 4/5/40.
87  FO 371/24831, To Black Swan for NO 1/2, Aand., Repeat C. in C. HF, from Admiralty.
88  R. de Dampierre, *L'équipée, op. cit.*, p. 81.
89  FO 371/24834, C. Dormer to the Viscount Halifax, 5/5/40.
90  Y. Hauge, *Kongen av Norge, op. cit.*, p. 167.
91  FO 371/24834, Sir C. Dormer to Halifax, *op. cit.*
92  J. Nygaardsvold, *Beretning om den Norske Regjeringens virksomhet, op. cit.*, p. 13.
93  FO 371/24834. HMS *Glasgow*. Report of proceedings to C. in C., HF. no. 0498/016, 4/5/40.

## CHAPTER X

1  W. Bullitt, *For the President, Secret and Personal*, Houghton & Mifflin, Boston, 1972, p. 411.
2  P. de Villelume, *Journal d'une défaite, op cit.*, p. 315.
3  FO 371/24831, R. Campbell to FO no. 161 DIPP, 28/4/40.
4  P. de Villelume, *Journal d'une défaite, op cit.*, p. 316.
5  *Documents secrets, op. cit.*, pp. 334–6.
6  Our italics.
7  UD. U 27-6/26; Minist. Colban til Lord Halifax, 29/4/40. See also D. Dilks, *Cadogan Diaries, op. cit.*, pp. 274–5.
8  FO 800/322, Keyes to WSC, 30/4/40.
9  CCAC, Keyes MSS, 13/12, Keyes to WSC, 28/4/40.
10  WO 106/1895, Massy to Paget, Absolute priority no. 2100, 29/4/40.
11  WO 106/1905, Report by Lt. Col. D. W. Clarke, *op. cit.*, pp. 2–4.
12  ADM 199/477, Naval officer in charge, Aandalsnes. Narrative Report of Proceedings, 7/5/40, p. 6.
13  See T. K. Derry, *The Campaign, op. cit.*, pp. 134–7.

14  Parliamentary Debates, House of Commons, vol. 360, May 1940, Col. 911–12, 2/5/40.
15  P. STEHLIN, *Témoignage, op. cit.*, p. 251.
16  R. DU PAVILLON, *Les dessous, op. cit.*, p. 249.
17  O. B. GETZ, *Fra Krigen, op. cit.*, p. 139.
18  P. STEHLIN, *Témoignage, op. cit.*, p. 252.
19  A. CARTON DE WIART, *Happy Odyssey, op. cit.*, p. 173.
20  P. STEHLIN, *Témoignage, op. cit.*, p. 252.
21  R. DU PAVILLON, *Les dessous, op. cit.*, p. 277.
22  P. STEHLIN, *Témoignage, op. cit.*, p. 253.
23  A. CARTON DE WIART, *Happy Odyssey, op. cit.*, p. 173.
24  O. B. GETZ, *Fra Krigen, op. cit.*, p. 139.
25  *Ibid.*, pp. 150–1.
26  T. K. DERRY, *The Campaign, op. cit.*, p. 143.
27  L. C. ROLSTAD, *April 1940, op. cit.*, p. 134.
28  Parliamentary Debates, H. of C. vol. 360, col. 912, *op. cit.*
29  CAB 65/12, WM 100 (40) 22/4/40.
30  *Ibid.*, WM 104 (41) 26/4/40.
31  CAB 65/12, WM 104 (41) *op. cit.*
32  *Ibid.*, WM 108 (40) 30/4/40.
33  M. GILBERT, *Winston S. Churchill*, vol. VI, *op. cit.*, p. 276.
34  N. NICOLSON, *Harold Nicolson, Diaries and Letters*, Collins, London, 1967, p. 74.
35  FO 371/24834. Memorandum by Mr R. Kenney, 3/5/40.
36  CAB 65/13, WM 109 (40) 1/5/40.
37  R. R. JAMES, *Chips, the Diaries of Sir Henry Channon*, Weidenfeld, London, 1967, p. 243.
38  N. NICOLSON, *Harold Nicolson, Diaries and Letters, op. cit.*, p. 74.
39  R. R. JAMES, *Diaries of H. Channon, op. cit.*, p. 244.
40  *Ibid.*
41  R. MACLEOD, *Ironside Diaries, op. cit.*, p. 293.
42  A. EDEN, *Memoirs, The Reckoning, op. cit.*, p. 96.
43  CAB 79/4, COSC no. 110, 4/5/40, 9.30 a.m.
44  ADM 199/1929, Lord Cork to Adm., Immed. TM. 11.55, 5/5/40.
45  CAB 120/3, 'Defence Organisation' no. 120 (40), 3/4/40.
46  R. R. JAMES, *Diaries of H. Channon, op. cit.*, p. 244.
47  N. NICOLSON, *Harold Nicolson, Diaries and Letters, op. cit.*, p. 75.
48  *Manchester Guardian*, 4/5/40.
49  BUL, NC 8/35, Norway debate, May 1940. Note on Intelligence for NC, 6/5/40.
50  D. DILKS, *Cadogan Diaries, op. cit.*, p. 276.
51  FO 371/24834, C. DORMER, To the Viscount Halifax, 4/5/40, *op. cit.*
52  H. KOHT, *Frå skanse til skanse*. Iden, Oslo, 1947, p. 116.
53  UD, U 27 – 6/26, H. Koht, Trumål, 10/5/40.

54 LSE, Dalton diaries, vol. 22, *op. cit.*, I, p. 65, 2/5/40.
55 Parliamentary Debates, H. of C., vol. 360, 7/5/40, col. 1075, 1078, 1081.
56 *Ibid.*, col. 1082-3.
57 R. R. JAMES, *Diaries of Sir H. Channon, op. cit.*, p. 244.
58 Parl. Debates, H. of C. vol. 360, *op. cit.*, col. 1088-94.
59 *Ibid.*, col. 1095.
60 *Ibid.*, col. 1102.
61 *Ibid.*, col. 1102-4.
62 *Ibid.*, col. 1104.
63 *Ibid.*, col. 1125.
64 *Ibid.*, col. 1126.
65 N. NICOLSON, *Harold Nicolson, Diaries and Letters, op. cit.*, p. 77.
66 H. MACMILLAN, *The Blast of War, op. cit.*, p. 69.
67 L. S. AMERY, *My Political Life*, vol. III, Hutchinson, London, 1955, p. 359.
68 *Ibid.*, p. 360.
69 Parliamentary Debates, H. of C., vol. 360, *op. cit.*, col. 1140-1.
70 L. S. AMERY, *My Political Life, op. cit.*, p. 361.
71 Parl. Debates, H. of C., vol. 360, *op. cit.*, col. 1149.
72 *Ibid.*
73 L. S. AMERY, *My Political Life, op. cit.*, p. 365.
74 Parl. Debates, H. of C., vol. 360, *op. cit.*, col. 1150.
75 N. NICOLSON, *Harold Nicolson, Diaries and Letters, op. cit.*, p. 77.
76 W. S. CHURCHILL, *The Second World War*, vol. I, *op. cit.*, p. 521.
77 H. MACMILLAN, *The Blast of War, op. cit.*, p. 69.
78 Parl. Debates, H. of C., vol. 360, *op. cit.*, col. 1265.
79 *Ibid.*, col. 1266.
80 *Ibid.*, col. 1283.
81 *Ibid.*, col. 1298, 1299-1300, 1322, 1335.
82 *Ibid.*, col. 1300.
83 H. MACMILLAN, *The Blast of War, op. cit.*, p. 72.
84 Parl. Debates, H. of C., vol. 360, *op. cit.*, cols 1129 and 1085.
85 *Ibid.*, col. 1337-9.
86 *Ibid.*, col. 1307.
87 *Ibid.*, col. 1283.
88 *Ibid.*, col. 1349-62.
89 H. MACMILLAN, *The Blast of War, op. cit.*, p. 75
90 Parl. Debates, H. of C., vol. 360, *op. cit.*, col. 1362.
91 W. S. CHURCHILL, *The Second World War*, vol. I, *op. cit.*, p. 522.
92 LSE, Dalton diaries, I 22, 8/5/40, p. 68.
93 D. DILKS, *Cadogan Diaries, op. cit.*, p. 280.
94 W. S. CHURCHILL, *The Second World War*, vol. I, *op. cit.*, p. 523.
95 BUL, NC 18/I. To Ida, 11/5/40.
96 D. DILKS, *Cadogan Diaries, op. cit.*, p. 280.
97 A. EDEN, *The Reckoning, op. cit.*, pp. 96-7.

98 W. S. Churchill, *The Second World War*, vol. I, *op. cit.*, pp. 523-4.
99 Viscount Templewood, *Nine Troubled Years*, Collins, London, 1954, p. 432.
100 W. H. Thompson, *Sixty Minutes with Churchill*, C. Johnson, London, 1953, p. 45.


## CHAPTER XI

1 UD, U 27-6/26, Trumål, 10/5/40, H. Koht, p. 5. Also H. Koht, *Frå Skanse*, *op. cit.*, p. 123.
2 T. K. Derry, *The Campaign*, *op. cit.*, p. 164.
3 A. Béthouart, *Cinq Années*, *op. cit.*, p. 48.
4 *Ibid.*, p. 50.
5 P. O. Lapie, *La légion étrangère à Narvik*, John Murray, London, 1941, p. 26.
6 A. Béthouart, *Cinq Années*, *op. cit.*, p. 51.
7 C. Favrel, *Ci-devant légionnaire*, Paris, Presses de la Cité, 1963, p. 162.
8. *Ibid.*, pp. 166-8.
9 A. Béthouart, *Cinq Années*, *op. cit.*, p. 53.
10 *Ibid.*
11 *Ibid.*, p. 55.
12 See J. L. Moulton, *The Norwegian Campaign*, *op. cit.*, pp. 237-9.
13 See in particular WO 106/1824, DMT to DMO and P, 7/5/40 and *Ibid.*, DMO & P to DDM O, 1/5/40.
14 CAB 65/7, WC 114 (40) 7/5/40.
15 SHAT. 4723 CEFS, Béthouart au Gen. Cdant en chef, no. 73, 15/5/40.
16 *Ibid.*, Tel. du Gen. Béthouart, no. 30, 30/40.
17 Col. Passy, *Souvenirs*, T.I., Raoul Solar, Monte Carlo, 1947, p. 17.
18 FO 371/24832, Naval message, chargé d'affaires to L. Collier, FO, N 5460/1130/30, 12/5/40.
19 FO 371/24833, Sir C. Dormer to Viscount Halifax, N. 5946/1130/30, 28/5/40.
20 T. Lie, *Leve eller dø*, *op. cit.*, pp. 220-2, 229-31.
21 X. Also T. Lie: *Leve eller dø*, *op. cit.*, pp. 212-13, and WO 106/1835, Lascelles to FO no. 830, 17/5/40.
22 O. Ruge, *Krigens dagbok*, *op. cit.*, p. 410.
23 WO 198/14. Gen. Ruge to WO on Rearmament and Reorganization of Norwegian troops, 15/5/40.
24 Passy, *Souvenirs*, T.I., *op. cit.*, p. 18.
25 O. Ruge, *Krigens dagbok*, *op. cit.*, p. 406.
26 UD, U. 27-6/26, E. Colban om Britisk hjelpeaksjon: et lite tilbakeblikk, 23/1/41.
27 P. de Villelume, *Journal d'une défaite*, *op cit.*, p. 337.

28 W. S. CHURCHILL, *The Second World War*, vol. II, *op. cit.*, pp. 38-9.
29 D. DILKS, *Cadogan Diaries, op. cit.*, p. 286.
30 H. ISMAY, *Memoirs, op. cit.*, p. 126.
31 W. S. CHURCHILL, *The Second World War*, vol. II, *op. cit.*, p. 42.
32 *Ibid.*, p. 43.
33 *Ibid.*, pp. 45-6.
34 CAB 65/7, WC 126 (40), 17/5/40.
35 *Ibid.*
36 CAB 65/7, WC 131 (40), 20/5/40.
37 CAB 65/7, WC 131 (40), *op. cit.*
38 *Ibid.*, WC 134 (40), 22/5/40.
39 *Ibid.*, WC 133 (40), 22/5/40.
40 CAB 99/3, SWC, 12th meeting, 11/10/40.
41 WO 106/1817, WP (40), 165, 22/5/40.
42 CAB 65/13, WM 135 (40), Confidential Annexe, 23/5/40.
43 *Ibid.*, WM 138 (40), Min. 4, Confidential Annexe, 25/5/40.
44 WO 106/1813, for COS from Lord Cork, no. 1558, 27/5/40.
45 A. BUCHNER, *Narvik*, K. Vowinckel, Heidelberg, 1958, p. 126.
46 A. BÉTHOUART, *Cinq Années, op. cit.*, p. 65.
47 J. M. TORRIS, *Narvik*, Brentano's, New York, 1943, p. 212.
48 P. O. LAPIE, *La légion, op. cit.*, p. 65.
49 C. FAVREL, *Ci-devant légionnaire, op. cit.*, p. 177.
50 J. M. TORRIS, *Narvik, op. cit.*, p. 212.
51 *Ibid.*, p. 213.
52 A. BUCHNER, *Narvik, op. cit.*, p. 135.
53 On Military operations for the capture of Narvik, see in particular
   J. MORDAL, *La campagne, op. cit.*, pp. 400-2; T. K. DERRY, *The Campaign,
   op. cit.*, pp. 207-11; A. BÉTHOUART, *Cinq Années, op. cit.*, pp. 59-69;
   J. L. MOULTON, *The Norwegian Campaign, op. cit.*, pp. 228-30, as well
   as WO 106/1859, Battle summary no. 17, *op. cit.*, pp. 70-3, and
   ADM 199/482, Report by Lt. Cmdr S. H. Balfour, RN, 7/6/40.
54 CAB 99/3, SWC, 13th Meeting, 31/10/40.
55 CAB 65/13, WM 141 (40), 27/5/40.
56 *Ibid.*, WM 146 (40), Minute 6, Confidential Annexe, 29/5/40.
57 FO 371/24833, Sir C. Dormer to Viscount Halifax, no. 2, 30/5/40
   (N. 594/1130/30).
58 *Ibid.*
59 H. KOHT, *Frå skanse til skanse, op. cit.*, p. 156.
60 FO 371/24833, C. Dormer to Halifax, 30/5/40, *op. cit.*
61 T. LIE: *Leve eller dø, op. cit.*, p. 229.
62 WO 106/1962. Gen. Auchinleck to CIGS, personal and secret, 30/5/40.
63 CAB 65/13, WM 149 (40), 31/5/40.
64 FO 371/56332, Report by Adm. of the Fleet Lord Cork, *op. cit.*
65 ABA, Referat fra Regjeringskonferenser, 1/6/40.

66 FO 371/24833, Sir C. Dormer to Viscount Halifax, no. 3, 4/6/40 (N. 5852/1130/30).
67 Den norske regjeringens virksomhet, *op. cit.*, bd. IV (Forsvarsdept.), *Rapport av. Min. B. Ljungberg*, p. 211.
68 FO 371/24833, Sir C. Dormer to Viscount Halifax, no. 3, *op. cit.*
69 SUD, HP 39 A I - 172, 1938–40, 59 A, 'Vissa händlingar'. Minister i London til U. min., Stockholm no. 624, 1/6/40.
70 *Ibid.*, no. 629, 1/6/40, 23–30.
71 AE, X, Amb. Corbin, Londres, à MAE, no. 2274, 1/6/40.
72 O. RUGE, *Krigens dagbok, op. cit.*, p. 408.
73 NRK 50495/1, 2/7/63 (Interview with King Olav V).
74 ABA, Referat, *op. cit.*, 3/6/40.
75 FO 371/32835, Sir C. Dormer to Viscount Halifax, no. 3, *op. cit.*
76 D. DILKS, *Cadogan Diaries, op. cit.*, p. 294.
77 FO 371/32835, Sir C. Dormer to Viscount Halifax, no. 3, *op. cit.*
78 ABA, Referat, *op. cit.*, 6/6/40, 16 h.
79 Arne Sunde, Anders Fjelstad.
80 T. LIE, *Leve eller dø, op. cit.*, p. 251.
81 H. KOHT, *Frå skanse til skanse, op. cit.*, p. 176.
82 NRK, 51963, 8/6/65, 'Sluttkampen i Nord-Norge'; Biskop Hansen om siste statsrådet i Tromsø.
83 T. LIE, *Leve eller dø, op. cit.*, p. 252.
84 WO 106/1963, CIGS to Gen. Auchinleck, 5/6/40.
85 CAB 65/7, WC 159 (40), 9/6/40.
86 O. LINDBÄCK-LARSEN, *Krigen i Norge, op. cit.*, pp. 171–2.

## LOOKING BACK

1 C. L. LUNDIN, *Finland in the Second World War*, Bloomington, Ind., 1957, p. ii.
2 T. K. DERRY, *The Campaign, op. cit.*, p. 230; J. L. MOULTON, *The Norwegian Campaign, op. cit.*, p. 259.
3 J. L. MOULTON, *The Norwegian Campaign, op. cit.*, p. 260.
4 F. KERSAUDY, *Stratèges et Norvège, op. cit.*, pp. 20–3, 42–4.
5 T. K. DERRY, *The Campaign, op. cit.*, p. 229.
6 K. J. VON PUTTKAMMER, *Die Unheimliche See*, Karl Kühne, Vienna, 1952, p. 11.

# SOURCES AND BIBLIOGRAPHY

## I. ARCHIVES

*Germany*
Auswartiges Amt (AA), Bonn.
Bundesarchiv (BA), Koblenz.
Institut für Zeitgeschichte (IFZG), Munich.
Militärgeschichtliches Forschungsamt (MGFA), Freiburg.

*Belgium*
Ministère des Affaires Étrangères (AEB), Brussels.

*Canada*
Archives Publiques du Canada (APC), Ottawa.
Ministère des Affaires Extérieures (MAE), Ottawa.

*Denmark*
Udenriksministeriet (UM), Copenhagen.

*France*
Fondation Nationale des Sciences Politiques (FNSP), Paris (Archives
    Daladier).
Ministère des Relations Extérieures, Paris (AE).
Service Historique de l'Armée de Terre (SHAT), Vincennes.
Archives du Commandant Cras, Paris (ACC).
Service Historique de la Marine (SHM), Vincennes.

*United States*
Franklin D. Roosevelt Library and Archives, Hyde Park, New York (FDR).
State Department, National Archives, Washington, DC (St. Dept.).
War Department, National Archives, Washington, DC (War Dept.).

*Great Britain*
Foreign Office, PRO, London (FO).
Birmingham University Library and Archive (BUL), Birmingham (Cham-
    berlain papers).
Admiralty, PRO, London (ADM).
Churchill College Archive Centre, Cambridge (CCAC).
Air Ministry, PRO, London (AIR).
London School of Economics (LSE), London (Dalton diaries).
War Office, PRO, London (WO).
Cabinet papers, PRO, London (CAB).

Prime Minister's papers, PRO, London (PREM).
Liddell Hart Centre for Military Archives, King's College, London (LHCMA).
Imperial War Museum, London (IWM).
Nottingham Regiment headquarters, Sherwood Foresters, Nottingham (NRHQ).
British Museum, London (BM).

*Norway*
Arbeiderbevegelsens Arkiv, Oslo (ABA).
Forsvarsdepartement, Oslo (FD).
Forsvarets Krigstidsarkiv, Oslo (FKA).
Hjemmefrontmuseet, Oslo (HFM).
Norsk Rikskringkasting, Oslo (NRK).
Riksarkiv, Oslo (RA).
Universitetsbibliotek, Oslo (UB).
Utenriksdepartement, Oslo (UD).

*Netherlands*
Ministerie van Buitenlandse Zaken (MVBZ), The Hague.

*Sweden*
Svensk Utrikesdepartement, Stockholm (SUD).

## II. INTERVIEWS

*Great Britain*
Lord Mountbatten of Burma (4 June 1979).
Sir Cecil Dormer, Minister of Great Britain in Norway, 1934–40 (14 August 1977).
Sir John Colville, Secretary to Neville Chamberlain and Winston Churchill (12 April 1980).
Sir Martin Lindsay of Dowhill, Chief of Staff to General Carton de Wiart at Namsos in 1940 (correspondence with author, September–October 1974).

*Norway*
General Wilhelm Hansteen, Norwegian Commander-in-Chief, 1942–4 (21 October 1976).
Rolf Fuglesang, Party minister in Quisling's movement (12 September 1976).
Colonel O. U. Munthe-Kass, Captain in Narvik, 1940 (22 October 1976).

*France*
General Béthouart, French Commander-in-Chief at Narvik, 1940 (12 May 1979).

SOURCES AND BIBLIOGRAPHY

Captain P. O. Lapie, Foreign Legion officer at Narvik (September 1979).

*Germany*

Rear-Admiral Karl Jesco von Puttkammer, naval ADC to Adolf Hitler (16 August 1974).

## III. OFFICIAL PUBLICATIONS

*Germany*

*Dokumente zur Englisch-Französischer Politik der Kriegsausweitung,* Auswärtiges Amt. w.b. no. 4 Zentralverlag (UB), Berlin, 1940.
*Weitere dokumente* (Geheimakten des Französischen Generalstabes), W.B. nos 5-6, Berlin, 1941.
*Akten zur Deutschen Auswärtigen Politik 1918-1945,* série D. 1937-1945 Bd. VIII, Frankfurt/Main, 1961.

*Denmark*

*Beretning til folketinget afgivet af den af tinget under 25 oktober 1950 nedsatte kommission* (Report to Parliament by the investigating commission named on 25 October 1950), annexe, Bilag Bd. XII, Copenhagen, 1951.

*United States*

*Nazi Conspiracy and Aggression,* USGPO, Washington, 1947, vol. VIII.

*France*

*Les événements survenus en France de 1933 à 1945. Témoignages et documents recueillis par la commission d'enquête parlementaire,* tome IX, Paris, 1952.

*Great Britain*

*Parliamentary Debates: House of Commons,* 1940, vols 359-60.
*Parliamentary Debates: House of Lords,* 1940, vol. 116.
*Brassey's Naval Annual,* 'Führer conferences on naval affairs', London, 1948.

*Norway*

*Innstilling fra undersøkelseskommisjonen av 1945,* vol. 1, +Bilag, vols I-VI, Storting, Oslo, 1946-7. *Stortings forhandlinger,* 1920-40.
Johann Nygaardsvold, *Beretning om den Norsk Regjeringens virksomet fra 9 april 1940 til 25 juin 1945,* Stortinget, Oslo, 1947.
*Regjeringen of Hjemmefronten under krigen,* Aschehoug, Oslo, 1948.
*Norges Forhold til Sverige under krigen,* vol. III, Oslo, Gyldendal, 1950.

*Sweden*

*Förspelet til det Tyska Angreppet på Danmark och Norge den 9 april 1940,* KGL Utrikesdept, Stockholm, 1947.

SOURCES AND BIBLIOGRAPHY

*International Military Tribunal*
*Procès des grands criminels de guerre*, Nuremberg, 1948, tomes XV, XVIII, XXVIII.

*USSR*
*Vnesnjaja Politika SSSR*, Sbornik Dokumentov, vol. IV (1935–40), Moscow, 1946.
*Dokumenty vnesnei politiki SSSR*, vol. VII, Moscow, 1963.


## IV. BIBLIOGRAPHY

### GENERAL STUDIES OF THE CAMPAIGN

MORDAL (Jacques), *La campagne de Norvège*, Self, Paris, 1948.
DERRY (Thomas K.), *The Campaign in Norway*, HMSO, London, 1952.
HUBATSCH (Walter), *Weserübung*, Musterschmidt, Götttingen, 1960.
LINDBÄCK-LARSEN (Odd), *Krigen i Norge 1940*, Gyldendal, Oslo, 1965.
MOULTON (J. L.), *The Norwegian Campaign of 1940*, Eyre & Spottiswoode, London, 1966.
ASH (Bernard), *Norway 1940*, Cassell, London, 1964.
MIDGAARD (John), *9 april 1940*, Aschehoug, Oslo, 1965.
SOMOTEJKIN (E. M.), *Ractoptannyi nejtralitet*, Mezhdunarodnye Otnoseniia, Moscow, 1971.
KERSAUDY (François), *Stratèges et Norvège 1940*, Hachette, Paris, 1977.
TRUFFY (Georges), *Narvik*, Atra, Paris, 1982.

### MEMOIRS, EYEWITNESS ACCOUNTS, SPECIAL STUDIES

*France*
MINART (Jacques), *PC Vincennes*, vol. 1, Berger-Levrault, Paris, 1945.
VILLELUME (Paul de), *Journal d'une défaite*, Fayard, Paris, 1976.
AUPHAN (Amiral Paul), 'A propos de l'expédition de Norvège', *Ecrits de Paris*, no. 47, 1948.
REYNAUD (Paul), *Au cœur de la mêlée, 1930–1945*, Flammarion, Paris, 1951.
GAMELIN (Général M.), *Servir*, Plon, Paris, 1947, t. 3.
BAUDOUIN (Paul), *Neuf mois au gouvernement*, Paris, Table Ronde, 1948.
WEYGAND (Général Maxime), *Mémoires*, t. 3, · 'Rappelé au service', Flammarion, Paris, 1950.
DUROSELLE (Jean-Baptist), *L'Abîme*, Imprimerie nationale, Paris, 1982.
BÉDARIDA (François), *La stratégie secrète de la drôle de guerre*, FNSP-CNRS, Paris, 1979.
BÉTHOUART (Général A.), *Cinq années d'espérance*, Plon, Paris, 1968.
STEHLIN (Paul), *Témoignage pour l'histoire*, Laffont, Paris, 1964.
PASSY (Colonel), *Souvenirs*, t. 1, Raoul Solar, Monte Carlo, 1947.

Du Pavillon (Raymond C.), *Les dessous de l'expédition de Norvège*, Arthaud, Paris, 1976.

Sereau (Raymond), *L'expédition de Norvège*, RAPO, Baden-Baden, 1949.

Lyautey (Pierre), *En Norvège, Narvik 1940*, Sequana, Paris, 1940.

Lapie (Pierre-Olivier), *La Légion étrangère à Narvik*, Flammarion, Paris, 1945.

Favrel (Charles), *Ci-devant légionnaire*, Paris, Presses de la Cité, 1963.

Torris (Marcel J.), *Narvik*, Fayard, Paris, 1941.

*Great Britain*

Woodward (L.), *British Foreign Policy in the Second World War*, vol. 1, HMSO, London, 1957.

Butler (J. R. M.), *Grand Strategy*, vol. II, HMSO, London, 1957.

Ismay (Lord Hastings), *The Memoirs of Lord Ismay*, Heinemann, London, 1960.

Kennedy (General Sir John), *The Business of War*, Hutchinson, London, 1957.

Gilbert (Martin M.), *Winston S. Churchill*, vol. 6, Heinemann, London, 1983.

Cooper (Alfred Duff), *Old Men Forget*, Hart-Davis, London, 1953.

Thompson (Laurence), *1940*, Collins, London, 1966.

Macmillan (Harold), *The Blast of War*, Macmillan, London, 1977.

Churchill (Winston S.), *The Second World War*, vol. I, Cassell, London, 1948.

Amery (Leo S.), *My Political Life*, vol. 3, Hutchinson, London, 1955.

Dilks (David), *The Diaries of Sir Alexander Cadogan*, Cassell, London, 1971.

MacLeod (R.), *The Ironside Diaries*, Constable, London, 1962.

Harvey (J.), *The Diplomatic Diaries of Oliver Harvey*, Collins, London, 1970.

Nicolson (Nigel), *Harold Nicolson, Diaries and Letters*, Collins, London, 1967.

James (R. R.), *Chips, the Diaries of Sir Henry Channon*, Weidenfeld, London, 1967.

Carton de Wiart (Adrian), *Happy Odyssey*, Jonathan Cape, London, 1950.

Clarke (Dudley), *Seven Assignments*, Jonathan Cape, London, 1948.

Buckley (C.), *Norway, the Commandos, Dieppe*, HMSO, London, 1952.

Maund (Rear Admiral L. E. H.), *Assault from the Sea*, Methuen, London, 1949.

Mountevans (Admiral the Lord), *Adventurous Life*, Hutchinson, London, 1946.

Fitzgerald (Major D. J. L.), *History of the Irish Guards in the Second World War*, Gale & Polden, Aldershot, 1949.

Hingston (Lt Col. Walter), *Never Give Up, a History of the K.O.Y.L.I.*, vol. 5, Lund-Humphries, London, 1950.

## Germany

WARLIMONT (Walter), *Im Hauptquartier der Deutschen Wehrmacht*, Bernard und Graefe, Frankfurt, 1962.

VON LOSSBERG (Bernard), *Im Wehrmachtführungsstab*, Hamburg, Nölke, 1950.

HALDER (Franz), *Kriegstagebuch*, HQ, US Army, Europe, Historical division, vol. 3.

PUTTKAMMER (Rear Admiral Karl Jesco von), *Die unheimliche See*, Karl Kühne, Vienna, 1952.

BOEHM (Admiral Hermann), *Norwegen zwischen England und Deutschland*, Lippoldsberg, Klosterhaus, 1956.

ASSMANN (Admiral Kurt), *Deutsche Schicksalsjahre*, Wiesbaden, Brockhaus, 1950.

DÖNITZ (Admiral Karl), *Memoirs, 10 Years and 20 Days*, London, Weidenfeld & Nicolson, 1959.

RAEDER (Admiral Erich), *Mein Leben*, Schlichtenmayer, Tübingen, 1957, bd. 2.

GEMZELL (Axell), *Raeder, Hitler und Skandinavien*, Gleerup, Lund, 1965.

SALEWSKI (M.), *Die Deutsche Seekriegsleitung*, Bernard und Graefe, Frankfurt, 1970.

ZIEMKE (E. F.), *The German Northern Theatre of Operations*, Washington, DC, DAP, 1959

ADMIRALTY, *Führer Conferences on Naval Affairs*, Whitehall, London, 1947, vol. 2.

LOOCK (Hans Dietrich), *Quisling, Rosenberg und Terboven*, DVA, Stuttgart, 1970.

SERAPHIM (Hans Günther), *Das politische Tagebuch Alfred Rosenbergs*, Musterschmidt, Göttingen, 1956.

HUBATSCH (Walter), 'Tagebuch Jodl', in *Die Welt als Geschichte*, Stuttgart, Heft 1/1952, Heft 2/1954.

DIETL (Gerda Luise) and HERMANN (Kurt), *General Dietl*, Münchner Buchverlag, Munich, 1951.

FEUERSTEIN (Valentin), *Irrwege der Pflicht*, Weisermühl, Munich, 1949.

FANTUR (Werner), *Narvik, Sieg des Glaubens*, Junker und Dünhaupt, Berlin, 1941 (Propaganda).

BUSCH (Fritz Otto), *Zehn Zerstörer, die Besetzung Narviks*, Sponholtz Vg, Hanover, 1959.

BUCHNER (Alex), *Narvik*, Kurt Vowinckel, Heidelberg, 1958.

BOTTGER (Gerd), *Narvik im Bild*, Gerhard Stalling Vg., Berlin, 1941 (Propaganda).

OKW, *Kampf um Norwegen*, Zeitgeschichte Vg., Berlin, 1940 (Propaganda).

DOLTRA (Esteban) and TARIN-IGLESIAS (José), *Narvik, una pagina para la historia*, Aguado, Madrid, 1941 (Nazi propaganda in Spain).

255

PRUCK (Erich), 'Abwehraussenstelle Norwegen', in *Marine Rundschau* no. 4, 1956, pp. 107-18.

*Norway*

HAMBRO (Carl J.), *7 Juni-9 April-7 Juni, Historiske Dokumenter*, Gyldendal, Oslo, 1956.

KOHT (Halvdan), *For fred og fridom i krigstid*, Tiden, Oslo, 1957.

KOHT (Halvdan), *Frå skanse til skanse*, Tiden, Oslo, 1947; *Norway, Neutral and Invaded*, Macmillan, New York, 1943.

LIE (Trygve), *Leve eller dø, Norge i Krig*, Tiden Norsk, Oslo, 1955.

HJELMTVEIT (Nils), *Vekstår og Vargtid*, Aschehoug, Oslo, 1969.

HARTMANN (Sverre), *Spillet om Norge*, Mortensen, Oslo, 1958.

RUGE (Otto), *Krigens dagbok*, Halvorsen og Larsen, Oslo, 1949.

ROLSTAD ( Leif C.), *April 1940*, Gyldendal, Oslo, 1980.

GETZ (Otto B.), *Fra Krigen i nord Trøndelag*, Aschehoug, Oslo, 1940.

FLEISCHER (Karl), *Efterlatte papirer*, Eget Forlag, Tønsberg, 1947.

NORSK FORSVARSFORENING, 'Fra Felttoget i Norge 1940', in *Til studium og eftertanke*, no. 98, April 1971, no. 4.

MUNTHE KAAS (Otto), *Evakueringen av Narvikavsnittet*, Gyldendal, Oslo, 1970; *The Campaign in Northern Norway*, RNIS, Washington, DC, 1944.

GLEDITSCH (N. og K.), *Glimt fra kampårene*, Oslo, Gyldendal, 1954.

WAAGE (Johann), *La bataille de Narvik*, Laffont, Paris, 1965.

ANDENAES (J.), RISTE (O.), SKODVIN (M.), *Norway and the Second World War*, Grundt-Tanum, Oslo, 1966.

*Poland*

ZBYSZEWSKI (Karel), *The Fight for Narvik*, Lindsay Drummond, London, 1940.

LITYNSKI (Zygmunt), *I Was One of Them*, Jonathan Cape, London, 1941.

BIEGANSKI (Witold), *Poles in the Battle of Narvik*, Interpress, Warsaw, 1969.

# INDEX